CITIES WITH INVISIBLE WALLS

CITIES WITH INVISIBLE WALLS

REINTERPRETING URBANIZATION IN POST-1949 CHINA

KAM WING CHAN

HONG KONG
OXFORD UNIVERSITY PRESS
OXFORD NEW YORK
1994

Oxford University Press
Oxford   New York   Toronto
Kuala Lumpur   Singapore   Hong Kong   Tokyo
Delhi   Bombay   Calcutta   Madras   Karachi
Nairobi   Dar es Salaam   Cape Town
Melbourne   Auckland   Madrid
and associated companies in
Berlin   Ibadan

Oxford is a trade mark of Oxford University Press

First published 1994

Published in the United States
by Oxford University Press, New York

British Library Cataloguing in Publication Data
available

Library of Congress Cataloging-in-Publication Data
Chan, Kam Wing.
Cities with invisible walls : reinterpreting urbanization in
post-1949 China / Kam Wing Chan.
p.   cm.
Includes bibliographical references (p.   ) and index.
ISBN 0–19–585764–X
1. Urbanization--China--History--20th century.   2. Cities and
towns--China--Growth--History--20th century.   3. Urban policy-
-China--History 20th century.   I   Title.
HT384.C6C43   1994
307.76'0951--dc20   93–40468
CIP

Printed in Hong Kong
Published by Oxford University Press (Hong Kong) Ltd
18/F Warwick House, Taikoo Place, 979 King's Road,
Quarry Bay, Hong Kong

To Ngan-chu, Wai-fung, and Ying-fung

Preface

THIS is a book about urbanization, written by one who as a child followed the family and shifted out of the countryside, only, after more than two decades, to begin to appreciate how important the event was. Direct migration experience, however, has not bestowed on me all the necessary ingredients to be a writer on urbanization using a second language. Instead, this study comes mainly from many years' work on a dissertation on Chinese urbanization, finally completed at the University of Toronto during 1988. So much has happened to urbanization and migration in China since the mid-1980s; there has also been a parallel explosion of information on the subject. While my doctoral dissertation focused primarily on the Maoist era, the present study extends the analysis to the 1980s and 1990s. The results of such a broader coverage in time, coupled with my continuous on-and-off re-thinking and re-working of my work since 1989, are extensive updates and revisions of the original work and two new chapters about the reform period. Hoping that it can speak to an audience larger than specialists in the field, this book has put more emphasis on policy and has limited technical material to the minimum possible without affecting the arguments.

This book was written with collected materials moved and reshuffled a few times, including thrice across the Pacific. I was blessed with luck, and almost all of them survived the short and, especially, long voyages and remained, though quite disorganized by now, usable and useful to this project. More importantly, the project has received the support and encouragement of many people. Among them I am indebted to Joseph Whitney and other members of my doctoral dissertation committee. Their counsel and expertise in different areas, coupled with the stimulating environment of the University of Toronto, were vital to my intellectual development and to the formulation of many of the ideas in this book. I am also grateful to Thomas Rawski, whose encouragement and guidance were especially crucial to my doctoral work in the early stages; to Dr Ronald Hill and Professor Reginald Kwok for their encouragement of my initial curiosity, which many years later launched me on this relatively challenging voyage; to

Professor C. K. Leung, who not only forged the crucial link with
the present publisher, but also supported my research work in
many other practical ways; to June Chan and Haihua Yan for
their unfailing, timely, and more-than-research assistance at different stages; to anonymous referees who provided constructive
criticisms and substantive advice; to Wing-shing Tang for his gen-
tle critique of a large portion of the manuscript and a supply of
useful materials with enthusiasm, though we may continue to dis-
agree on some of the points; to Yunguan Yang for his invaluable
materials drawn from the 1990 Chinese Census; and to Lawrence
Ma and Tim Oakes for reading Chapter 4 and providing valuable
comments and suggestions.

Various editors at Oxford University Press participated in the
project at different phases, and I am grateful to them for their
editorial suggestions, coordination of the project, and enormous
understanding for an author who has struggled to meet deadlines,
often under unfavourable conditions. The cartography staff at the
Department of Geography and Geology, University of Hong Kong,
drew most of the graphs on short notice. My sister, Jean, deserves
special mention for the crucial, though often indirect, help she
provided. Not only could she be always counted on for transferring research materials between Hong Kong and Seattle, but she
was also most generous in giving her time to handling matters I
could not attend to due to involvement in the project. The Canadian
Commonwealth Scholarship provided five years of critical financial support for my Ph.D. programme, including dissertation
research. The University of Hong Kong and the Jackson School
of International Studies, University of Washington, offered me
grants to continue research on the same subject in the reform era.
I wish to record my sincere thanks to all of them. Chapter 2 incor-
porates my articles published in *Urban Geography* (1988), *Modern
China* (1994), and *Urbanizing China*, edited by Gregory Guldin
(1992). An early version of Chapter 3 appeared in *International
Journal of Urban and Regional Research* (1992, vol. 16, no. 2). I
thank the publishers for permission to use this material.

Finally, a book such as this puts heavy demands upon a family. The sacrifice mine had to offer is enormous, especially as the
period of giving birth to this book coincided with those of our
two children. The book was first conceived about the same time
as Wai-fung, now a jolly and able two-year-old, who has since the

toddler stage been curious about Dad's work in front of a flashy colour machine but has remained largely co-operative throughout to allow my writing tasks be completed. The completion of correcting the first galleys was celebrated almost immediately with the birth of the youngest Chan, Ying-fung. Needless to say, but necessary to record, this book would have never seen the light of day without the understanding, patience, and forbearance exhibited by my wife, Ngan-chu, who bore much of the housework and parenting burdens to ease my involvement in the research and writing while I had a regular, if not heavier, teaching load. It is to Wai-fung, Ying-fung, and especially, Ngan-chu that this book is dedicated.

K. W. C.
Seattle, USA

Contents

Tables

Figures

Abbreviations

e	non-working population multiplier
GIL	percentage of output in industry
Li	industrial employment
LIL	percentage of employment in industry
Ln	non-agricultural employment
Ls	service employment
Q	industrial output
r(X)	average annual (instantaneous) growth rate of X
s	service employment multiplier
u	degree of urbanization of non-agricultural employment
UL	percentage of population living in urban areas
UM	urban multiplier
UP	urban population (=TPCT)

Introduction

> Walls have been so central to the Chinese idea of a city that the traditional words for city and wall are identical, the character *cheng* standing for both. In imperial times the great bulk of China's urban population was concentrated in walled cities; an unwalled urban center was at least in some senses not a proper city. (Chang 1977, p. 75)

URBANIZATION—taken to mean the concentration of population in urban centres—has accompanied economic development in many countries during their early stages of industrialization (Davis 1965, 1966; United Nations 1980). That some amount of urbanization is an almost inevitable result of economic growth is evident in the experiences of most countries where development has occurred. Urbanization is a complex, multi-faceted process, but fundamentally it is the spatial manifestation of the economic structural shift of labour away from agricultural- to industrial-based activities in the production structure.[1] Crucial to this shift are the output gains associated with resource transfers from the low-productivity agricultural sector to the high-productivity industrial sector.

Rapid growth of urban population in developing countries has been one of the world's most critical development problems in the decades since the Second World War. At least, that is a widely accepted proposition in academies and among government policy-makers (Gugler 1988); Tolley and Thomas 1987; Preston 1988). In many studies urban population growth in the Third World in this period is shown to deviate from the general pattern of what was observed in the Western world during a comparable time. Those studies have argued that urban population explosion has taken place over a much shorter period because of very high rates of both natural increase and net rural–urban migration (e.g. World Bank 1980; United Nations 1980; Stren *et al.* 1992). While there is a debate in the literature about the rapidity of the process and the social and economic factors which have caused it, most accept that the systematic urban bias in policy has been the main contributor to rapid urban growth and rural exodus. Furthermore, the phenomenal demographic growth of Third World cities is considered dysfunctional, posing many serious, at least short-run urban problems such as unemployment or underemployment, congestion, and environmental deterioration, alongside an impoverished rural sector (see e.g. Lipton 1977, 1984). The notion of 'over-urbanization', despite a destructive critique by Sovani (1964), when used in its original formulation by Hauser (1958) to characterize the diachronic match between high urban population growth and relatively slow industrial employment growth, remains useful when comparing industrial and urban growth in development.[2] The well-known Harris-Todaro (1970) migration model is also developed to explain the existence of chronic urban unemployment, due to sluggish creation of industrial jobs, and the continuing urban inflows implied in the 'over-urbanization' thesis.

Equally important is that despite the efforts of governments and international agencies in the last decades to slow down urban growth, the momentum of population growth in most of the Third World continues to run unaltered (Yeung 1990; Stren *et al.* 1992). This has led to a number of studies and projections, painting a 'gloom and doom', unsustainable urban future for the Third World, especially in view of the financial and natural resources that will be required (e.g. Brown 1976a). The most oft-cited urban projection produced by the United Nations (1987) suggests that by the turn of the century, sixteen out of twenty-two of the world's largest metropolises with populations of over ten million will be in today's developing countries, an awesome challenge to many Third World governments even if not all of the population forecasts of individual cities are realized.[3]

Compared with the sprawling squatters, expanding shanty towns, and rising poverty of the Third World urban scene, the orderly Chinese cities under Mao Zedong's rule, allegedly devoid of many of those urban ills, were presented as a shining counter-example to the world in the 1970s by a number of Western scholars (e.g. Chen 1972; Murphey 1975, 1980; Kojima 1978), even though concrete information about China at the time was extremely difficult to assemble. This image was reinforced by the Chinese government's revolutionary rhetoric about building a new society to a plan different from Western capitalist development prescriptions. The supposedly unique and successful Chinese Maoist experience has since generated a great deal of publicity and provoked huge scholarly interest, as can be expected from the perceived promise of the Chinese approach. In the words of one of the most experienced China hands of the time (Murphey 1975, p. 167), the Chinese approach to urbanization stands

as one of the truly significant and innovative achievements of this century. The Chinese effort since 1949 to develop a new approach to urban development holds, I believe, great promise not only for China, but for the rest of the world still grappling or floundering with the problems which the modern commercial and industrial city . . . has brought with it.

What has been characterized as the uniqueness of the China approach is that China's patterns and policies seem to be counter to historical trends in other countries. While contemporary urbanization has accompanied industrialization in almost all countries during their early stages of economic development, China's post-1949 pattern appears to be quite different. Even based on the lowest estimate of China's industrial output and the highest urban population figures, China's presumed success, as seen in the late 1970s, in simultaneously fostering rapid industrialization and keeping urban expansion under control was enormous.[4] This is just the reverse of what has been characterized as 'over-urbanization'. The low level of urbanization in China has been imputed to a series of distinguishing Chinese 'anti-urban' policy measures, featuring mass urban population removal to the countryside, strict bans on urban in-migration, suppression of urban consumption, and rural industrialization programmes that professedly attacked the problems of development at the root.

To leap one step forward, conventional wisdom on China had it that Mao Zedong had rejected the traditional Soviet model of unbalanced urban-industrial growth after 1957, opting instead for the simultaneous development of agriculture and industry (e.g. Gurley 1976; Weisskopf 1980; Van Ness and Raichur 1983). In this view, the aforementioned 'anti-urban' measures were seen as the logical results of Mao's scheme to promote greater rural–urban balance and agricultural growth. Development under Mao constituted a genuine, alternative model to the common 'urban-biased' Western classical or Soviet 'industrially biased' development models. It was believed, albeit again on the basis of mostly sketchy and impressionistic accounts, that China during the Maoist period between 1957 and 1978 achieved balanced industrial and agricultural development and reduced rural–urban disparities while stabilizing urban growth. This was contrasted not only with the rapid and uncontrolled urban growth and its accompanying problems of urban poverty in the Third World but also with the massive dislocations in the USSR that resulted from Stalin's rapid urban-industrial development and collectivization (see e.g. Meisner 1974; Frolic 1976). Thus, to many writers, especially non-China specialists as recent as Smith (1989), the 'Chinese model' of urban development has been viewed as intrinsically dissimilar to the Soviet or the Western model. The Chinese development experience represents an alternative worthy of emulation, or at least envy, by other developing countries.

The avalanche of information about China's population and economy since the late 1970s, accompanied by a greater degree of transparency in the system, has ushered in a new era of research. Based on the new information, a growing body of recent research has rejected the above interpretation of the Maoist development strategy. For example, Lardy (1983) has demonstrated that policies under Mao consistently discriminated against agriculture in allocating investments and setting industrial and agricultural commodity prices. Kirkby (1985, p. 18) repudiated his earlier (1977) observation of an increasing rural–urban balance in China and suggested that the most important factor behind the portrayal of 'anti-urbanism' in China has been 'our own Western susceptibility to agrarian utopian and oriental fantasy' rather than the hard Chinese reality. Chan and Xu (1985) helped straighten out serious misinterpretations of Chinese urban population statistics, upon which many previous studies were erroneously based. Clearly, there have been grim misunderstandings of China's development in the Chinese urbanization literature. A number of major studies have worked with the wrong analysis paradigm. So the conventional interpretations of urbanization in mainland China over the Maoist decades have also been highly skewed. This has, in turn, distorted our understanding of policies in the post-Mao era.

Several reasons for this state of contemporary Chinese studies can be gleaned from Johnson (1982), Myers (1986), Kuo and Myers (1986), and Leung (1987). The long period of information blackout after the failure of the Great Leap Forward posed almost insurmountable obstacles to systematic, empirical investigation by outsiders. The 'pilgrimage mentality' that caused Western intellectuals to see the ideal in foreign cultures also impeded objective evaluation of Chinese development. Many overlooked the usual dichotomy between rhetoric and reality that also exists in the Chinese system. Official statements of ideals and principles, supported by field information drawn from showcase factories and communes, were often taken as reliable indicators of the ways policies were implemented in China. In short, as Johnson (1982) said, 'too often the myth was accepted at face value'. Adding to this bias is the Sino-centric and 'area studies' approach that has often caused China specialists to become parochial. This is an outlook that has prevented them from fully exploiting new insights from a comparative perspective, and has led to an over-emphasis on the idiosyncrasies of China's development to the neglect of developments in other related fields (Leung 1987)[5].

This book is an attempt at remedying the shortcomings of previous literature: the current endeavour reinterprets and reanalyzes China's post-1949 urbanization and the explicit and implicit policies affecting it from a new perspective. The present endeavour not only draws on significantly richer empirical information about Chinese urbanization unavailable to outsiders in the past, but also analyses the material within a broader urbanization and economic system/development framework. This was mostly absent or poorly conceived in the past literature on Chinese urbanization. I have sought to apply an interdisciplinary approach to the urbanization question and have used models and analytical tools accordingly. The focus of the present study is on Chinese urbanization at the national aggregate level. While the regional dimension of urbanization and urban systems is an important topic rightly favoured by geographers, the sheer size of the current task, if it is to be treated at any depth, easily fills a volume such as this. A more disaggregated treatment of Chinese urbanization will have to be prepared separate from this one.

Following a review of the existing research on Chinese urbanization in the next chapter, Chapter Two tackles one major hurdle in recent Chinese urbanization studies, the problem of urban population definitions, and provides an account of the trends of urban growth and rural–urban migration in various periods, upon which further assessments can be made. Chapter Three then examines the Maoist policies of controlling urban growth within a theoretical framework linking the socialist system and industrialization strategy with policies affecting urbanization. It will be argued that overall urbanization policies in China have been motivated primarily by the considerations of rapid industrialization, similar to those in other Soviet-type economies, instead of China's special ideological commitment to rural development. Chapter Four takes the reader to the reform period and examines the various forms of urban inflows and their relationships with the state's recurrent objective to economize on urbanization costs. The final chapter summarizes the main points of this book and concludes by looking into China's urbanization future and the challenges ahead.

Notes

1. This is through changes in demand occasioned by what is known loosely as Engel's 'law', which states that income shares spent on food decrease with income, but those spent on industrial products and service rise with income. That is, the income elasticity of food demand is low.
2. See a reconsideration of this concept in Gugler (1982) and application of the concept in United Nations (1980, pp. 17–9) and Smith (1989).
3. The alarmist projection is based partially on misinterpreted (inflated) 'urban' population figures of at least two cities, Shanghai and Beijing (see a survey of urban definitions used in China in Chapter Two).
4. While the industrial sector alone already accounted for close to 40 per cent of the country's gross national product in the late 1970s, the percentage of population living in urban areas in China remained relatively low, only about 20 per cent. The industrial figure is the lowest estimate in use (adjusted for international prices) produced by the World Bank (1983a). A higher figure based on domestic prices will indicate that about half of China's gross national product came from the industrial sector in 1979 (SSB 1991a). The urban population figure is from the State Statistical Bureau (1991a).
5. A detailed and controversial account of American misperceptions of the Chinese reality can be found in Mosher (1990).

1 A Review of Contemporary Research

CHINA's post-1949 urbanization has been studied by scholars in disciplines ranging from anthropology and history, to sociology and urban planning. The literature accumulated thus far is huge and is still growing rapidly. For instance, an earlier bibliography on cities and city planning in the People's Republic of China compiled by Ma (1980) included some 200 titles, largely produced by Western scholars of different backgrounds during the two decades prior to 1980. Yeh's recent catalogue (1989) on a similar subject lists more than 600 English items, mostly published in the 1980s. With the post-Mao revival of urban-related disciplines such as urban planning and urban geography in China, far greater access to information, and vibrant urban economic activities, recent scholarship on Chinese urbanization has been developing at an unprecedented rate.

It is beyond the scope of this chapter to cover all the works on post-1949 urbanization. So, for the purpose of this study, the review is confined to the literature on China's urbanization since 1949 and related policies at the national level.[1] Even such a narrow focus will have to be highly selective. This review is divided into two parts because of the different stages of development and emphases in research. It covers Western then mainland Chinese scholarship.

Western Research on China's Post-1949 Urbanization

Urbanists in the West have long been fascinated by the urban scene in contemporary and traditional China. Western studies of China's urbanization under socialism were initiated in the late 1950s and the early 1960s by a number of analysts working in, or closely associated with, the US Government. Studies in this period were largely concerned with assembling demographic data on China's cities from various sources and describing the urbanization trends in the first decade of the People's Republic. Some of the better known works include those by Orleans (1959), Shabad (1959), Ni (1960), and Ullman (1961). Skinner (1964–5) also provided an analytical account of rural marketing and its relationship with the fate of small towns. In general, however, only limited progress was achieved in theorizing Chinese urbanization patterns at this early stage of research development.

The 1970s represents the formative stage in the development of Western research on China's post-1949 urbanization. Following the interest in Third World development and urban research during the 1960s and 1970s, China's urbanization and urban policy came under increasing scrutiny from Western scholars, some of whom were intensely captivated by the new Chinese socialist development experience. Important works in this decade included specialized monographs by Howe (1971) and Tien (1973) analysing urban employment and population, respectively, in the 1950s. Bernstein (1977) also studied in great depth the urban rustication movement. Chen (1973) and Chang (1976) painstakingly pieced together urban population data from a variety of sources to create a basis for many ensuing quantitative studies.[2] This was accompanied by an extensive body of literature, notably by Murphey (1975), Ma (1976, 1977), and Cell (1980), which studied China's urban development from a perspective emphasizing the socialist or Maoist ideology of equality and concern with rural–urban differences. These developments led to more thematic works in the early 1980s, such as Murphey (1980) and various volumes of collected papers by Leung and Ginsburg (eds.) (1980), and Ma and Hanten (eds.) (1981), among others.

The advancement of the field was heavily shaped by new paradigms on China's post-1949 economic development. Partly outraged by the US involvement in the Vietnam War, and partly impressed by the striking and 'revolutionary' events in China during the Great Leap Forward and the Cultural Revolution, a new generation of China specialists began to view the Chinese communist regime as 'the modernizing communist regime' or, even further, 'the revolutionary socialist regime' (Kuo and Myers 1986). Policies under Mao were generally perceived as aiming at the creation of a new socialist society and a new man. For instance, Gurley (1970), one of the most influential protagonists of this view, had this to say in an article entitled 'The New Man in the New China':

Perhaps the most striking difference between the capitalist and Maoist views concerns goals. Maoists believe that . . . to raise the level of material welfare of the population . . . should be done only within the context of the development of human beings . . . And it should be done only on an egalitarian basis.

On economic development, many China specialists emphasized that the new regime, faced with very unfavourable resource endowment, had been able to feed and support a huge population without the common pathologies of modern development, such as unemployment and starvation (Myers 1986). On sectoral priorities, it was commonly alleged that the Maoist approach rejected conventional approaches, which were characteristically skewed toward industrial development and 'urban-biased', and opted for a more balanced development of both industry and agriculture by according heavy weight to rural development (see e.g. Wheelwright and McFarlane 1970; Gray 1972; Gurley 1976; Eckstein 1977). In retrospect, because of the information blackout in China after the late 1950s, 'hard' evidence and economic data were scant. Support for the above argument relied heavily on selective Chinese official assertions and skimpy statistics, together with interpretations of pronounced government policies, the ideology and history of the Chinese Communist Party, and events taking place in the 1960s and 1970s in China.

For example, official price indices released in the 1970s, which indicated a narrowing of the price gap between agricultural and industrial goods, and the policy of freezing urban-sector wages, were cited in support of the Maoist 'pro-rural' approach (Lardy 1978; Gurley 1979).[3] In addition, the communization and all-out drive for industrialization during the Great Leap Forward, which led to the establishment of hundreds of thousands of small iron-smelting plants in the countryside, were seen as Mao's (unsuccessful) attempt at rural development. Mao's (1956) famous statement of 'simultaneous development of industry and agriculture', his criticism of the Soviet approaches, and the official line of 'taking agriculture as the foundation of the economy'[4] were frequently cited as strong evidence of Mao's policy of giving priority to the countryside (e.g. Schwartz 1973). As Kirkby (1985, p. 5) commented later, China's 'pro-ruralism also seemed to be writ large in the enormous weight accorded to self-reliant agricultural development in the propaganda messages of the day'. Furthermore, China's commitment to agricultural development was also attributed categorically to the Chinese communists' peasant roots and the rural-based Chinese Revolution. By contrast, the Soviet Bolshevik Revolution was said to be urban-based, and Stalin's industrialization and collectivization programmes were heavily biased against the peasantry. The Sino-Soviet split in the late 1950s and armed conflicts in the 1960s reinforced the perception that China was embarking on a road different from the USSR's[5] (e.g. Meisner 1974).

This perspective gradually gained dominance in the mainstream of Chinese studies in the mid-1970s (Myers 1986). The Chinese development model, with its central tenet of priority development of agriculture,[6] was firmly established in the literature and received immense publicity in the development field (e.g. Friedmann and Douglass 1978; Amin 1981). Literature extolling the virtues of Chinese-type socialism proliferated during the decade. It was generally believed that the distinctive Chinese model attacked the problem of development at its root and offered greater promise as a unique, alternative approach for other underdeveloped societies (e.g. Oksenberg 1973; Maxwell 1979; Weisskopf 1980).

A 'logical' extension of the 'pro-rural' thesis was the notion that the Maoist development strategy was 'anti-urban', in the sense that policies favoured the countryside over the city and aimed at ultimately eradicating the differences between the two (Meisner 1974). This central theme in the study of contemporary Chinese urbanization led Ma (1976, p. 114) to conclude that 'any serious study of China's urban evolution since 1949 must take Mao Tsetung's explicit anti-urban and pro-rural policies into consideration'.

Several major features of China's urbanization policies can be gleaned from major writers who followed this thread of thought (Murphey 1975, 1980; Ma 1976, 1977; Kojima 1978; Lewis 1971; Chen 1972; Chiu 1980; and Cell 1980). They include the transformation from consumer to producer cities; establishing industrial enterprises in rural communes, and improving services in rural areas; limiting the growth of urban population by controlling inflows to cities, especially to big cities; resettling urban intellectuals and youth in the countryside to promote rural development; and developing urban industries that support agriculture.

These features constituted a brand-new 'revolutionary' model of rural–urban co-operation, their protagonists argued. Not surprisingly, the Chinese 'anti-urban' stance in urbanization was also said to contrast with Stalin's urban-industrial bias. Statements like 'Soviet and Chinese patterns of urban development are so intrinsically dissimilar' were common and arguably due to the different concepts of urbanism and sectoral priorities adopted by the two communist regimes (Frolic 1972, p. 306; Meisner 1974). In the early 1980s, the prevailing interpretation of Chinese urbanization policies may be summarized as follows:

1. The level of urbanization was comparatively low by world or Third World standards. Urban growth stabilized or only increased slightly during the 1960s and 1970s.

2. China's ability to foster rapid economic (industrial) growth in the 1960s and 1970s with little urban growth was a remarkable achievement in contrast to the common 'over-urbanization' in many other Third World countries during the process of economic growth. China was said to have avoided problems of unemployment, squalor, and squatters in cities.

3. Practices of resettling urban residents in the countryside and restricting migration contributed significantly to slow urbanization, rural development, and equalization of resources between the urban and rural sectors. Elaborate migration controls were seen as a mechanism to keep skilled labour on the farm and to foster the well-being of the peasants. To many observers a new organic unity of rural and urban seemed to be emerging in China.

4. China also succeeded in promoting the development of smaller settlements and greater spatial equality.

The death of Mao and the arrest of the 'Gang of Four' ushered in a new era of relative liberalization and openness, with the most welcomed explosion of information about many aspects of Chinese society and economy. Many Western students of China were amazed to learn of official or quasi-official revelations of wide disparities between the urban and rural areas, the massive famine in the early 1960s, and the generally unfavourable treatment of the peasantry under Mao. Studies in the 1980s by Western scholars have increasingly questioned and refuted many of the past assertions and presumptions about the Maoist development model (e.g. Prybyla 1982; Stone 1986; Leung and Chan 1986). In the field of economic development, careful research by Lardy (1983) and others (e.g. Tang 1984) convinced many that the Maoist strategy was heavily skewed in favour of industry, thus removing the past Maoist 'pro-rural' smoke-screen that had clouded the view of almost a generation of scholars.

As more information about China's population and economy became available, especially after the publication of the first *Zhongguo tongji nianjian* (*Statistical Yearbook of China*) in 1982 and the third Census results, in-depth studies of a number of aspects of China's urbanization have been possible. While the reassessment of China's past economic development experience continued in the 1980s, Western urbanists interested in China, especially geographers trained in the empiricist tradition, were busily exploiting the newly expanded opportunity to produce a flurry of studies, many of which were included in the several collections edited by Sit (1985), Kwok *et al.* (1990), Yeung and Hu (1990), and Guldin (1992), in addition to those described earlier. Others were preoccupied with analyzing China's urban population statistics and urbanization trends, a subject that had long suffered from enormous confusion and lack of pertinent data (e.g. Chan and Xu 1985; Kirkby 1985; Sit 1985; Ma and Cui 1987; Kojima 1987). Many previously neglected aspects of Chinese urban development have also come under the scrutiny of Western scholars. These include urban and rural population growth (e.g. Hsu 1986), migration (Chan 1988a), small town development (e.g. Tan 1986; Lee 1988), urban systems (e.g. Pannell 1984; Henderson 1986), 'symptoms' of unbalanced development in Chinese cities (Chang 1983), and the socio-political aspects of urban life (Whyte and Parish 1984). A handsome volume with a wealth of detailed information about individual cities was recently put together by Schinz (1989). While these largely empirical studies have clarified many aspects of Chinese urbanization, fundamental theoretical questions remain unanswered. A coherent set of explanations has yet to be developed. Contradictory, dated, and superficial interpretations of China's urbanization policies continued to be made in the 1980s.

The general remarks by Stren *et al.* (1992) about many urbanization studies showing a lack of understanding or, at least, giving an insufficient treatment of the macro-economic issues that have profoundly affected urban population growth, also apply to the scholarship on Chinese urbanization. For instance, despite the revealing findings of Lardy (1983), Tang (1984), and many others about China's sectoral strategy, there is no shortage of urbanization studies still adhering to the dated 'pro-rural', 'anti-urban', and 'rural–urban balance' interpretations of Chinese urban policies (see e.g. Parish 1987; Yeung and Zhou 1987; Ebanks and Cheng 1990). On the other hand, reforms carried out by post-Mao leaders in the 1980s have led some researchers to turn around and conclude that the post-1979 urbanization policies have shifted from the Maoist 'anti-urban' stance to one that favours rapid urbanization (Banister 1986; Kwok 1987). A more careful review of the evidence, as will be provided in Chapters Three and Four, suggests that neither of the above views is accurate. The Maoist approach is certainly not in favour of rural development; nor can one categorically label the post-Mao policy as 'pro-urban'. The reality is more mixed and full of apparent contradictions.

Nevertheless, recent Western scholarship has produced a number of insightful works that address fundamental empirical and theoretical issues. Despite some serious errors in handling Chinese urban population statistics, Kirkby's (1985) encyclopedic work on urbanization, for example, has made an important advance in the field. He refutes the argument that the Chinese Communist Party embodies a philosophy of favouring development of the country-side over the city. Instead, he argues that the practice of restricting urbanization in China was a result of the pursuit of high rates of industrialization and accumulation rather than ideological 'anti-urbanism'. This is an important dimension of China's urbanization patterns and policies.[7] This line of analysis was further advanced by Chan (1988b), Perkins (1990), and Zhang (1991), as well as studies focusing on the impact of the household registration system on migration (e.g. Christiansen 1990; Li 1992), and comparative urbanization studies (e.g. Douglass 1988). This new understanding of China's development strategy and politico–economic system has provided crucial links for building a more coherent and comprehensive framework.

Although most agree that economic sectoral change is an important driving force of urbanization and that urbanization in China is closely related to the performance of industry and agriculture, treatments of these macro relationships, especially under the socialist system, have so far largely been casual, if not superficial. This leaves many important questions unresolved. Most fundamentally, many sinologists in the West have tended to treat China as a large, developing, or 'Third World', country and have ignored (or failed to see) the fact that China also has political, social and economic characteristics in common with the so-called 'Soviet-type economies'. Even if comparisons with the Soviet experience are made, they tend to stress the contrast between the Chinese and Soviet policies and patterns (e.g. Frolic 1972, 1976; Whyte and Parish 1984). A more careful survey of Soviet economic development and urbanization literature reveals many similarities between Soviet and Chinese systems of migration and urbanization in the early industrialization stage (see Chan 1990; Ronna and Sjoberg

1993). The allegedly 'unique' elements of Chinese urbanization patterns, such as the control of rural–urban migration based on administrative measures of residence and employment permits, the preponderance of 'temporary' migration to cities, the confusing multiplicity of definitions of urban population, the policy to limit large city growth, and the neglect of investment in urban infrastructure, are all part of the system one finds in the former Soviet Union and many other East European countries at comparable stages of development (see e.g. Smith 1989). These similarities challenge students of China's urbanization to investigate whether they are mere coincidences.

Urbanization Research in Mainland China

While Western studies focusing on urban development have a relatively long history, urban research in China before the late 1970s was limited (Shen and Cui 1990). The fields within which the majority of urbanization research is conducted in the West, such as urban geography, urban sociology, urban economics, and urban planning, did not exist as university subjects in pre-1972 China (Xu 1983; Xu and Chu 1986). Nor was urban geography treated as a separate branch of geographical research. A survey of the *Acta Geographica Sinica*, the only journal of geographical research circulated nationally and internationally before the mid-1970s, identifies only six articles between 1949 and 1965 that would fall into the category of urban geography (Xu and Chu 1986; *Acta Geographica Sinica* 1984). Except for the article by Yan *et al.* (1964), all are concerned with the geography of one or two mostly empirical aspects of a particular city. Although there was a gradual resurgence of urban research in the 1970s, it was heavily tilted toward urban design, mainly catering to the needs of national economic construction (Shen and Cui 1990).

Urban research was formally resurrected in the late 1970s in a renewed effort by the government to modernize the country giving more attention to urban development. The number of papers that have since been produced, even within the sub-field of urban geography, is exceedingly large (Shen and Cui 1990; Yeung and Zhou 1991). Wang's (1993) review of the sub-field of population geography also includes a large number of works concentrating on urban topics. More narrowly focused studies on urbanization at the aggregate level are pursued under one or more of the following themes: (i) urban population definitions; (ii) urbanization trends and future projections; (iii) urbanization policies and planning; and (iv) rural development and small towns. The urban definitional intricacies generated by the seemingly erratic practices of the statistical authorities in the early 1980s prompted a flurry of studies on classifying rural and urban populations, which provided an important basis for many later works (e.g. Hu 1983; Yao and Wu 1982; Wu 1983) and attracted intense attention from Western scholars.

Other studies in the early 1980s have also generated fresh insights into China's urbanization process and have proposed useful working hypotheses for further exploration. For instance, Wu's (1981) pioneering study of urban employment structure showed that China's urban population has a higher percentage of employment in industry than those of other major cities in the world. Wu (1983) also led the study of the relationship between the level of urbanization and the availability of 'commodity grain' (urban grain supplies), a popular postulate held by the government and many scholars. Yao and Wu (1982) were among the first scholars to turn their attention to the rural–urban movement of the 'yinong yigong' (peasant-worker) migrants and suggested that this was a 'special' form of China's urbanization. Fei (1984), on the other hand, revived the study of small towns.

Works since the mid-1980s have undoubtedly surpassed previous endeavours in both quantity and quality. A few highly selective, and not necessarily representative examples, are used below as illustrations. On the empirical side, Xu et al. (1987) produced a detailed descriptive study of China's small urban settlements. Tin and Lin (1986), Ma (1987), Wei (1989), and Zhang (1988) furnish revealing accounts of China's internal migration from different vantage points. A number of large-scale urban population and migration surveys have also been conducted under the auspices of various government departments and institutes, generating an enormous body of rarely seen first-hand information. A series of papers emanating from these migration investigations (e.g. CASS 1989; Zhang, Q. 1989; Li and Hu 1991) provide some more good summary analysis. On the theoretical aspect of urbanization and policy, the collected volume by Ye et al. (1988), based on an urbanization project under the auspices of the State Commission on Science and Technology, contains many useful attempts to understand Chinese urbanization policies (e.g. Zhao 1988). Recent works employing a dualistic socio-economic framework, notably by Cheng (1990), Guo and Liu (1990), Gao (1991), and Gu (1991), have generated the most exciting insights by focusing on the importance of China's household registration system in bifurcating Chinese society. Parallel to similar works by Western scholars, these perceptive studies have greatly advanced our understanding of the impact of the politico-economic system and its development strategy on urban population growth. They are also important starting points for probing into the deeper structure of China's urbanization.

Concluding Remarks

From this survey of literature on Chinese urbanization, what can one draw to help direct research to advance our understanding of China's urbanization and build a more coherent and informative framework? Here I would like to make three points:
1. Researchers need a thorough understanding of Chinese empirical information (factual accounts and statistics), including the fundamental terminology used. One almost needs to be a sinologist to be able to handle all the subtleties embedded in the linguistic nuances. As reviewed before, definitional issues, trivial as they seem to be at first sight, have affected in a significant way the quality of past scholarship on urbanization.
2. The study of urbanization, as a demographic manifestation of economic structural change, must be tackled within a larger economic development framework. In this respect, the Chinese economic system, the development strategy, and many macro-economic policies have had a serious impact on urbanization. The insufficient attention paid to these aspects in the past Chinese urbanization literature tended to cloud important linkages and explanations that could otherwise be sought. To sort out the uniqueness and communality of Chinese urbanization, a comparative approach, as opposed to a narrowly focused areal, sinological approach, is necessary. From this perspective, the large body of literature on generally better-researched socialist countries, such as those by Ofer (1977), Fallenbuchl (1977), Murray and Szelenyi (1984), Forbes and Thrift (1987), Ronna and Sjoberg (1993), and Third World urbanization, all become relevant materials for China urbanization analysts.

3. More generally, as urbanization relates not only to sectoral development, but also to a whole array of socio-economic and political variables (such as population policy, food grain distribution, household registration, political campaigns, and city planning) in China, a multi-disciplinary approach, instead of a single disciplinary approach, to the Chinese urban question would be most promising. In fact, it is very much in the geographers' tradition to mount a multi-disciplinary approach, though they tend to be more interested in meso- or micro-level (regional or sub-regional) studies and tend to overlook more fundamental political and socio-economic constraints.

It is with these points in mind that a systematic investigation of the patterns and policies of Chinese urbanization will begin in the next chapter.

Notes

1. For recent reviews of a broader field, China's urban geography, please refer to Shen and Cui (1990), Pannell (1990), and Yeung and Zhou (1991).
2. With the benefit of hindsight, most of the urban population figures presented in those studies mixed different, incomparable urban categories. See Chan and Xu (1985) for a review of this problem. Chen's (1973) set of 1970 city population figures have been widely used (a recent example is Ebanks and Cheng [1990, p. 45]).
3. Lardy (1983) repudiated his earlier view. Surprisingly, the obsolete interpretation has continued to gain acceptance in the writings on the subject in the late 1980s (e.g. Wu 1987; Smith 1989; Bhalla 1990).
4. This pronouncement was made in the wake of the famine in the early 1960s, a short period when 'standard' Maoist policies retreated to the back-bench (see Chapter Three).
5. Ironically, one of the major causes for the Sino-Soviet split was Mao's disagreement over Khrushchev's exposition of Stalin's serious errors and condemnation of his personal cult (see Renmin ribao and Hongqi Editorial Boards 1963; Gittings 1968).
6. Other features of the Chinese model include pursuits of egalitarianism, self-reliance and spatial equality, and emphasis on 'mass democracy' and ideological purity (Wheelwright and McFarlane 1970; Gurley 1976; Eckstein 1977).
7. However, probably because of the many foci in his study, he has not yet given adequate attention to investigating this postulate. While he has

recognized the importance of the economic development strategy in affecting China's urbanization, he has not taken full advantage of new findings and insights generated by recent Chinese economic studies and urbanization studies in Soviet-type economies. Furthermore, errors in handling Chinese urban population statistics have also undermined the accuracy of his findings (see Chan 1986).

2 Urban Definitions and Urban Population Growth since 1949

UNDERSTANDING post-1949 China's urbanization patterns and policies requires first establishing a reasonably accurate set of urban population statistics, upon which urban growth trends and their components can be meaningfully analysed. This is the main purpose of the present chapter, which serves as a background for the analyses in later chapters.[1] Urban population definitional problems, trivial as they might appear at first glance, have seriously plagued the study of China's urbanization since as early as researchers started to tackle urbanization issues (Ullman 1961). The nearly complete blackout of demographic and economic statistics in the 1960s and 1970s posed almost insurmountable obstacles to any serious attempt, at least by outsiders, to understand urbanization since the late 1950s. Even with the resumption of statistical work in the early post-Mao period, the size of the 'urban' population remained an 'enigma' to Western China-watchers (Orleans and Burnham 1984). It was not until 1985, with the assiduous work of many scholars, that the baffling mysteries surrounding China's urban population size between 1949 and 1982 were made clear to outsiders (Chan and Xu 1985; Ma and Cui 1987).

However, new developments in the definition of 'urban' and of urban boundaries since 1983 continued to create problems that plagued any evaluation of China's urbanization trends in the 1980s. While some authors were willing to accept one of the then two existing urban population series as being reasonable,[2] many others, including this author, considered neither of them satisfactory for any analytical work (e.g. Chan 1987; Zhou 1989). Only with the introduction of new urban criteria in the 1990 Census has a reasonable consistency been restored. This chapter evaluates the various 'urban' definitions in use and points out problems in the existing literature. As reviews of the pre-1982 situation are readily available elsewhere, the emphasis here is on developments since 1982. This chapter goes on to provide an account of urban population growth, based on a set of estimates of net rural–urban migration and other information available, and establishes a baseline for urban population growth in the 1980s.

Urban Definitions

Two types of officially designated urban places are recognized in China: cities (*shi*) and towns (*zhen*).[3] A city is generally the larger in population and is definitely higher in the Chinese administrative hierarchy. Designation of a settlement as a town, or a town as a city, means that the place moves up one level in the hierarchy, giving it greater access to financial support from the state for infrastructure, food subsidies for its residents, and industrial investment. It also gives the local government greater autonomy to raise certain taxes such as the 'urban maintenance and construction tax' and, in some cases, to approve foreign investment projects (Koshizawa 1988; Yeh and Xu 1989).[4] Three major factors, the urban designation criteria, the urban boundary, and the household registration classification, affect the calculation of the size of urban population in China. These factors have changed a number of times over the years, combining in different ways to produce one of the world's most complex systems of urban population definition. It is a system that has baffled many analysts and disorientated most others. One only needs to have a glimpse of the mass of literature written on the subject to appreciate this. Given the space here, the remaining part of this chapter will only concentrate on the most important aspects directly related to the objectives of this book. Greater details of the issues that arose in the earlier periods can be found in Tien (1973), Chan and Xu (1985), Kojima (1987), Scharping (1987), and Ma and Cui (1987).

Within the cities category, places are differentiated with reference to the levels they occupy in China's spatial administrative hierarchy (Figures 2.1 and 2.2). Three cities directly under the central administration (*zhixiashi*), Beijing, Shanghai, and Tianjin are provincial-level units, holding the highest positions in the urban hierarchy. Next down are prefectural-level cities (*dijishi*), which are under provincial administration. One special feature of provincial-level and prefectural-level cities is that their urban areas are subdivided into city or urban 'districts' (*shiqu* or *shixiaqu*). This is not found in generally smaller county-level cities (*xianjishi*), which are in the lowest echelon of the city hierarchy. There is no further subdivision of the urban areas into districts within these smallest cities. As at the end of 1989, there were 3 provincial-level cities, 185 prefectural-level cities, and 262 county-level cities (Ministry of Internal Affairs 1990).

Figure 2.1 China's Spatial Administrative Hierarchy in the Pre-1983 Period: A Generalized Schema

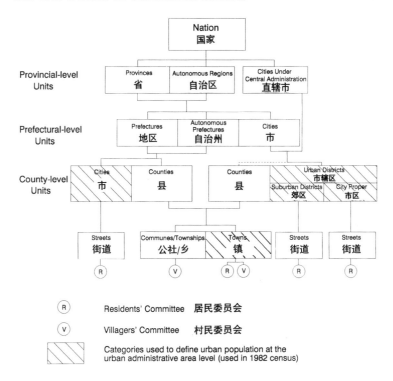

In addition, all provincial-level cities and many prefectural cities such as Guangzhou and Chongqing also administer a number of counties called 'suburban counties' (*jiaoxian* or *shixiaxian*) outside their urban areas. This practice of putting suburban counties under municipal administration was initiated in the late 1950s in response to problems with the supply of vegetables in major metropolises such as Shanghai (Fung 1981). Hence, administratively, as Figures 2.1 and 2.2 depict, a prefectural-level city may be subdivided into two parts: the 'city districts' and the 'sub-urban counties'. Only the city districts are considered 'urban'. The sub-urban counties, being predominantly agricultural in nature, are not designated 'urban', except for the designated towns in these counties (see below). However, many journalistic reports (e.g. *Ta Kung Pao* 1984) and some studies, especially those commissioned by the United Nations (1980, 1987), have often erroneously used

Figure 2.2 China's Spatial Administrative Hierarchy in the Post-1983 Era: A Generalized Schema

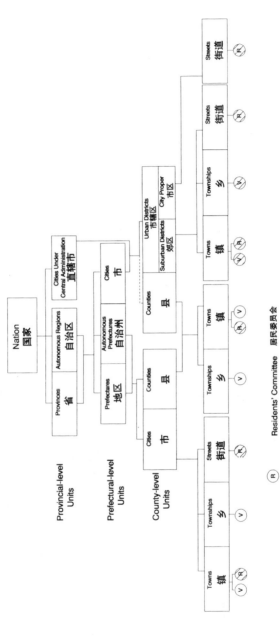

the population of this 'urban-based administrative region'—counties included—to represent China's urban population, resulting in a skewed assessment of China's urban growth rate or forecast for the future (Chan and Xu 1985).

Pre-1990 Definitions

In 1982, for a settlement to be designated as a city, it had to have a population of at least 100,000. Those whose populations were less than 100,000 had to command special administrative, strategic, or economic importance to qualify for city designations (Yeh and Xu 1989; Zhou 1989).

The town designations were even more complicated. The criteria used in the 1982 Census, which are considered reasonable by many analysts (Hu 1983; Chan and Xu 1985), accepted either a settlement with a population of more than 3,000, of whom more than 70 per cent are 'non-agricultural', or a settlement with a population of 2,500–3,000, of whom more than 85 per cent are 'non-agricultural' (SSB 1983a, p. 576; Chan and Xu 1985). The 'agricultural' and 'non-agricultural' classification was based on household registration, another important issue requiring further examination later. The above set of town designation criteria was used between 1964 and 1982. Prior to 1964, slightly broader urban designation criteria were adopted, but the difference they made to the aggregate size of urban population was very small and can be considered negligible (Chan and Xu 1985, p. 593). Under this set of criteria, China's urban population was 211 million at the end of 1982, accounting for 21 per cent of the total population (Table 2.1, Column 2).

When the boundaries of urban administrative areas defined according to the above criteria—that is, the administrative boundaries of all urban districts and towns—roughly coincide with the boundaries of areas of urban activity (for example, built-up areas at an urban density and factories), in the urbanist's parlance, the urban administrative areas are neither 'overbounded' nor 'underbounded'. In such circumstances the total number of *de facto* residents in these urban administrative areas is a reasonable representation of the size of the urban population (United Nations 1974, p. 9). This was largely the case between 1949 and 1982, and the Total Population of Cities and Towns (*shizhen zongrenkou*) statistics, which include only the resident population in designated

Table 2.1 Urban Population in China, 1949–1990

Year End	National Total (Mill.)	TPCT (UAA) Size (Mill.)	TPCT (UAA) Growth Rate (%)	TPCT (UAA) % of Nation	TPCT (UC) Size (Mill.)	TPCT (UC) Growth Rate (%)	TPCT (UC) % of Nation	NPCT (UAA) Size (Mill.)	NPCT (UAA) Growth Rate (%)	NPCT (UAA) % of Nation	Implied APCT (UAA) Size (Mill.)	Implied APCT (UAA) Growth Rate (%)	Implied APCT (UAA) % of Nation
	1	2	3	4	5	6	7	8	9	10	11	12	13
1949	541.67	57.65		10.6									
1950	551.96	61.69	7.0	11.2									
1951	563.00	66.32	7.5	11.8									
1952	574.82	71.63	8.0	12.5									
1953	587.96	78.26	9.3	13.3									
1954	602.66	82.49	5.4	13.7									
1955	614.65	82.85	0.4	13.5									
1956	628.28	91.85	10.9	14.6									
1957	646.53	99.49	8.3	15.4									
1958	659.94	107.21	7.8	16.2									
1959	672.07	123.71	15.4	18.2									
1960	662.07	130.73	5.7	19.7									
1961	658.59	127.07	-2.8	19.3				106.03		16.1	21.04		3.2
1962	652.95	116.59	-8.2	17.3				98.19	-7.4	15.0	18.40	-12.6	2.8
1963	691.72	116.46	-0.1	16.8				100.07	1.9	14.5	16.39	-10.9	2.4
1964	704.99	129.50	11.2	18.4				98.85	-1.2	14.0	30.65	87.0	4.3
1965	725.38	130.45	0.7	18.0				101.70	2.9	14.0	28.75	-6.2	4.0
1966	745.42	133.13	2.1	17.9				103.01	1.3	13.8	30.12	4.8	4.0
1967	763.68	135.48	1.8	17.7				106.09	3.0	13.9	29.39	-2.4	3.8
1968	785.34	138.38	2.1	17.6				104.72	-1.3	13.3	33.66	14.5	4.3
1969	806.71	141.17	2.0	17.5				104.01	-0.7	12.9	37.16	10.4	4.6
1970	829.92	144.24	2.2	17.4				105.26	1.2	12.7	38.99	4.9	4.7
1971	852.29	147.11	2.0	17.3				107.09	1.7	12.6	40.02	2.7	4.7

Table 2.1 (cont.)

Year End	National Total (Mill.)	TPCT (UAA) Size (Mill.)	TPCT (UAA) Growth Rate (%)	TPCT (UAA) % of Nation	TPCT (UC) Size (Mill.)	TPCT (UC) Growth Rate (%)	TPCT (UC) % of Nation	NPCT (UAA) Size (Mill.)	NPCT (UAA) Growth Rate (%)	NPCT (UAA) % of Nation	Implied APCT (UAA) Size (Mill.)	Implied APCT (UAA) Growth Rate (%)	Implied APCT (UAA) % of Nation
1972	871.77	149.35	1.5	17.1				110.70	3.4	12.7	38.65	-3.4	4.4
1973	892.11	153.45	2.7	17.2				113.49	2.5	12.7	39.96	3.4	4.5
1974	908.59	155.95	1.6	17.2				114.58	1.0	12.6	41.37	3.5	4.6
1975	924.20	160.30	2.8	17.3				116.09	1.3	12.6	44.21	6.9	4.8
1976	937.17	163.41	1.9	17.4				117.92	1.6	12.6	45.49	2.9	4.9
1977	949.74	166.69	2.0	17.6				119.56	1.4	12.6	47.13	3.6	5.0
1978	962.59	172.45	3.5	17.9				124.42	4.1	12.9	48.03	1.9	5.0
1979	975.42	184.95	7.2	19.0				133.12	7.0	13.6	51.83	7.9	5.3
1980	987.05	191.40	3.5	19.4				138.63	4.1	14.0	52.77	1.8	5.3
1981	1000.72	201.71	5.4	20.2				143.20	3.3	14.3	58.51	10.9	5.8
1982	1016.54	211.31	4.8	20.8	214.80		21.1	147.15	2.8	14.5	64.16	9.7	6.3
1983	1030.08	241.50	14.3	23.4	222.74	3.7	21.6	152.35	3.5	14.3	89.15	38.9	8.7
1984	1043.57	331.36	37.2	31.8	240.17	7.8	23.0	166.89	9.5	14.6	164.47	84.5	15.8
1985	1058.51	384.46	16.0	36.3	250.94	4.5	23.7	179.71	7.7	15.8	204.75	24.5	19.3
1986	1075.07	441.03	14.7	41.0	263.66	5.1	24.5	181.91	1.2	16.7	259.12	26.6	24.1
1987	1093.00	503.62	14.2	46.1	276.74	5.0	25.3	191.17	5.1	16.6	312.45	20.6	28.6
1988	1110.26	543.69	8.0	49.0	286.61	3.6	25.8	200.82	5.0	17.2	342.87	9.7	30.9
1989	1127.04	574.94	5.7	51.0	295.40	3.1	26.2	211.70	5.4	17.8	363.24	5.9	32.2
1990	1143.33	604.47	5.1	52.9	301.91	2.2	26.4	202.53	-4.3	18.5	401.94	10.7	35.2

Notes and Sources:

TPCT (UAA): Total Population of Cities and Towns (Urban administrative areas-based). SSB (1990a); CASS (1991).

TPCT (UC): Total Population of Cities and Towns (UAA/Committees-based). SSB (1991a)

NPCT (UAA) Non-agricultural Population of Cities and Towns (UAA-based) and CASS (1990; 1991). Note that the figures are different than those in Ma and Cui (1987). NPCT was not used prior to 1962 (Hu and Chen 1984; Chan 1987).

APCT (UAA) Agricultural Population of Cities and Towns (UAA-based). APCT (UAA) = TPCT (UAA) − NPCT (UAA).

towns and in urban districts of cities, are relevant (Table 2.1, Column 2) (see also Chan 1987). Many also agree that the urban administrative area-based Total Population of Cities and Towns statistics in this period are internationally comparable (Hu and Chen 1984; Chan and Xu 1985; Banister 1986).

The consistency and usefulness of these statistics have, however, been profoundly altered by changes in the criteria for urban designations and in the delimiting of the physical urban boundaries since 1983. Following the post-Mao policy of promoting urban-based development (examined in Chapter Four), many more towns and cities were allowed to be designated (Yeh and Xu 1989). The State Council in November 1984 promulgated a new set of criteria for designating towns, which greatly relaxed the requirements (Appendix 2.1). A number of provincial governments, which controlled actual town designations, also exercised a significant degree of flexibility in the 1980s in carrying out this task (Xu et al. 1985; Lee 1989, p. 779). The result was that the number of designated towns rose precipitously from 2,781 in 1983 to 6,211 in 1984, and continued to rise to about 9,000 in 1987 and stabilized at that level until 1990 (Table 2.2). Most of these newly designated towns were established along the lines of 'the town leading (administering) the development of the countryside'. The boundary of the newly designated town (hence, the urban administrative area) covered exactly that of the previous township (xiang). Inevitably, the newly designated towns include large stretches of rural areas and a huge proportion of the rural population. Such an arrangement was based on the consideration that existing township bureaucracies could readily be transformed into town bureaucracies without much change to the existing setup and areas under their administration (see Appendix 2.1).

In a similar move, as part of the same effort to promote rural–urban development, many counties since 1983 have been allowed to be reclassified as 'cities' under certain conditions. A revised State Council directive, promulgated in 1986 and still in use, stipulated that, for instance, a county with a total population of less than 500,000, a county-town of 'non-agricultural' population of at least 100,000, and an annual output of at least RMB¥300 million also qualifies for city designation (Appendix 2.1). The important change here was that the complete county, not just the town, would be reclassified as the city. As expected, the newly designated cities, almost all at the county level, contain large

Table 2.2 Number of Officially Designated Urban Places

Year-end	Cities	Towns	Total
1953	166	5,402	7,068
1956	175	3,672	3,847
1961	208	4,429	4,637
1964	169	2,877	3,046
1970	176	na	na
1976	187	3,261	3,448
1978	191	2,850	3,041
1980	217	2,874	3,091
1981	229	2,845	3,074
1982	239	2,819	3,058
1983	271	2,781	3,052
1984	295	6,211	6,506
1985	324	7,511	7,835
1986	347	8,464	8,811
1987	381	9,121	9,502
1988	432	8,614	9,046
1989	446	9,088	9,534
1990*	456*	11,935*	12,391*

Notes: *   mid-year census figure
          na not available
Sources: Mainly from CASS (1990, pp. 300 and 302); also from Chan and Xu
          (1985 Table 2); State Council (1991, pp. 33–5). The figures used here
          for cities are slightly different from those tabulated by the Ministry of
          Internal Affairs.

expanses of rural areas and a huge rural population within their urban administrative areas. Yulin, Qinzhou, and Bose in Guangxi are good examples.[5]

   The new developments, though administratively convenient and probably desirable in promoting 'lateral' (spatial) integration in many respects,[6] have upset totally the relatively reasonable statistical consistency of defining urban population based on urban administrative areas prior to 1983. Figure 2.2 presents a graphic generalization of the newly revised spatial administration structure. Many villages have since 1983 been included within the urban administrative areas of cities and towns. Thus, the Total Population of Cities and Towns tabulated on the urban administrative areas has since been greatly inflated: it more than doubled from 211 million in 1982 to 574 million in 1989 (Table 2.1, Column 2). The common sources of inflation come from many newly designated county-level cities and towns (Zhou 1989). This has rendered the urban administrative area-based Total Population of Cities and Towns completely unusable as a measure of China's urban population since 1983.

Furthermore, the definition of urban population is complicated by a simultaneous usage of another 'urban' population definition, the Non-agricultural Population of Cities and Towns (*feinongye chengzhen renkou*), which is based primarily on household registration classification status. The Chinese household registration (*hukou*) system categorizes the entire population as 'peasants' and 'non-peasants', or more commonly 'agricultural' and 'non-agricultural'.[7] Members of the latter group are distinguished by their entitlement to 'commodity food grain' (*shangpinliang*) rations from the state. The system has over time changed from serving primarily as a classification scheme for differentiating occupational or residential affiliations to a mechanism for determining entitlements to state-supplied foods ('commodity grain'), employment, housing, and other benefits (Chan and Tsui 1992). While the 'agricultural' population was most probably made up of *bona fide* agriculturists in the 1950s, many peasants from townships and previously, communes, working in non-agricultural jobs as contract workers (*hetong gong*), temporary workers (*linshi gong*), or in the category of 'both workers and peasants' (*yigong yinong*) in urban areas have been classified under the household registration as 'agricultural' population because they are still considered as township/commune members and are not eligible for commodity grain or other urban rations. Such an agricultural/non-agricultural classification of the population is essentially of a *de jure* nature.

The dual system of agricultural/non-agricultural classification based on household registration and urban/rural classification by residence results in a grouping of the country's entire population into four major categories: 'urban agricultural' (A), 'rural agricultural' (B), 'urban non-agricultural' (C), and 'rural non-agricultural' (D). Their composition and relationships are detailed in Table 2.3. Various statistics serving different planning and policy purposes are used based on different combinations of these categories. For example, the Total Population of Cities and Towns is formed by aggregating (A) and (C); the Non-agricultural Population of Cities and Towns refers only to (C). The Non-agricultural Population of Cities and Towns was often referred to as *chengzhen renkou*, which

Table 2.3 Composition and Relationships of Urban, Rural, Agricultural, and Non-agricultural Populations

	By Household Registration Status	
	Agricultural (826.6, 82.6%)	Non-Agricultural (174.1, 17.3%)
By Residence		
	A (58.5, 5.8%)	C (143.2, 14.3%)
DESIGNATED URBAN AREAS (201.7, 20.2%)	i. 'temporary' and contract workers ii. 'peasant-workers' iii. 'peasants' in urban petty trades iv. agriculturalists v. dependents of all above	i. staff and workers, and their dependents (including retirees, etc.) ii. workers in individual enterprises and their dependents
	B (768.1, 76.8%)	D (30.9, 3.1%)
RURAL AREAS (799.0, 79.8%)	i. agricuturalists except in state farms ii. labourers in various enterprises run by communes and brigades in rural areas iii. dependents of (i) and (ii) iv. settled youths from urban origins	i. workers in state-run agro-enterprises, and their dependents ii. state cadres and scientific personnel in rural areas, and their dependents

Note: Figures in parenthesis represent the sizes (in millions) and percentages of national population totals of the respective groups in 1981.

Population Statistics	Composition
1. *Shizhen zongrenkou* (Total* Population of Cities and Towns)	= A+C
2. *Xiangcun zongrenkou* (Total* Rural Population)	= B+D
3. *Feinongye chengzhen renkou* (Non-agricultural Population of Cities and Towns)	= C
4. *Xiangcun renkou* (Rural Population)	= A+B+D
5. *Nongye renkou* (Agricultural Population)	= A+B
6. *Feinongye renkou* (Non-agricultural Population)	= C+D

* Note that the word 'total' here is a direct translation of the Chinese word '*zong*'. It does not necessarily mean a more inclusive concept in the context of rural population (compare 'Total Rural Population' and 'Rural Population').

Source: Chan and Tsui (1992); CASS (1991, p. 425)

means 'the population of cities and towns'. A major confusion here is that Chinese statistical authorities and many researchers, especially before 1982, used the Non-agricultural Population of Cities and Towns to represent the 'urban' population without stating this point explicitly (Chan and Xu 1985).

In general, when the urban administrative areas are not over-bounded or underbounded, the Total Population of Cities and Towns is preferred to the Non-agricultural Population of Cities and Towns because the former includes the so-called 'urban agri-cultural' population, which not only represents part of the *de facto* urban population,[8] but also has been the most active component of urban growth since the early 1960s. However, the enormous 'overbounding' of many, especially newly designated, cities and towns since 1983 has invalidated the usefulness of the Total Population of Cities and Towns as an urban population indicator. As a result, information about the 'urban' population—based on the above definition—generated by the State Statistical Bureau (1988b) and the Chinese Academy of Social Sciences (1988) becomes less useful for any analytical work. Studies of 'urban' in-migrants and population (e.g. Goldstein 1990) based on these two sources inevitably suffer the same problem. Other researchers have returned to use the Non-agricultural Population of Cities and Towns statistics as representing the urban population, but the result is not satisfactory either. The most important reason for this is that the Non-agricultural Population of Cities and Towns, while being less sensitive to the urban bounding problems, has excluded totally the 'urban agricultural' population, which has been the fastest-growing segment in most Chinese urban centres in the last two decades. The exclusion of the 'urban agricultural' segment from the urban count significantly under-represents the actual temporal change in recent decades. The near impossibility of meaningfully defining the Chinese urban population prompted a series of critiques and proposals by scholars in the late 1980s (e.g. Chan 1987; Feng 1988; Wang and Han 1989).

1990 Definitions

Apparently in response to the many criticisms lodged against the unsatisfactory urban/rural classification schemes used in the 1980s, the Chinese statistical authorities, without altering the existing administrative structure, introduced with the 1990 Census another

dimension to the definition of urban and rural populations—
smaller, sub-settlement divisions (State Council 1991). This new
system has restored, to a significant degree, the temporal and
international comparability of the Chinese official urban population counts, though still not in the way demanded by scholars (e.g.
Zhou and Sun 1992). Admittedly, the task of differentiating urban
from rural areas has been much harder in the post-Mao era as
the previous policy of rigidly segmenting the rural and urban sectors has given way to a more lenient policy, resulting in surges in
the population mobility and expansion of industrial production in
the countryside (see Chapter Four). Urban boundaries are no
longer as clear-cut as they used to be.

Since large administrative boundaries at the settlement (cities
and towns or urban administrative area) level do not necessarily
differentiate in a satisfactory manner between the urban and rural
populations in these settlements, the 1990 Census used smaller,
sub-settlement administrative jurisdictions based on 'residents'
committees' (*jumin weiyuanhui*) and 'villagers' committees' (*cun-
min weiyuanhui*) and combined them with the existing settlements
(cities and towns) to set up a new scheme of urban and rural population. Residents' committees, almost all in urbanized areas, have
a high proportion (about 72 per cent in 1990[9]) of the residents in
these areas holding 'non-agricultural' household registration status and an even higher proportion, probably over 80 per cent, in
urban occupations (Zhou and Sun 1992). Villagers' committees,
on the other hand, set up in villages and run by villagers themselves, are theoretically rural based (State Council 1987a).

Precisely, the urban population in the 1990 Census is composed
of the following (refer to Figure 2.2):

1. for provincial/prefectural-level cities (which are subdivided
into urban districts), the entire resident population of urban districts;

2. for county-level cities (without further division into urban
districts), only the resident population of 'streets' (*jiadao*), which
are constituted by residents' committees;

3. for towns, with the exception of those within provincial/pre-
fectural cities (in practice, only prefectural-level) cities, the population of all residents' committees.

The population size of each category reported by the 1990
Census is detailed in Appendix 2.2. Following the previous practice of defining Total Population of Cities and Towns, the new

census has adopted the *de facto* principle (as contrasted to the *de jure* criterion in the Non-agricultural Population of Cities and Towns) in defining urban population, which is still referred to as the '*shizhen zongrenkou*'. In the provincial/prefectural cities where serious overbounding tends to be limited to a number of highly industrial cities (e.g. Zipo and Liupanshui), the urban population is defined by the resident population of the urban administrative areas. In the categories of county-level cities and towns, where overbounding is serious and pervasive, the urban administrative areas principle is abandoned. Instead, a finer criterion is introduced to exclude non-urbanized areas, mostly under villagers' committees, from the urban population counts. Overall, a mixture of criteria based on urban administrative areas and local committees of governance is used. To differentiate this new set from the previous purely urban administrative area-based Total Population of Cities and Towns, I will refer hereafter to the new series as the urban administrative area/Committee-based Total Population of Cities and Towns. The urban population size tabulated on the above definition came to 296.5 million, or 26.2 per cent of the nation's total in mid-1990.[10] This figure comes very close to previous estimates made by researchers using the urban administrative area-based Total Population of Cities and Towns statistics after adjusting for overbounding (Wei 1989; Chan 1992a).

Despite some minor problems (Zhou and Sun 1992; He *et al.* 1992; Ding 1991), the aggregate urban population figure at the national level produced by the 1990 Census is regarded by many as reasonable and comparable to the Total Population of Cities and Towns figure generated by the 1982 Census. The reasons for this approval are as follows.

1. The serious overbounding problem in the population figures of towns and county-level cities since 1983 has been overcome by applying the residents' committee criterion.

2. Provincial/prefectural-level cities in the 1990 Census still include a 65.4 million, mostly rural, population in areas under village committees, thus causing overbounding in the 1990 definitions (Appendix 2.2). However, witnessing the prevalence of rural non-agricultural enterprises in many of these villages in the peri-urban zone at the fringe of major metropolises of coastal China in the late 1980s, one can make a strong case for treating a significant portion of this administratively 'village population' in the peri-urban zone as an urban or 'proto-urban' population (Cui and Wu

1990; Gu 1993). These areas are what McGee (1991) has termed *desa kota* regions, where existing agricultural activities are densely mixed with rapidly expanding non-agricultural production, which is intricately linked to factories in, and investment from, the cities. Furthermore, some of the villagers in these regions actually worked in jobs in the 'informal' economy in the cities.

3. Equally important, the overbounding caused by the above has been offset in aggregate terms by the undercounting of a *de facto* urban population of at least 45 million in the *zili kouliang hu* ('households with self-supplied grains') category and an unknown population in market towns (*jizhen*) which had already met the town designation criteria but had not yet been so classified (Ding 1991; Zhou and Sun 1992).

4. Though the designation criteria used since 1983 are broader than those used before, the 1983 criteria are more reflective of the true urbanization level in the 1980s in view of the prevalence of non-agricultural activities occurring in many rural settlements, especially in the coastal regions in the post-1983 era (Gu 1993).

Indeed, considering all these factors and the fact that most of the 'floating population' (examined below) have not been counted in the above definition, one is inclined to think that the urban population count based on the 1990 Census definition is slightly on the low side. Nevertheless, apparently owing to the greater acceptance of this definition, the State Statistical Bureau has recently reworked retrospectively the urban administrative area-based Total Population of Cities and Towns statistics of 1982–90 to produce an urban administrative area/Committee-based Total Population of Cities and Towns series for this period (Table 2.1, Column 5). This series has greatly facilitated the following analysis of the urbanization trends in the post-Mao period.

Overall Urbanization Trends

The various urban population figures from Table 2.1 appear in graph form in Figure 2.3. One can easily appreciate from the figure the importance of sorting out the three series, as they depict very diverse trends. Based on the above discussion, the Total Population of Cities and Towns is used here for studying urban population growth trends since 1949. Precisely, the urban administrative areas-based Total Population of Cities and Towns

Figure 2.3 Urbanization Levels in China, 1949–1990

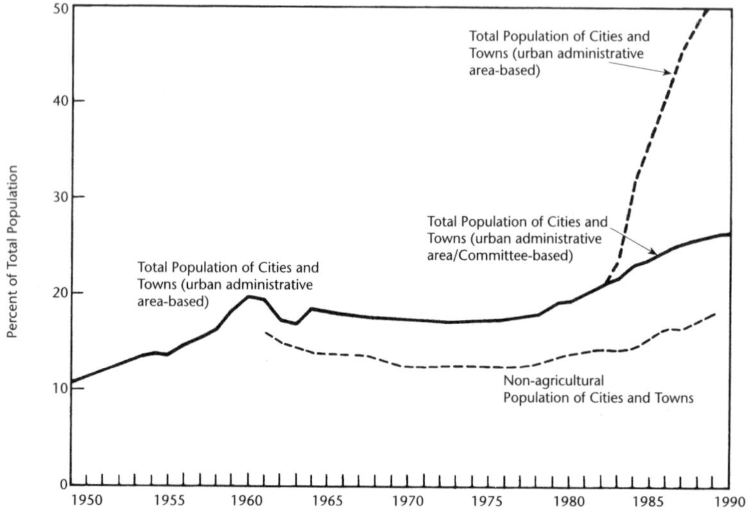

Source: Table 2.1

is used for the period 1949–82 and the urban administrative area/ Committee-based Total Population of Cities and Towns for 1983–90 (Table 2.1). The calculated average annual growth rate of urban population between 1949 and 1990 is then 4.0 per cent, relatively high by world standards, and similar to those of other developing countries (United Nations 1980). A close examination of Figure 2.3 indicates that there were a number of twists and turns in China's post-1949 urbanization path, unlike the relatively smooth and evolutionary trails taken by many other developing countries. For example, there was a precipitous drop of two points in the urban population percentage between 1961 and 1962. Within the fifteen years from 1962, the level of urbanization remained scarcely changed. The stability is more striking in view of the rapid industrialization during the same period. These special features reflect the population dynamics as well as the effects of political and economic forces at work in this period.

As a first step in studying urbanization, the components of urban population growth, urban natural increase and net urban in-migration, need to be decomposed. The former is a natural population growth process related to the aspatial aspect of population dynamics. The latter, however, is a process of spatial re-distribution of population contributing directly to urbanization. For our purpose, the focus is on migration of longer-term significance. Following standard practices, short-term circulators, such as visitors, tourists, business travellers, and commuters, are not defined here as 'migrants', though they have also an important impact on many large cities in China today and are potentially migrants as well.

Most of the migration statistics generated by the Chinese household registration system suffer from several problems, rendering them inaccurate and incomplete records of rural–urban migration flows.[11] Nor is the migration information collected by two surveys carried out in the second half of the 1980s (SSB 1988b; CASS 1988) directly usable for our purposes here, because of the inappropriate 'urban' definition used around that time. Hence, the present study is forced to work mainly with implied net urban in-migration figures derived indirectly by the so-called 'residual methods' based on vital rates (United Nations 1974). Since systematic and detailed information on the reclassification of urban boundaries is not available,[12] as in many other similar studies, figures about net rural–urban migration presented in this chapter also include net population gain or loss due to urban reclassification. As long as the urban population (Total Population of Cities and Towns) statistics used here reasonably reflect the population size in truly urbanized areas, population gains due to the expansion of physically urbanized terrain are arguably part of the urbanization process and similar to urban in-migration (United Nations 1974).

Estimates of annual net urban in-migration presented here for 1950–81 come from my earlier study (Chan 1988a). Those after 1982 are newly constructed estimates based on the same principle and procedures. The derivations and estimates are detailed in Appendix 2.3. A summary of the components of urban growth by period is presented in Table 2.4. These periods correspond roughly to the different phases of political and economic development in China, reflecting the underlying premise that urban growth and political and economic factors are closely associated in the Chinese context. The remaining part of this chapter is primarily concerned with urban demographic growth and rural–urban migration in different periods. A thorough examination of the policies affecting urbanization is deferred to the next two chapters.

Table 2.4 Components of Urban Growth by Period, 1950–1990

Period	No. of Years Covered 1	Average Annual Urban Growth Absolute Size (Mill.) 2	Average Annual Urban Growth Rate (%) 3	Average Change in Urban % per year (%) 4	Natural Increase Av. Annual (Mill.) 5	Natural Increase Size (%) 6	Net In-migration Av. Annual (Mill.) 7	Net In-migration Size (%) 8
I 1950–57	8	5.6	7.2	0.59	2.26	40	3.35	60
II 1958–60	3	10.4	9.1	1.45	1.91	18	8.50	82
III 1961–65	5	-2.6	-2.1	-0.63	2.99	#	-5.62	#
IV 1966–77	12	3.0	2.0	-0.04	2.09	69	0.93	31
V 1978–82	5	9.0	4.8	0.66	2.01	22	6.96	78
VI 1983–90	8	10.9	4.3	0.66	2.85	26	8.04	74
1950–90	41	5.6	4.0	0.39	2.36	42	3.28	58

Notes: Col. 1: This refers to the period inclusive of the years specified e.g. 1950–57 covers the time span from the beginning of 1950 to the end of 1957.

Col. 2: Adjustments have been made for changes in urban definition.

Col. 3: Average annual growth rates (r) is computed by use of an exponential growth formula: $r = \ln \{[P(t+n) - R]/P(t)\}/n \times 100\%$ where $P(t)$ and $P(t+n)$ are the populations at years t and $t+n$, respectively; and R is the population change due to urban reclassification.

Col. 4: This refers to the average annual gain in urban percentage points.

Col. 6 and 8: Expressed as percentage of Col. 2; # = cannot be computed due to negative net migration.

Sources: Chan (1988a) and Appendix 2.2

Period I: 1950-1957

The period 1950-7 was one of rapid urban population growth, averaging 7.2 per cent a year, more than twice the natural urban increase (about 3 per cent). This period coincides with the economic recovery in the Rehabilitation Period (1950-2) following the end of the civil war, and the phase of rapid industrialization under the First Five-year Plan (1953-7). Both high urban rates of natural growth, resulting from the post-war baby boom and reduced urban mortality, and high rates of net urban in-migration were responsible for the rapid urban population growth in this period. To be exact, in the first two or three, still unstable, years of the People's Republic, while millions of previous urban employees and their families returned to cities after the war, there was a massive campaign to remove vagrants, prostitutes, the unemployed, ex-nationalist officials, and soldiers from major cities. Shanghai provides an example of this type of migration. Reportedly, it lost about 620,000 people to out-migration in 1950 against only 570,000 in-migrants during the same year (Zhang, K. 1989).

The relative social stability in urban areas and the massive industrialization programme during the First Five-year Plan period (1953-7) turned cities into magnets for labourers from the countryside (Ma 1987). Millions of rural workers were recruited by rapidly mushrooming state industrial enterprises all over the country as part of the centrally planned industrialization. Others came looking for urban jobs on their own initiative, or were driven out by instability in the countryside as collectivization accelerated in 1956 (Howe 1971). Such movements were lawful under the freedom of migration clause in the freshly drawn up Constitution in 1954 (*Constitution of the PRC* 1954). At times, when the number of self-initiated rural migrants threatened to clog up railroads and strain urban infrastructures, the government took action to stop the so-called 'blind flows' (Tien 1973). About the same time, urban-educated youth were mobilized to remote regions like Xinjiang to participate in agricultural production (*Tongji gongzuo* 1957; Tien 1973), marking the beginning of China's youth rustication programme (Ma 1977).

By and large, however, comprehensive coercive administrative measures to restrict migration, through a system of household registrations and employment or study permits,[13] were not implemented until December 1957 (Zhang, Q. 1989), by which time serious outflows triggered by the rural communization programme starting in that year threatened to engulf Chinese cities. With relatively few effective controls on internal migration, the pattern of urban growth prior to 1958 resembled in many ways that in other economies undergoing rapid industrialization.

Period II: 1958–1960

The Great Leap Forward, begun in the spring of 1958, however, threw many of the regular setups, including the newly established migration control system, into disarray. This was a time when the Chinese leadership headed by Mao Zedong was willing to carry out massive internal purges of outspoken senior party officials and banish tens of thousands of intellectuals, in pursuance of the urgent and overriding task of industrialization to catch up with capitalist countries like Great Britain. In urbanization terms, the Great Leap Forward set in motion an unprecedented, explosive urban inflow. The government's all-out mobilization of popular enthusiasm to accelerate industrialization, particularly in iron and steel production, led to a dramatic increase in industrial employment in both state enterprises and hundreds of thousands of small industrial workshops all over the country almost overnight (Lardy 1987). The number of female workers in state enterprises rose from 3.3 million to 8.1 million in 1958 alone (All China Women's Federation and Shaanxi Provincial Women's Federation 1991). Despite earlier concerns about 'blind flows' to cities, millions of peasants were recruited by various types of urban enterprises at the local level to participate in the frantic industrialization drive. Rural–urban migration peaked in 1959 with an estimated annual net inflow of about 15 million. The influx of rural peasants pushed China's urban percentage from 16.2 per cent in 1958 to 19.7 per cent in 1960, the all-time high in the pre-1980 era.

Period III: 1961–1965

In sharp contrast to the previous period, the early 1960s was a time of continued net urban outflows. The extraordinary pace of rural–urban labour shift during the Great Leap Forward later contributed to labour shortages in the food-producing sector, which, combined with natural calamities and economic mismanagement, resulted in nationwide famine, claiming more than 20 million lives

(Ashton *et al.* 1984), with the heaviest casualties in the country-side. The catastrophic consequences of the Great Leap Forward made it clear to policy-makers in Beijing in 1961 that, at the pre-vailing level of agricultural productivity, China's grain production capacity was unable to sustain such a huge urban industrial pop-ulation.[14] To redress the dislocation, about 18 million urban work-ers and another 6 million dwellers, most of whom had migrated to the cities during the Great Leap Forward, were returned to their home villages during the period 1961–3 on the grounds that this move would help relieve both the burden commodity grain requisition imposed on the peasants and urban unemployment caused by the economic depression (Chen 1961; Zhao 1988).

The supply of grain to the urban population was further improved by an immediate and large increase in grain imports in 1961, which turned China into a net importer of food grain for the ensuing two decades. Furthermore, controls on cityward migration were made extremely stringent. Urban grain ration distribution was also tightened, making it difficult to buy food grain outside the state system. In 1964, the official definition of urban population was also restricted to the 'non-agricultural' segment of urban residents (that is, the Non-agricultural Population of Cities and Towns) (Chan and Xu 1985; Koshizawa 1988, p. 186; Zhou and Sun 1992). In the aftermath of the economic dislocation, the government fur-ther tightened urban consumption. The Daqing model of 'putting production first and living second' when building cities was also publicized for emulation by the whole nation (Zhao 1988). At the same time, to deal with the unemployment problem, the government made plans to relocate new graduates from the urban areas.

The number of urban residents resettled from the cities during the period 1961–3 is roughly equal to the number of urban entrants in 1958–60. In net terms, between 1961 and 1963 the country experienced a sustained decrease in urban population size for three years in a row. As a result, the urbanization level in 1963 reverted to the pre-Great Leap Forward level (17 per cent). The lessons learned from the Great Leap Forward and its aftermath have since had a profound impact on subsequent urbanization policies in that maintaining a manageable urban population, espe-cially with regard to food supply, became a prime concern for the government's strong interventionist policy in the urbanization process in the 1960s and 1970s (see Chan 1989).

Period IV: 1966–1977

This period covers the Cultural Revolution decade (1966–76) and saw the launch of the *shangshan xiaxiang* ('up to the mountains and down to the villages') movement. The movement was in response to the urban youth unemployment problem created by the political unrest, although revolutionary rhetoric claimed that it was an effort to narrow rural and urban differences and an opportunity for the urban youth 'to be re-educated by the peasants' (see, for example, Beijing Revolutionary Committee 1968). The movement was later institutionalized and enforced in an extensive and prolonged manner. With another resettlement campaign of *xiafang* (sending down) targeting cadres and intellectuals, the publicity from these resettlement campaigns created an impression for outsiders that this was a period of predominantly urban outflows (Chan and Xu 1985).

My calculations, however, show that taking 1966–77 as a whole, there was a net urban in-migration of about 11 million, or 30 per cent of the total urban population increase during this period (Table 2.4). The urban population grew at a rate slightly below that of the national population, resulting in a small decline in the urban percentage from 1965 to 1977. More importantly, given the known urban outflows, the small, but positive, net migration figure implies that there were voluminous two-way movements between urban and rural sectors in this period. Estimates put the gross urban out-migration at between 30 and 50 million[15] (Xu, J. 1986; Zhao 1989). By inference, the gross in-migration figure would be larger. This was a period of huge exchange (*da duiliu*) of urban and rural labour.

The reported stringency of migration controls in the 1960s and 1970s immediately prompts the question how such a massive inflow was possible. According to Chan and Xu (1985) and Chan (1992a), first, the groups of urban in-migrants during this period were largely peasant labourers recruited as 'temporary' and 'contract' workers (13–14 million in 1966–76), 'peasant-workers' and, in the 1970s, people returning from the rustication programme (urban youth returnees amounted to 4.4 million between 1974 and 1977) (see Table 2.5 and Feng and Zhao 1982). Second, with the return of order from the chaos of 1967 and 1968, urban industrial production began to gradually recover and generated demand for labour, especially in the Third Front region where new enterprises were

Table 2.5 Migratory Flows Generated By Rustication of Urban Youth, 1962–1979 (Size in 1,000s)

Year	Rusticated Youth	Returned Youth	Net Flows to Countryside
1962–66	1,293		
1967–68	1,997		
1969	2,674		
1970	1,064	4,014	5,332
1971	748		
1972	674		
1973	896		
1974	1,725	604	1,121
1975	2,369	1,398	971
1976	1,880	1,353	527
1977	1,717	1,030	687
1978	481	2,553	−2,072
1979	248	3,954	−3,706
Total	17,766	14,906	2860

Source: State Statistical Bureau (1987c, pp. 110–111)

being established. The rigid policy of those days, however, did not allow these enterprises to recruit from existing urban youth. Instead, able labourers had to be brought in from outside for urban capital construction and low-skilled industrial jobs. Third, most of the peasant in-migrants were not given 'non-agricultural' household registration status and were not officially considered as 'urban' residents entitled to urban benefits; nor were they counted under the restrictive definition of the Non-agricultural Population of Cities and Towns. These migrants thus provided a supply of cheap labour which urban industrial managers welcomed and which local urban authorities tolerated. There was also a small number of in-migrants who had circumvented the migration controls and came 'through the back door' by illicit means (State Council 1982a, 1982b).

Period V: 1978–1982

In the early 1970s, the unpopularity of the youth rustication programme had already forced the government to tacitly allow the return of some youth under various guises (Feng and Zhao 1982). Table 2.5 indicates that the average annual volume of return flows was about 1 million in the mid-1970s. The pressure for changing the rustication policy became much greater amidst the spontaneous outpouring of demands for redress of personal grievances from all sectors of society and corrections of errors in policy formulation in the early post-Mao years (Gold 1980). Pressed also by demonstrations of frustrated youths in Shanghai, in 1978 in particular, the government finally let almost all the rusticated urban youth and most sent-down intellectuals return to their original places of urban residence. At the same time, the inflow of rural peasant migrants in the form of 'temporary', 'contract' workers, and 'peasant-workers' continued. The return flows of rusticated youth—according to Table 2.5, amounting to 2.6 million in 1978 and 4 million in 1979—created serious unemployment problems in many cities from 1978 onward. Official statistics show that close to 6 per cent of the urban labour force was unemployed in 1978 and 1979 (Chan 1988a). The Chinese government has since made strenuous efforts to expand urban employment, particularly by revitalizing the urban collective service sector. About 38 million urban jobs were created from 1978 to 1982. In 1981 and 1982, the urban unemployment rate had dropped to less than 3 per cent, a level that would be considered normal in a market economy with full employment.

The sudden upsurge of return flows of rusticated youth and the government's more tolerant attitude to urban inflows led, as expected, to rapid urban growth, especially in 1979, which saw an urban inflow of 10 million, mostly of a 'recovery' nature. A total net rural–urban migration of 33 million was estimated for this five-year period. However, permanent in-migration to cities was still subject to many controls. The annual average net urban in-migration rate, 3.3 per cent, for 1980–2 was modest. Much of the urban in-migration in the 1980s also fell into the category of the 'urban agricultural' population.

Period VI: 1983–1990

Unlike the previous period, which was dominated by the sudden and relatively short-lived event of the return of urban educated youth, the post-1983 period was characterized by steadily high urban population growth, buttressed by increased urban and rural prosperity and more open policies brought about by the post-Mao economic reform. The urban administrative area/Committee-based Total Population of Cities and Towns data shows that the urban population soared by 87 million, or about 40 per cent, to reach 302 million, within eight years (Table 2.1). The average annual urban growth rate was maintained at the high level of 4.3 per cent. With a bigger urban population base, this meant larger annual increases, averaging 11 million a year. This sustained urban growth was bolstered by high levels of urban inflows and extensive expansion of urbanized areas, including an addition of thousands of newly designated small towns. The component of net rural–urban migration (including urban reclassification) accounted for about three-quarters of the urban population increase despite a moderate rise in the urban rate of natural growth in the mid-1980s.

The net rural–urban migration figure generated by the present study gives a larger, and probably more accurate, indication of the volume of rural–urban flows than has been reported by a State Statistical Bureau (1988b) national survey used by Goldstein (1990) and Li (1992). The State Statistical Bureau (1988b) counted a total net rural–urban migration of only 13 million in the five-year period between mid-1982 and mid-1987.[16] This figure is much smaller than the total net rural–urban migration volume (35 million) in the previous five-year period (1978–82), implying a significant drop in rural–urban mobility. Such an observation is obviously at variance with what has been observed and reported by many other studies conducted at different geographical scales (e.g. Wakabayashi 1990; Liu et al. 1990; Combined Research Group of Eight Cities 1990). Alternatively, the present study suggests a substantially higher figure of net rural–urban migration between 1982 and 1987, amounting to 49 million (tabulated from Appendix 2.3). Of this figure, about 20 million were generated simply by the establishment of roughly 6,000 additional designated towns (from undesignated market towns) during this period.[17] The reclassification component identified here represents mostly physical expansion of urbanized areas, and therefore is part of urbanization. Many of these newly designated towns also grew mainly by migration from villages prior to their designations.

To this stream of net rural–urban flows computed from the official urban administrative area/Committee-based Total Population of Cities and Towns statistics, one must also add a portion of the so-called '*liudong renkou*' (floating or mobile population), which has become prevalent in big cities since the early 1980s. The 'floating population' (as opposed to what the Chinese call *qianyi renkou* or 'migrants') refers loosely to the population staying in places where they do not have a permanent household registration status (Li and Hu 1991). This category includes tourists, people on business trips, traders, sojourners, peasant workers contracted from other places, vagrants, and other unemployed people (Table 2.6). Floating population, as the term suggests, is elusive and seasonal. Within any year, the size tends to be larger in the winter season when demand for work on farms is low, and usually reaches its peak in February or March immediately after the Spring Festival (see e.g. *Wen Hui Po* 1989a; *Ming Pao* 1992).

The period of stay ranges from a couple of days to a few years. Therefore, a portion of the floating population is made up of short-term visitors or seasonal circulators and should be excluded from any reasonable urban resident count. Some of those who stay longer may have registered with the authorities as '*jizhu*' or '*zhanzhu renkou*' (temporary population).[18] But there are people who, though staying for a relatively long period, for various reasons do not register their stay and, hence, are not included in the official records. Though the 1990 Census attempted to include everyone who stayed in urban places for at least one year in its urban counts, it is reasonable to expect that many of those without temporary residence certificates, especially those coming from the countryside, had evaded the enumeration, partly because of their mobility (many of them did not have fixed abodes) and partly because of their fear of subsequent evictions if they became known to the authorities (see also *Ming Pao* 1990a).

The elusive nature of the floating population thus hinders any serious attempt to derive an accurate count of them. Among the many surveys undertaken in the second half of the 1980s, the most comprehensive nation-wide study of floating population was carried out under the auspices of the Ministry of Construction (Li and Hu 1991). It covered eleven of the largest cities between 1988 and 1990 and reported that they had a total floating population of 8 million. The number of floaters ranged from 70,000 in Jilin to 2.09 million in Shanghai (Table 2.6). If the average ratio of floating population to the total population of the eleven cities is extrapolated to the entire urban population,[19] the total size of the floating population in the urban areas would have been around

Table 2.6 'Floating Population' in China, 1988–1990

A. Size of Floating Population in Selected Cities (in Millions)

Cities	Year	Size	Cities	Year	Size
Shanghai	1988	2.09	Beijing	1988	1.31
Guangzhou	1989	1.30	Wuhan	1990	1.20
Chengdu	1989	0.42	Hangzhou	1989	0.50
Taiyuan	1989	0.36	Zhengzhou	1989	0.37
Harbin	1989	0.23	Anshan	1989	0.16
Jilin	1989	0.07			

(i)   Total population size of above cities = 33.79 million
(ii) Aggregated Floating Population = 8.01 million
(iii) Floating Population as a percentage of population size of cities = 23.7%

B. Floating Population: Reasons for Moves

	%	Average Length of Stay (no. of days)
Seeking employment		
Nannies	9.0	307
Technicians	0.6	302
Construction workers	14.6	297
Other employment	10.5	236
Self-employed vendors	10.7	225
Self-employed repairers	2.9	207
	48.3	
Family/friends-related		
Seeking support from relatives	2.4	324
Visiting relatives and friends	8.0	224
	10.4	
Using Urban Facilities		
Study and training	4.0	210
Receiving medicare	3.2	136
On business	11.7	66
Attending conferences	1.8	16
Tourists	3.4	10
In transit	9.5	3
	33.6	
Others		
Vagrants	0.5	173
Unclassifiable	7.4	133
	7.9	
All	100.0	195

Sources: Li and Hu (1991)

70 million in 1989. The figure appears to be in line with others that have cited estimates of 50 million in 1985, 70 million in 1987, 70 million in 1989, and 50 million in November 1990 (*Wen Wei Po* 1989b; Li 1991; *Ming Pao* 1990b; Huang 1992).

Whatever its size, it is clear that not all of the floating population comes from the countryside. Based on a nation-wide survey of large cities, Li and Hu (1991, p. 12) report that 60 per cent of the floating population was from the countryside and the rest from inter-urban flows. Furthermore, two-thirds of 'floaters' are short-term visitors such as tourists and people on business trips staying from only a couple of days to less than a year and would not qualify as 'migrants' according to the 1990 Census criteria. Again, if these ratios are applied to the entire 40–70 million floating population, one arrives at a figure of between 24 and 42 million for those from the countryside.[20] Within those from the countryside, only one-third or 8–14 million were considered genuine urban residents (in contrast to short-term visitors). These 8–14 million (net) rural–urban migrants raise the overall urban population size in 1990 by 3 to 5 per cent and the overall urban percentage by about one point. These figures represent the maximum because some of the floating population has already been counted in the Total Population of Cities and Towns statistics produced by the 1990 census. If these 8–14 million urban dwellers represent additional gains in urban population between 1983 and 1990, then the average annual growth rate of the urban population would be raised from the 4.3 per cent calculated earlier to 4.7–4.9 per cent. The highest estimate of urban population at the end of 1990, therefore, would be about 316 (302+14) million.

The real impact of the floating population on urban centres was much more than is suggested by the number of 'permanent floaters' estimated above, especially in big cities where these floaters congregated. Two-thirds of the floaters were short-term visitors, but the perpetual existence of this sizeable group means another huge addition to the permanent *de facto* urban population. As mentioned before, the size of the floating population also fluctuated over time. The extant literature suggests that it increased from the early 1980s and peaked some time in 1987 and 1988. The size of the floating population dropped in 1989 and 1990 due to the implementation of an austerity programme that started in late 1988 and the political turmoil in 1989 (Li and Hu 1991). Higher flows reappeared in 1991 and especially 1992 following the return of stability and more open economic policies (*World Journal* 1992h). The trend in the second half of the 1980s appeared to have followed that of the overall net rural–urban migration.

In general, the high rate of urban inflows was generated by a host of factors. While these will be treated in depth in Chapter Four, a brief account is in order here. The success of rural reforms generated millions of footloose rural labourers, only to be absorbed by the expanding urban, especially non-state, sector, made possible by the relaxation of migration and employment controls. New provisions made by some provincial authorities in 1983 and by the State Council in 1984 allowed peasants engaged in non-agricultural work in market towns (*jizhen*[21]) to obtain residence status if they supplied their own food grain and had secured accommodation (*Renmin ribao* 1984). These people, classified as '*zili kouliang hu*' (households with self-supplied grains), were allowed to migrate not only to market towns, but also to designated towns, mining areas, city suburbs, and smaller cities, at least in Guangdong (*Nanfang ribao* 1984; Chan, J. 1990), but were ineligible for low-priced food grain and such urban benefits as housing and job security guaranteed by the state. The convergence of these changes with thousands of new town designations around 1984 help to explain the sudden upsurge of urban growth in 1984, as is shown in Appendix 2.3.

Besides, as part of the decentralization of administration, provincial and other local authorities were also granted more powers to approve conversions of agricultural households to non-agricultural status. This has also contributed to the rapid expansion in the number of non-agricultural households. Since there are no comparable urban administrative area/Committee-based Non-agricultural Population of Cities and Towns statistics for the post-1983 period to make an accurate assessment of its contribution to overall urban growth, a rough estimation indicates new conversions to urban non-agricultural population between 1980 and 1989, excluding those caused by natural population growth, were probably about half of that of the total net rural–urban migration in the same period.[22] *Guangmin ribao* (1989) reports that about half of the 40 million people whose household registration status was converted from 'agricultural' to 'non-agricultural' in 1980–8 gained approval from local authorities. Some local officials were also quick to capitalize on this opportunity to attract money and skills, as well as to make personal gains. Various *ad hoc* measures enabling

migration of varying degrees of permanency to urban places outside the narrow conventional channels have also been tried in a
few localities (these are examined in Chapter Four).

The only significant curb on the rising urban influx took place
temporarily following the government's austerity programme, which
started in late 1988 and was exacerbated by the urban unrest in
1989. Many small urban enterprises were closed down and numerous construction projects cancelled. Millions of temporary
workers were reportedly laid off. According to one source, in the
first nine months of 1989, several million of them had to be turned
back to the countryside (*Ming Pao* 1989b). The Chinese government estimated that by the end of 1990, the urban unemployment
rate would rise to 4 per cent (*Wen Wei Po* 1990c). Appendix 2.3
shows that the annual net urban in-migration rate dropped to less
than 1.9 per cent in 1989 and 1.1 per cent in 1990, as compared
to over 3.5 per cent in the mid-1980s.

Summary

This chapter has reviewed at length the various 'urban' definitions
in use and has tackled the problems that have emerged since 1983.
Based on a set of representative urban population statistics and
estimates of net rural–urban migration, an account of urbanization since 1949 has also been provided. After the rapid urban
growth and rural–urban migration experienced in the 1950s, the
early 1960s saw a major but brief reversal of the process with net
outflows from the urban to the rural areas. This was followed by
low rates of net urban in-migration during the latter half of the
1960s and most of the 1970s. A substantial increase in net urban
migration gains was witnessed in the post-1978 period, with the
increased migration of 'temporary population', though the average annual rate per unit of urban population during this period
was still lower than the average for the First Five-year Plan period in the 1950s.

Given the strong pressures for urbanization in China and
Zelinsky's (1971) prediction of rising rural–urban mobility at this
stage of development, the low rates of migration in the 1960s and
1970s suggest the efficacy of government policy in restricting migration. Without such controls, much higher inflows to cities would
have certainly been recorded. Urban natural growth rates have

decreased since the mid-1960s and also contribute, to a smaller degree, to the decline in urban growth rates. A comprehensive examination of policies affecting urbanization in the Maoist and post-Mao eras is the main focus of the following two chapters.

Notes

1. On pre-1949 urbanization, refer, for example, to Chang (1963), Skinner (ed.) (1977), Mann (1984) and Chao (1986).
2. For example, Ma and Cui (1987) adopt the 'Non-agricultural Population of Cities and Towns' as urban population, while Banister (1986) and Luo and Pannell (1991) choose to use the Total Population of Cities and Towns. Problems with these series are explained later.
3. *Shi* is also translated as 'municipality'. For consistency, the term 'city' is used here throughout. Precisely, officially designated cities and towns are formally termed '*jianzhishi*' and '*jianzhizhen*' in Chinese. Many of the smallest urban settlements, often referred to by the Chinese as '*jizhen*' (market towns), are not officially designated as 'urban'.
4. See also Table 3.4 and regulations regarding 'urban maintenance and construction tax' in 1978 and 1985 (Editing Committee 1989, pp. 123–4). City governments are allowed to retain 7 per cent of the profits from enterprises within their administrative area, and town governments, 5 per cent for building and maintaining urban infrastructures. In rural areas, the tax rate is only 1 per cent. (For private and collective rural enterprises, the 5 per cent tax might actually serve as a disincentive to move from rural areas to towns [Xu *et al.* 1985]). According to Koshizawa (1988), other sources, such as grants and investments from the central government and funds raised through user charges, are more important in financing urban construction. From his survey in Shandong, Gao (1991) also reports that each (presumably 'permanent') resident receives RMB¥8 (per month) as food subsidies from the state while those in cities receive RMB¥10 each. Rural residents are not entitled to the food subsidies.
5. A few existing cities also expanded their 'suburban district' boundaries to include some townships and towns.
6. Instead of simply being an 'administrative flat', as Goldstein (1990, p. 697) suggested.
7. Strictly speaking, there is a minor difference between the 'peasant/non-peasant' and 'agricultural/non-agricultural' classification of population as

defined by the Chinese statistical authorities. State farm workers are 'non-peasants' but are part of the 'agricultural' population according to the State Statistical Bureau (see Zhang 1987; Chan and Tsui 1992). In this chapter, Table 2.3 included, 'agricultural' population is treated as synonymous with 'peasants'.

8. In 1982, the 'urban agricultural' population accounted for about 30 per cent of the total urban population—see (C) in Table 2.3. Only a very small portion of the 'urban agricultural' population was engaged in farming; most of it also catered to nearby urban markets. Most Chinese analysts consider the 30 per cent a reasonable approximation of the 'genuine' urban population who have not been given 'non-agricultural' registration status in urban areas (see also Zhang 1989; Tian 1989).

9. This compares favourably with 68 per cent in the 1982 Total Population of Cities and Towns counts (Zhou and Sun 1992).

10. Based on a purely urban administrative area criterion, the urban population would be 601.4 million, or 53.3 per cent of the total population of the nation (see Appendix 2.2).

11. These statistics—at their 'face value'—however, have been used by Li (1992). See a review by Chan and Yang (1992).

12. Even Goldstein (1990), who, as the title of his paper suggests, purports to study the effect of reclassification on urbanization, provides little concrete information on this aspect. CASS (1988), bearing in mind caveats of this study examined below, reports that natural increase, net migration, and urban reclassification accounted for 4.2 per cent, 46.3 per cent, and 49.5 per cent respectively, of the population growth of towns (based on the urban administrative area classification) between 1982 and 1987.

13. More details are given in Chapters Three and Four. The migration restriction policy promulgated in late 1957 is technically a violation of the 1954 Constitution. The clause about migration freedom was eliminated in the later constitutions (PRC, *Documents of the . . . 1975; Constitution of the PRC* 1982).

14. A party meeting held in May and June 1961 accepted Chen Yun's proposal to implement a programme to reduce the size of the urban population by at least 20 million in the coming three years from 129 million at the end of 1960 (Chen 1961; Liu 1989, pp. 252–3).

15. Zhao (1988) suggested that about 15 million urban youth were resettled. Added to this were another 20 million resettled through the *xiafang* campaigns and 15 million through other means.

16. In heavily overbounded urban administrative areas, migration from non-urbanized (rural) areas to urbanized areas within the same administratively 'urban' boundary was not tabulated as 'urban-to-urban' migration, as in SSB (1988b) and CASS (1988). If those urban places had not been 'overbounded', the above type of migration would have been counted as rural–urban migration.

17. Assuming that each has a population of slightly above 3,000.

18. The Chinese household regulations require one to obtain a 'temporary residence certificate' for any stay over three days in a place different from where one has registered one's household (*Hukou dengji tiaoli* 1958). In the 1980s, it was fairly easy to pay for and obtain a temporary residence certificate in many cities provided one already had a job and a place to stay (or at least, an address to report). The certificate provided some legality to temporary residence status.

19. Assuming that floating population is 23.7 per cent of the urban population, as in the eleven-city survey.

20. This is also in line with what is reported in *Ming Pao* (1989, p. 10), which cites a figure of about 30 million peasants migrating to work outside their home villages in the second half of the 1980s.

21. Normally, *jizhen* refers to towns without official designations. However, judging from the text of the State Council's notice in which the policy was made known (*Renmin ribao* 1984), it appears that *jizhen* here also includes designated towns except for the county towns (*xiancheng*).

22. Computed from Table 2.1, assuming that 80 per cent of all the urban natural population growth was in the Non-agricultural Population of Cities and Towns category.

3 Policies to Restrict Urbanization in the Maoist Era

> Like many city walls in Europe and the Middle East, those in China were built essentially to protect palaces, temples, granaries, residences, and certain natural resources against barbarian invasion, tribal uprising, and peasant rebellions.
>
> (Chang 1977, p. 77)

THE low urban growth rate and stagnation in the urbanization level in the 1961–77 period, documented in the previous chapter, has in the past been hailed as a great achievement of Chinese policy. According to the so-called 'pro-rural' explanation, Maoist ideology gave priority to agricultural development, leading to a series of 'anti-urban' consumption and 'anti-urbanization' policies. Low urban growth and restriction of rural–urban mobility formed central components of the supposedly unique Maoist 'pro-rural' model of development. In what is to follow in this chapter, however, an explanation sharply different from the previous one is advanced. The proposition put forth is that Chinese (anti-)urbanization policies in the Maoist era were based upon a 'closed-city' strategy common to economies under classical socialism, a strategy that depended upon economic development policies heavily biased against agriculture and consumption.

It is important to make clear at the outset my emphasis in this chapter. Given that urbanization is a complex multi-faceted process, a comprehensive understanding would require considering all the relevant factors, including historical, political, socio-economic, and geographical aspects. While the indispensability of a multifactorial approach cannot be underlined too strongly, the attention in this chapter is nevertheless confined to a single set of explanatory factors associated with the socialist system and related industrialization strategy. The concentration here is on the lasting, long-term features of practices and policies, instead of the short-term vacillations, which have been dealt with to some degree in Chapter Two and elsewhere (e.g. Chan 1989). No one can argue that such an approach will account for every aspect of urbanization, but the set of elements identified below is the single most important dimension of China's urbanization in the period under study.[1] Following such an approach, the first part of this chapter identifies the major principles governing socialist urbanization based on a synthesis of the existing literature on urbanization in Soviet-type economies in the relevant stage. The stylized framework outlined then permits in the second part an analysis and evaluation of the Chinese situation in the Maoist era.

Urban Population Growth under Classical Socialism: A Generalized Framework

Urbanization in the early stage of industrialization[2] is, in essence, the spatial manifestation of the economic 'structural transformation', and is characterized by a massive shift of labour away from agricultural to non-agricultural activities in the production structure. At the risk of over-simplification, a framework permitting some quantitative and temporal comparisons between industrial development and urban population growth is set up below. This is based on the numerical relationship implied in the classical 'basic/non-basic' formulation, treating the size of urban population as a function of the size of industrial or 'basic' population (Ullman and Dacey 1962; Clark 1982), though, industrialization is possible, at higher costs, with limited or even no urbanization.[3] To produce a certain amount of industrial output, Q, the minimum amount of urban population (UP) required depends on the 'urbanization multiplier' of the industrial labour directly required in the production.[4] The multiplier is determined in turn by a host of variables, ranging from the ancillary service population needed, the proportion of dependent population, and so on. The details are explained below. UP is expressed as follows:

$$UP = Li \times UM \tag{1}$$

or

$$UP = Li \times (s \times u \times e) \tag{2}$$

where Li: industrial employment; UM: 'urbanization multiplier' of Li ('urban multiplier' for short); s: the service employment-multiplier (>1); u: the degree of urbanization of non-agricultural employment (<1); and e: the non-working population multiplier (>1).

Furthermore, 's' can also be expressed as Ln/Li, where $Ln = Li + Ls$, and Ls is the labour providing the services (for example, administration, transportation, and research) for the production of Q, as well as for other consumption-oriented activities such as retail and catering. Such a formulation emphasizes the demand side and the propulsive role of manufacturing, as well as the derivative or auxiliary role of services and, as will be shown later, concurs broadly with the priority accorded to industry in a socialist economy. The relationship between manufacturing and services is here expressed in terms of economic multipliers.

The value of 'u' rests on the definition of urban areas, the industrial locational patterns (whether or not concentrated), and the degree of commuting by urban labour (the so-called 'migration substitution'). The multiplier 'e' measures the number of people (including the worker himself or herself) supported by one worker in the non-agricultural sector. It is a function of the family size (the number of children per household), the labour participation rate, and the unemployment rate of the working population. As will be made clear later, socialist central planners at the macro-level were able to introduce measures or manipulate conditions that directly or indirectly affected the various multipliers to achieve their objectives. This is paralleled to some degree at the micro-level by the behaviour of local bureaucrats and managers.

'Classical socialism,' after Kornai (1992), refers to the practice by a number of socialist (Soviet-type) countries premised on two central components: a centralized command planning system based on nationalized or socialized economic enterprises and a Stalinist-type economic development strategy. Broadly speaking, historical experience indicates that classical socialism is a phase following the 'revolutionary-transitional system' (characterized by nationalization and socialization of economic sectors, and redistribution of property and income), and preceding 'reform socialism' (Kornai 1992). This has been the case in China and the Soviet Union.

While processes of sectoral transfer and population concentration similar to those in market economies occur under classical socialism (Musil 1980), the form of urbanization is distinct from that of market economies because of the following two factors. First, population mobility in the classical socialist system is to a high degree regulated by state planning in accordance with the needs of national economic development. Under the socialist system, individual labour mobility is subjected to many constraints imposed by the state, such as issuance or denial of a residence permit (Bornstein 1985; Smith 1989). Furthermore, urban employment and recruitment are also under full or almost full bureaucratic control of the state as the urban economy is demonetized and nationalized. Although there may be demand for sectoral transfers of population, this demand may be suppressed or met by 'substitution'. The degree of internal population mobility between socialist and market economies is a major factor in shaping the two different types of urbanization patterns. Socialist urbanization is often seen by researchers in socialist countries as 'a planned and managed process' in contrast to the 'voluntary', 'unplanned', 'anarchic' urban expansion occurring under capitalism (Kansky 1976; Musil 1980).

Second, socialist economies established during the immediate post-Second World War period have adopted economic systems and industrialization programmes under classical socialism (mostly in the 1950s and the 1960s), similar to those implemented in the USSR under Stalin. Because of the close link between the system, industrialization, and urbanization, this has also produced a 'standardized' socialist urban development pattern. The economic growth strategy under classical socialism, combined with 'soft' budget constraints at the individual industrial enterprise's level (Kornai 1986, 1992), lead to three main characteristics that have significant implications for urbanization dynamics and policies. First, consumption is squeezed to achieve high accumulation rates and high rates of output growth (Table 3.1). Second, the government pursues an unbalanced growth based on industry, especially heavy industry, often leading to the neglect of other aspects of the economy. There is a strong ideological bias among central planners against the service sectors, which are considered to be 'non-productive' and consumption oriented (Ofer 1973). Third, discriminatory policies are set against agriculture: massive 'tribute' from the agricultural sector is designed to finance rapid industrial growth[5] through collectivization and setting of commodity prices (Fallenbuchl 1970; Bideleux 1985). The Soviet growth strategy is, in essence, as Lipton (1977) has noted, a more extreme form of the classical growth model based on industrial growth (as postulated by Lewis 1954). The main differences between these two types of models lie in the much higher targets of growth and investment rates of the Soviet growth strategy, and the 'coercive' manner in which the strategy is executed.

The Soviet growth strategy leads to widely divergent growth rates between industry and agriculture, and a more labour-intensive agricultural sector than that of market economies (Weitzman 1970; Ofer 1976). The heavy emphasis on rapid industrial output

Table 3.1 Investment Patterns of Socialist Countries

A. Average Shares of Accumulation (% of National Income)

	1929	1937	1940	1951–55	1956–60	1961–65	1966–70
USSR	18.7	25.9	19.2	25.1	26.3	27.1	27.4

	1951–53	1954–56	1957–59	1960–62	1963–65
Bulgaria	27.1[a]	18.4	23.2	29.7	34.2
Czechoslovakia	14.5	12.3	18.1	20.5	14.3
Hungary	25.1	15.6	21.4	25.9	26.8
Poland	24.0	22.7[b]	23.0	24.3	26.0
Rumania	25.0	20.0[b]	20.5[c]	20.0[d]	26.0[e]

B. Agriculture's Shares in State Capital Investments (%)

USSR	1928–32	1933–37	1938–40	1941–45	1946–50	1951–55	1956–60	1961–65
Agriculture	15.6	11.8	10.8	9.4	11.8	14.2	14.3	15.5
Heavy Industry	31.7	30.5	28.5	39.5	33.4	36.5	30.4	31.7
Light Industry	6.3	6.8	5.9	3.4	5.2	4.5	5.3	4.8

Agriculture	1951–55	1956–60	1961–65	1966–70	1971–74
Bulgaria	13	21	22	16	18
Czechoslovakia	11	16	14	11	10
Hungary	17	15	17	20	20
Poland	10	13	14	16	15
Rumania	9	16	19	16	14
Albania	12	18	15	16	12

Notes: a 1952–53 b 1955 c 1957 & 1959 d 1960 & 1962 e 1963 & 1965
Sources: Cohn (1970); Fallenbuchl (1970); Bideleux (1985) and Wang (1981)

expansion in the overall adopted strategy, combined with the unsatisfiable demand for expansion of socialist industrial enterprises (Kornai 1986), generates high industrial employment growth, especially during the early years of 'extensive' growth. Industrial expansion and agglomeration create a strong tendency toward urbanization. At the same time, the wide gaps in wages, consumption, and economic opportunity between the industrial and agricultural sectors are maintained. There are immense incentives for peasants to move out of the rural areas because state policies toward agriculture, including the collectivization and compulsory delivery of agricultural goods, are mostly unfavourable.

On the consumption side, however, urbanization is considered 'costly' because it increases aggregate consumption by raising the migrants' consumption levels relative to their previous (rural) levels. There is a higher 'feasible' minimum in the urban areas because of the political clout of the urban class (Ofer 1976; Linn 1982). Urban population also requires a much higher per capita investment in infrastructural facilities. Many amenities, like housing, transport, garbage and sewage disposal, are expensive in urban agglomerations but cheap or not required in rural areas.[6] Housing, for example, is often self-supplied in rural areas by peasants during winter and off-work hours. Under classical socialism, as the urban sector is more or less totally under the state's direct control, all these costs also become the responsibility of the state and expenses to the state budget. However, high consumption costs are at variance with the paramount objective of high accumulation necessary for rapid industrial growth.

Furthermore, if urban industrial labour has to be imported from the countryside, it may also be increasingly more expensive due to the rise in the opportunity cost to the farm sector following the depletion of 'surplus' rural labour (as hypothesized by Lewis [1954, 1958] and Ranis and Fei [1961]).[7] As socialist agriculture is more heavily dependent on labour input, there may be critical times when rapid rural–urban labour transfer poses serious problems to economies having a low level of per capita agricultural output, such as China.[8]

Ideologically, attitudes of early socialists towards urbanization were at best ambivalent, as a careful review of Marx's and Engel's writing suggests (see Kirkby 1985). It can be argued that socialist states do not have strong attitudes to urbanization *per se*, at least initially (Forbes and Thrift 1987; Regulska 1987). What has later shaped their urbanization policy stems mostly from their prime, if not only, concern—rapid industrial output growth. When industry takes priority, urban development simply becomes subjected to industrial development policy.

In the first phase (roughly the first decade) of classical socialism, according to Fallenbuchl's (1970) analysis, rapid industrialization proceeds along an 'extensive' growth path through massive infusion of labour and capital, and leads to rapid urban growth. This was witnessed in the Soviet Union during the 1930s (Harris 1970; Musil 1980) and many East European countries in the 1950s (Compton 1976). Among the factors contributing to this trend are the relative shortages of capital in the initial years, the long gestation periods of investment in producer industries, and, in the European case, initial urban labour shortages caused by population losses during the Second World War. At the same time, the rise in consumption costs of the swelling urban population is held down by curbing consumption (for example, under the name of sacrificing for a better life in the future) and in the intensification of use of urban infrastructures (through measures such as redistributing housing property and rationing consumer products) (Kornai 1992).

More generally in the later phases, as intensifying use of urban infrastructures and curtailment of consumption cannot be pushed indefinitely (there are politically or physiologically defined limits), high levels of industrial growth must be met by rising aggregate consumption costs of the expanding industrial population. Thus, socialist planners at different levels try various means to maximize industrial growth while at the same time keeping both rural and urban consumption costs as low as the population will tolerate. In the urban sector, while further urbanization cannot be totally avoided with industrial growth, planners try to keep urban consumption costs down by minimizing per capita costs of urbanization and increasing the industrial output per urban resident. This is what Ofer (1976) has called 'economizing' on urbanization in socialist economies. Over time, this means continuing the growth of industrial output, Q, and decelerating the growth of urban population, UP, or maximizing the relative growth rate of Q/UP, under the condition of unchanged per capita urbanization costs.

A range of measures has been used to achieve t his objective. As will be exemplified by the Chinese case below, these measures concentrate on maintaining a low level of urban consumption, raising the industrial output–labour ratio, and reducing the urban multiplier effect of industrial labour based on a system of migration controls (Chan 1990). Owing to these, classical socialist economies generally exhibit lower urban growth rates once the first phase is passed. At the same time, the levels of urbanization in these countries are lower than those of comparable market economies based on similar per capita gross national product (Ofer 1976). Konrad and Szelenyi (1977) have coined the term 'under-urbanization' to describe the pattern of slow urban growth in socialist countries because of the deliberate state policy of under-investing in urban infrastructure.

The Economic Growth Pattern in Maoist China

The period of classical socialism in China covers approximately the period between 1953 and 1978, coinciding with what is generally referred to as the Maoist period. The year 1953 marks the beginning of the First Five-year Plan, which saw China adopt in more or less wholesale form the orthodox Soviet growth strategy and its centralized command system of economic planning. At the other end, the year 1979, following the momentous Party meeting held at the end of 1978, began Deng Xiaoping's era of economic reform. It may also be noted that in between 1953 and 1978, there were two brief aberrations from classical socialism: the period 1963–5 saw a number of Dengist reformist elements in command, and the chaotic early years of the Cultural Revolution (1966–9) resembled more the 'revolutionary-transition' phase of the early 1950s (Kornai 1992). The above classification is at variance with the conventional Western wisdom that treats the post-1958 period as one when the Soviet approach was replaced by the Maoist balanced growth strategy based on simultaneous development of agriculture and industry.[9]

Basic Components of China's Economic Growth Strategy under Mao

Despite Mao's oft-cited (1956, 1961–2) critique of Soviet industrialization strategy, the Chinese economic growth strategy throughout the Maoist period, as argued here, included all the macro-economic components of the Soviet growth strategy outlined before. Modifications to the Soviet industrialization strategy only occurred in the brief period of post-Great Leap Forward retrenchment (1961–5) and the post-Mao (after 1979) period. In fact, as will be seen in Chapter Four, even in the reform period of the 1980s, the influence of the Soviet growth strategy has still been dominant in Chinese macro-economic management. Hence, it is not too surprising to find that the First Five-year Plan, though well known for its close imitation of the Soviet model, is still regarded by current Chinese leaders like Chen Yun (1986) and the prominent economist Xue Muqiao (1980) as the 'golden era' of 'balanced' growth in Chinese socialist economic history.

Maximum Output Growth through High Accumulation

The Chinese government gave an overriding commitment to achieving high levels of output growth by devoting a large share of the country's output, measured by net material product, to investment at the expense of current consumption and standards of living. A slogan favoured by the leadership, '*xian shengzhan, hou shenghuo*' (putting production first, standard of living second), suggests unequivocally this strong, narrow productionist mentality. Not only did China begin its First Five-year Plan with a comparably high investment rate—averaging about 24.2 per cent of the country's net material product (Table 3.2)—but this rate was also pushed to extremes on many other occasions such as in 1958 and 1959 (the Great Leap Forward) when the rate leapt to 33.9 per cent and 43.8 per cent respectively (Wang 1981). The catastrophe of the Great Leap Forward forced Chinese leaders to 're-adjust' and be more lenient in the period 1961–2. But the tendency for high accumulation soon re-emerged. The rate of investment rebounded to close to the First Five-year Plan-level, reaching 22.7 per cent in 1963–5. High levels of accumulation (31–4 per cent) were maintained throughout the post-1970 period.

   A comparison of the investment statistics in Tables 3.1 and 3.2 reveals that China had higher accumulation rates than other socialist countries in comparable phases. For example, in the USSR this rate averaged about 25 per cent for the first ten five-year plans, with a maximum of 28.1 per cent (based on five-year averages); but in China, for most of the years since 1949, the investment rate has been above 25 per cent, with the highest five-year average reaching 33 per cent in the pre-1980 period (Wang 1981).

Table 3.2 China's Investment Patterns and Output Growth, 1952–1990

	1953–57	58–60	61–62	63–65	66–70	71–75	76–80	81–85	85–90
Shares of Net Material Product based on Current Price (%)									
Consumption	75.8	60.7	85.0	77.3	73.7	67.0	66.8	68.7	65.7
Accumulation	24.2	39.3	15.0	22.7	26.3	33.0	33.2	31.3	34.3
Sectoral Shares of State Capital Investment (%)									
Productive Sectors	67.0	85.4		79.4	83.8	82.5	73.9	57.4	67.1
Non-productive Sectors	33.0	14.6		20.6	16.2	17.5	26.1	42.6	32.9
Heavy Industry	36.2	54.0		45.9	51.1	49.6	45.9	38.5	44.3
Light Industry	6.4	6.4		3.9	4.4	5.8	6.7	6.9	7.5
Agriculture	7.1	11.3		17.6	10.7	9.8	10.5	5.0	3.3
Transport & Communications	15.3	13.5		12.7	15.4	18.0	12.9	13.3	13.0
Commerce & Services	3.6	2.0		2.5	2.1	2.9	3.7	5.9	3.2
Housing	9.1	4.1		6.9	4.0	5.7	11.8	21.3	12.7
Population and Output (Net Material Product) Growth Rates (Average Annual Increase in %)									
Industry	17.9	26.5	–35.3	19.3	11.8	8.2	8.8	9.7	9.7
Agriculture	3.7	–12.1	3.0	10.9	2.6	3.0	0.7	8.2	4.0
All Sectors	8.5	8.8	–21.0	13.7	8.0	5.3	5.9	9.5	7.2
Population	2.35	0.79	0.81	2.50	2.69	2.15	1.32	1.40	1.54

Source: computed from State Statistical Bureau (1991a)

Selected Growth Based on Heavy Industry

The long-accepted notion that Mao departed from the Soviet lop-sided concentration on industrial development does not stand up to empirical scrutiny either. Table 3.2 shows that the allocation of state funds in China is characteristically skewed in favour of heavy industry. The heavy reliance of the tax base on industry reinforced the importance of the industrial sector (Naughton 1992a). Total state investments in 'agriculture', including those in related branch-es of forestry, water conservancy, and meteorology, remained rela-tively low, which contributed, *inter alia*, to the slower agricultural growth in the later periods (Perkins and Yusuf 1984). While agri-culture accounted for more than half of the country's net mater-ial product in the pre-1980 period, it received a mere 7.1 per cent of total state capital investment in the First Five-year Plan. This percentage increased slightly to 10.5 per cent in 1958 and 1959. Only in the wake of the catastrophic famine was the government forced to come to the aid of agriculture, and the investment in agriculture rose to 14.4–24.6 per cent between 1961 and 1964 (Lardy 1987). Once the agrarian crisis was over, it dwindled to about 10 per cent for the 1966–80 period and even more dismal levels between 3.3 and 5.1 per cent in the 1980s.

Industry, particularly heavy industry such as basic metals and machine building, received most of the state investment funds throughout. During the First Five-year Plan period, investments in heavy industry made up 36.1 per cent of the total, a propor-tion higher than that in the First Five-year Plan under Stalin in the USSR (Table 3.1). During the Great Leap Forward years of 1958 and 1959, the investment share of heavy industry was pushed to extremely high levels: 57.0 and 56.7 per cent respectively (Wu 1987). Although this rate was moderated in the 1960s and 1970s, it nevertheless remained high at 46–51 per cent (based on the five-year plan averages).

Discriminatory Policies against Agriculture

Collectivization and compulsory state procurement of farm prod-ucts from the peasantry were the two major instruments that Soviet-type economies employed to forcibly induce unequal exchange between agriculture and industry, siphoning off savings from the farm sector to fuel the extraordinary high speed of indus-trial growth, especially in the initial stage (Lardy 1983). Scholars in China (e.g. Xue 1980) since the late 1970s have admitted that China under Mao adopted similar agricultural economic policies. As in the early years of Soviet industrialization, faced with the problem of having to raise the marketed surplus of grain, the Chinese government in 1953 resorted to a system of 'unified purchase' (*tonggou*), which meant compulsory procurement of farm products by the state, to ensure that the needed food grain for urban industrial growth was available from the peasantry at low prices (Chen 1954; Perkins 1966). The unified purchase system was extended later to cover all other major farm products, such as cotton, soya beans, tea, and cattle. Although agricultural prices were raised on several occasions since the 1950s, these increases were barely enough to cover the increased costs of production (Tang 1984; Zhang 1981).[10]

Collectivization of the farm sector, beginning in 1952, was hurriedly completed in 1956. The programme escalated to another new high during the communization drive between 1957 and 1959. Much larger and newly bestowed with government administrative functions, communes, coupled with the simultaneous implementation of migration controls enacted under the household registration law, assured a high degree of state control over the rural populace (and hence farm produce). Such control was another essential mechanism for inducing terms of trade favourable to industry.[11] It was also hoped that larger collectives would help raise agricultural output through institutional changes and economies of scale, without increasing state investment in agriculture (Chen 1955; Bernstein 1984). Acute production problems in larger communes, however, soon forced these collectives to downsize in the early 1960s. The commune system was maintained till the early 1980s.

Economic Performance by Sector in the Maoist Period

To bring out the broad pattern of sectoral changes over time, Table 3.3 and Figure 3.1 present the general pattern of sectoral growth in the post-1949 period. The output figures refer to net material product based on 1952 prices published by the State Statistical Bureau (1991).[12] Four points, which have an important bearing on urban growth rate and policies, should be made:

1. A wide divergence in the output growth rates between industrial and agricultural sectors was inevitable under the industrialization-biased policy (Lardy 1983). Agriculture in the 1960s and

Table 3.3 Sectoral Economic Performance, 1952–1982

	INDUSTRY (I)						AGRICULTURE (A)							
Year	Q	L	K	Q/L	Q/K	K/L	Q	G	L	K	Q/L	G/L	Q/K	K/L
ABSOLUTE VALUE														
1952	11.50	1528	148.8	75.3	772.8	973.8	34.00	163.92	17316	1129.2	19.6	94.7	301.1	652.1
1957	28.12	2115	350.0	133.0	803.5	1654.8	40.83	195.05	19300	1308.4	21.2	101.1	312.1	677.9
1960	62.26	4059	783.7	153.4	794.4	1930.8	28.42	143.50	16996	1245.5	16.7	84.4	228.2	732.8
1962	30.75	2033	864.5	151.3	355.7	4252.5	30.16	160.00	21259	1260.4	14.2	75.3	239.3	592.9
1965	54.94	2376	1032.5	231.2	532.1	4345.4	41.79	194.53	23372	1710.3	17.9	83.2	244.3	731.8
1970	99.25	3479	1310.8	285.3	757.2	3767.7	47.53	239.96	27786	1989.3	17.1	86.4	238.9	715.9
1975	149.19	5075	1861.7	294.0	801.4	3668.4	55.18	284.52	29415	2606.0	18.8	96.7	211.7	885.9
1980	231.46	7736	2662.2	299.2	869.4	3441.3	57.26	320.56	29117	3183.3	19.7	110.1	179.9	1093.3
1982	249.56	8377	2930.5	297.9	851.6	3498.2	68.54	354.50	30853	na	22.2	114.9	na	na

INDEX (1957 = 1)

Year													
1952	0.41	0.72	0.43	0.57	0.96	0.59	0.83	0.84	0.90	0.86	0.93	0.94	0.96	0.96
1957	1.00	1.00	1.00	1.00	1.00	1.00	1.00	1.00	1.00	1.00	1.00	1.00	1.00	1.00
1960	2.21	1.92	2.24	1.15	0.99	1.17	0.70	0.74	0.88	0.95	0.79	0.84	0.73	1.08
1962	1.09	0.96	2.47	1.14	0.44	2.57	0.74	0.82	1.10	0.96	0.67	0.74	0.77	0.87
1965	1.95	1.12	2.95	1.74	0.66	2.63	1.02	1.00	1.21	1.31	0.85	0.82	0.78	1.08
1970	3.53	1.64	3.75	2.15	0.94	2.28	1.16	1.23	1.44	1.52	0.81	0.85	0.77	1.06
1975	5.31	2.40	5.32	2.21	1.00	2.22	1.35	1.46	1.52	1.99	0.89	0.96	0.68	1.31
1980	8.23	3.66	7.61	2.25	1.08	2.08	1.40	1.64	1.51	2.43	0.93	1.09	0.58	1.61
1982	8.87	3.96	8.37	2.24	1.06	2.11	1.68	1.82	1.60	na	1.05	1.14	na	na

ANNUAL RATE OF GROWTH (%)

Period													
52–57	17.88	6.50	17.11	11.38	0.78	10.60	3.66	3.48	2.17	2.95	1.49	1.31	0.72	0.78
57–75	9.27	4.86	9.29	4.41	-0.01	4.42	1.67	2.10	2.34	3.83	-0.67	-0.24	-2.15	1.49
65–80	9.59	7.87	6.31	1.72	3.27	-1.56	2.10	3.33	1.47	4.14	0.63	1.86	-2.04	2.68
52–80	10.72	5.79	10.30	4.93	0.42	4.51	1.86	2.40	1.86	3.70	0.01	0.54	-1.84	1.85

Notes: Q = output (Net Material Product in RMB¥billion, 1952 constant prices)

G = grain output (in million tons)

L = employment (in 10,000)

K = capital stock (in RMB¥100 million, 1952 constant prices); they are mostly estimates. K (A) includes capital stock in rural industry

na = not available

Sources: Q, G, and L from State Statistical Bureau (1991b)

K from State Statistical Bureau (1985b), Chen *et al.* (1988), and Tang (1984)

Figure 3.1 Sectoral Growth Rates, 1952–1980

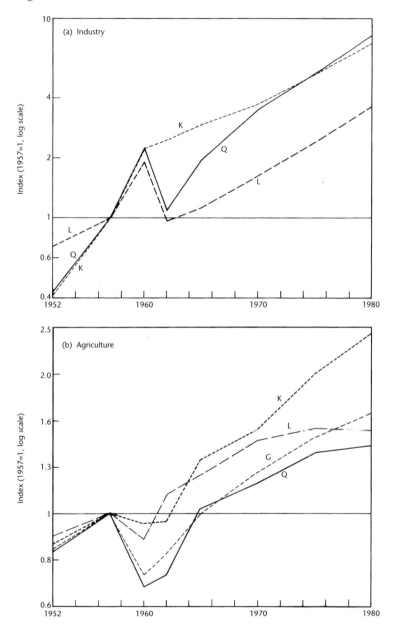

Notes: Q = Output, G = grain output, L = employment, K = capital stock
Source: Table 3.3

1970s also suffered from mismanagement and misguided regional self-sufficiency policies. The industrial sector expanded at an average annual rate of 10.7 per cent between 1952 and 1980 while the agricultural sector registered only 1.9 per cent growth per year. The output of grain (G), the principal product of the agricultural sector, increased by only 2.4 per cent per year during the 1952–80 period (and only 1.9 per cent between 1957 and 1977), slightly above the population growth rate (1.9 per cent).

2. Though a significant slackening in the output growth rate of the industrial sector was evident in the post-1957 period, there was no significant decline in the growth rate of industrial employment between the First Five-year Plan period (6.5 per cent per annum) and the 1965–80 period (7.9 per cent). Industrial production in 1965–80 was more capital intensive due to a rapid expansion of industrial capital stock in the previous period, but the industrial output growth was still mainly of the 'extensive' type, that is to say based on massive infusions of both labour and capital rather than on improvements in productivity (see also Wang 1981).[13]

3. Given the different priorities assigned to agriculture and industry, it is to be expected that the expansion rate of capital in the agricultural sector was lower compared to that of the industrial sector. Accurate assessments of the capital stock in China are extremely difficult to derive, but estimates attempted by Tang (1984) and Chen et al. (1987) used in Table 3.3 provide some broad trends. The relative neglect of agriculture, whose principal output was food grain, had serious implications for sectoral labour transfers, an important issue that deserves a separate treatment.[14] With relatively limited capital funds available, agriculture had to fall back more and more on the traditional input of labour (Lardy 1983). In fact, a shift toward more labour-intensive farm production was witnessed during the 1960s and 1970s (Rawski 1979).[15] Growth of labour productivity (Q/L) in the agricultural sector was thus held back; there was hardly any increase in the grain output per agricultural worker, G/L, between 1957 and 1978. This posed a serious constraint on inter-sectoral labour transfer.[16] A huge and widening gap in labour productivity between the agricultural and industrial sectors became inevitable. Based on roughly comparable prices, the World Bank (1983a) estimated that the sectoral crude labour productivity ratio[17] of China in 1979 was 6.1:1, compared to the average of 4:1 for most other Third World countries. A similar observation is also made by Wang (1981 p. 93).

4. The Great Leap Forward, widely portrayed before as 'the Chinese road to socialism' (e.g. Wheelwright and McFarlane 1970) or 'the alternative to Stalinism' (e.g. Gray 1976), has been interpreted as Mao's refutation of the Soviet growth model. However, judging from the investment and sectoral policies of the Great Leap Forward, it was more an intensification of the Stalinist programme to pursue high targets of steel production and high accumulation than anything else.[18] Such a 'leap' was premised on heavy extraction from the agricultural sector, where output was projected to increase substantially through institutional changes (namely communization and the mobilization of peasants' 'enthusiasm and initiatives for socialism'), rather than increases in capital investment.[19] The extreme squeeze of the farm sector put it at high risk; in some Chinese observers' words, it was analogous to 'draining the pond to catch the fish'. When hit by unfavourable climatic conditions in 1959–61, the overburdened agricultural sector collapsed, causing widespread hunger and millions of premature deaths during the 1960–2 period (Ashton *et al.* 1984).

Implications for Urban Growth

Industrial Employment Growth

As outlined earlier, industrial output growth in the period 1949–82 was largely of the 'extensive' type, despite the increase in the capital–labour ratio in industry in the post-1965 period. As a result, the high growth rate of industrial employment, averaging 5.8 per cent per year throughout the Maoist period, indicated a strong demand for labour and enormous pressures for urban growth.

Rural–Urban Disparities

The relative neglect of agriculture led to divergent output growth rates between agriculture and industry, and a wide gap in sectoral labour productivity and rural–urban disparities. These disparities showed few signs of narrowing between 1957 and 1977 under the Maoist policy.[20] Lardy (1983) and Whyte and Parish (1984) have amply documented the increasing rural–urban disparities in real income and consumption. Estimates by Parish (1981), Rawski (1982), and Lardy (1983) show that in terms of 'real income' disparity between the rural and urban populations, the ratio was in the range of 3:1 to 6:1 in 1976. This compares to ratios ranging from 2:1 to 3:1 in most other developing countries in the 1960s and 1970s (Lipton 1977, pp. 430–3).[21]

These huge disparities were orchestrated by two interrelated instruments: on the economic side, state investment and pricing policies in favour of industry, and, on the population side, restrictions on rural–urban migration (Lipton 1984; Zweig 1987; Chan 1988b; Zhang 1991). Post-Mao Chinese scholars have admitted that the 'scissors gap' that characterized the Soviet policy also appeared in China under Mao (Ma 1982; Chen 1982). According to the former Ministry of Agriculture's estimate, by selling over-priced industrial goods to the rural areas and buying under-priced agricultural produce from the peasantry, the government was able to reap a huge profit, for example, of between RMB¥20 to 30 billion in 1978 (cited in Yang and Li 1981). As the gap between the urban and rural areas, or the 'migration-gradient' widened, the 'natural' impulse for rural-to-urban migration intensified. Other factors such as high rural population density and the mostly unpopular rural collectivization only added strength to the centripetal force.

Urbanization Costs

Increases in urban population are 'costly' when the aim is maximizing production for two major reasons.

The Difference in Urban and Rural Consumption and Costs

As suggested before, in Soviet-type economies, where the state serves as the controller of the entire economy, an increase in consumption naturally cuts into the total funds available for industrial investment. Consumption is often curbed or postponed to make room for accumulation. However, urban per capita consumption is still significantly higher than in rural areas due to the urban way of life and the political clout of the urban population. The clout stems partly from the Marxist ideology of claiming that urban-industrial workers, the 'proletariat' class, are the masters of the socialist state, but more importantly, from the greater capability of the urban population to organize politically to voice their complaints or protect their interests. The urban way of life also requires much higher per capita expenditures in social services and infrastructural facilities than that in the countryside, partly due to the higher quality of urban services.

Table 3.4 Average Costs of Social Services in Rural and Urban Areas, 1979

Items	Average Costs (RMB¥)			Ratio		
	Cities (C)	Towns (T)	Rural (R)	C/T	C/R	T/R
Borne by the State:						
Maternity Care	40	15	5	2.7	8.0	3.0
Child Care	178	89	0	2.0		
Maternity Pay	78	78	15	1.0	5.2	5.2
Education	560	550	365	1.0	1.5	1.5
Medical Care	241	241	49	1.0	4.9	4.9
Capital Investment in Infrastructure	480	0	0			
Maintenance of Infrastructure	640	0	0			
Sub-total	2,217	973	434	2.3	5.1	2.2
Borne by the Family:						
Living Expenses	4,224	3,466	1,100	1.2	3.8	3.2
Medical Care	240	240	24	1.0	10.0	10.0
Education	225	150	72	1.5	3.1	2.1
Sub-total	4,689	3,856	1,196	1.2	3.9	3.2
Total	6,906	4,829	1,630	1.4	4.2	3.0

Notes: * Direct costs incurred from birth to age 16

Source: Based on household surveys carried out in 1979 and information on urban construction (Liu 1984)

Table 3.4 reports one study of rural–urban differentials in the costs of bringing up a child from birth to sixteen in China. We do not need to be too concerned about the precision of these figures; it is enough to show the huge difference between what one would receive from the state in the cities and in the countryside in terms of direct and indirect economic support. On a per capita basis, the state paid about five times as much in the cities as in the countryside. As in many countries, investment in, and maintenance of, urban infrastructures (roads, utilities, and so on) were chiefly responsible for the large differentials in per capita expenditure borne by the state between the cities and other types of settlements. While the state on average chipped in about RMB¥1,000 per head on the construction and maintenance of the infrastructures in cities, literally nothing was paid to towns and the rural areas.[22] In addition, the state also handed out every year RMB¥120 per head on subsidies for food grain and edible oils to the urban non-agricultural population (*Guangmin ribao* 1989; see also Chapter Two, note 4). Since the urban sector is almost totally owned and administered by the state, and urban residents are the state's direct responsibility, household consumption in urban areas has to be paid from the state budget directly. Given the huge urban–rural differentials in consumption, the additional urban consumption per capita due to rural–urban transfer must be considered as extra costs from the state's point of view (Naughton 1992a).

Costs to the Agricultural Sector

The Lewis (1954) model suggests that where there is 'surplus' rural labour, as in the initial stage of most underdeveloped economies, the economic costs of inter-sectoral labour transfer to agriculture are zero. Such was probably the case in China in the early 1950s. Under the rapid industrialization and urbanization drive of the First Five-year Plan, however, the 'surplus' rural labour was likely to quickly disappear. Towards the late 1950s, massive transfers of labour from the farm sector within a short time began to affect agriculture, putting the food producing sector at stake. With little regard for this risk and believing that agricultural labour productivity could be raised by ideological appeals and institutional reorganization, Mao launched a leap-type industrialization drive in 1957 to achieve socialist construction at 'high speed'. This generated explosive rates of industrial growth and urbanization. The Great Leap Forward ultimately ended in a complete dislocation of the farm economy and widespread famine. One of the major factors of the failure of the grain sector was the shortage of labour in the farms (Lardy 1987; Chan 1989). The failure of the Great Leap Forward prompted the government to immediately launch a massive 'clearing-out' campaign to bring down the urban population size and take a very conservative, in fact, very hostile, attitude toward rural–urban migration in the remaining period under Mao.

Policies to Economize on Urbanization Costs

Given the overwhelming priority accorded to rapid expansion of production (*vis-à-vis* consumption) by the government and the inevitability of some, however modest, urban growth, planners sought to resist the expansion of 'non-productive' consumption expenditures (mainly urban housing, transport facilities, commerce, and public utilities) occasioned by industrial growth and the augmentation of urban population, especially through migration (Perkins 1990). In many ways, this approach served to use the urban population and urban facilities more 'efficiently' (Kirkby 1985), or in Ofer's words, to 'economize' on the costs of urbanization. While Chinese planners have never made known their intentions as precisely as those stated above, there is no shortage of evidence, as detailed below, from Chinese policy documents and actual practice in support of this interpretation.

As pointed out earlier, economizing on urbanization costs can be met by suppressing urban consumption, or raising the ratio between industrial output and urban population size. Specifically, the following three groups of policy measures contributed in one way or the other to the Chinese anti-urbanization policy in the Maoist era, though they probably also served other state economic and political aims.

Minimizing the Growth of Per Capita Urbanization Costs

Advocacy of sacrifice of consumption was broadly subsumed under the Maoist revolutionary rubric of 'transforming consumer cities to producer cities', a point Mao (1949) first made on the eve of the founding of the People's Republic and later elaborated by others (see e.g. Liu *et al.* 1949). In terms of specific policy statements, a 1955 Party Central Committee's directive regarding state investment called for 'steadfastly lowering the provision standards of non-productive construction' (Zhao 1988; Wang 1990). According to Zhao (1988), the policy initiative contained in this central directive formed the basis of many subsequent urban-industrial investment plans, in which infrastructural standards were compressed ('*yasuo*') to make room for directly productive industrial investments. Furthermore, the Daqing Oilfield, where miners toiled in a hostile, cold, swampy environment and lived in dispersed settlements of temporary housing with limited facilities, was held up in the 1960s as a model for the rest of the country to follow (Xu 1983).

In practice, increase in urban personal consumption during the Maoist era was curbed by a *de facto* wage freeze and by various forms of rationing of consumer goods and services, although there were increases in mainly work-related benefits (such as medical and child care, and pension funds) and subsidies for food prices. Between 1957 and 1977, the average wage for workers in the state sector, for example, remained at a low level. Measured in constant terms, they actually declined from RMB¥142 to RMB¥135 per worker (SSB 1984a). This also served as a great inducement for females to work to raise family incomes (see below). On a per urban resident basis, both direct and indirect grain consumption only increased marginally by 10 per cent over the two decades since 1957 (Lardy 1983).

A formal urban rationing system, first put in place in 1953, covered almost all foodstuffs and many other consumer goods from cloth to bicycles, during almost all the Maoist era. Ration coupons were handed out to urban residents registered with the household registration authorities (Government Administration Council 1953; State Council 1955). Typically, standards laid down by the central authorities determined monthly or annual quotas for each urban 'non-agricultural' resident (Chan and Tsui 1992). Often, food rations could only be redeemed at the place of household registration and became an effective tool in tying down the population to where they had registered their households.

Other items of urban consumption also suffered from the policy to minimize 'non-productive' expenditures. Urban housing was neglected, with (mainly urban) housing's share of total state capital investment remaining low until the late 1970s (Table 3.2). A survey of 192 cities in 1978 indicates that the per capita floor area in those cities dropped from 4.5 m² in 1950 to 3.6 m² in 1978 (SSB 1986b). The housing problem in the late 1970s was more acute than is revealed by these floor-area figures. Mainly owing to the lack of adequate maintenance, more than half of all urban residences in 1979 were described as 'in urgent need of repair', and buildings containing more than 30 million m² of floor space were 'in danger of collapse'. The urban housing shortages became so severe that when the post-Mao leadership took over in the late 1970s, it had to admit the housing problem was a 'crisis' and began to invest more in the urban housing sector (Lalkaka 1984).

A similar story of neglect can be told for almost any kind of urban consumer service. Deterioration of service delivery in cities is most forcefully demonstrated by the decline in the absolute number of workers in the retail and service sectors between 1952 and 1978 despite increases in urban population. This resulted in a drastic jump—from twenty-three to forty-three—in the number of persons served per retail and service employee in the urban areas (Table 3.5). The consequence of the under-provision of service and retail facilities translated into widespread consumer complaints and long queues for consumer goods, a familiar scene in Maoist China and most pre-reform socialist countries. The low level of consumer service provision also forced urban residents to spend a long time outside their regular work hours in the self-provsion of these services,[23] hence alleviating the state's financial burden.

Given the significant cost differentials between cities and towns in the provision of infrastructural facilities by the state (Table 3.4), downward migration (and to some extent, 'horizontal' movements along the same level) in the settlement hierarchy was allowed and, at times, encouraged.[24] This was part of a more general policy of urban development, oft-touted by outsiders (see e.g. Buck 1981; Kwok 1982), that has run through both the Maoist or Dengist eras. This policy has involved controlling the growth of large cities, rationally developing medium cities, and actively promoting the growth of small cities. It evolved from a 1955 central directive to curb non-productive construction (Zhao 1988; Wang 1990). This is obviously not the right place to tackle the complex subject of the differential treatment of cities by size in China, a huge body of literature has been accumulated around this theme. It is only necessary to point out that there was a close link between the overall tendency to control urban consumption and the urban settlement strategy—a fact that has not yet been sufficiently attended to in the current literature on Chinese urban development.

Increasing the Industrial Labour–Output Ratio

Inducing a rise in industrial labour productivity, Q/Li, was an important means of achieving industrialization without urbanization in most European socialist economies (Ofer 1976). Rapid

Table 3.5 Size of Retail, Catering, and Personal
Services Sectors

	1955	1957	1963	1978	1982
Urban Areas					
No. of employees in R,					
C, and S sectors (1000)	na	na	na	3574.00	7676.00
No. of persons served					
per employee	na	na	na	33.56	18.62
No. of employees in R					
and S sectors (1000)	3709.90	3551.8	na	2806.60	6144.00
No. of persons					
per employee	18.45	23.14	na	42.73	23.26
No. of service					
outlets (1000)	1860.00	1000.00	na	180.00	na
No. of persons served					
per outlet	36.79	82.18	na	666.33	na

	1952	1957	1963	1978	1982
National (R, C, and S)					
No. of enterprises (1000)	5500.00	2703.00	1439.00	1255.00	3832.00
No. of persons served					
per enterprise	104.51	239.19	480.69	767.00	264.98
No. of employees (1000)	9529.00	7614.00	5152.00	6078.00	12921.00
No. of persons served					
per employee	60.32	84.91	134.26	158.37	78.59

Notes: R = retail, C = catering, S = personal services, na = not available
Sources: compiled from Yu (1981) and SSB (1984a)

growth in Q/Li in the initial phase of industrialization was favoured
by the post-war recovery and the low initial level of productivity. However, in the longer run, continual and speedy increase in
Q/Li required raising capital intensity in industrial production.

Table 3.3 shows that a steep rise in the Q/Li ratio was observed
in China during the 1950s, similar to what happened in other
socialist economies. The Q/Li ratio doubled between 1952 and
1960, averaging 9 per cent growth per year. However, there were
problems in raising the Q/Li ratio in the second phase, especially after 1965. Growth in the Q/Li ratio between 1965 and 1982
was far lower, averaging only 1.7 per cent per year. This could be

associated with the disruption caused by the Cultural Revolution, inefficient investment in the Third Front in south-west China, and the peculiar managerial behaviour of hoarding labour resources in industrial enterprises (Field 1986; Kornai 1986; Luo 1987). The slow increase in industrial-worker productivity implies that the high growth rate of industrial output (9.6 per cent per year) during this period had to rely on a high rate of expansion of industrial employment (7.8 per cent per year).

Decreasing the Urban Multiplier

While depressing basic consumption in the urban areas might have been a direct way to contain the urbanization costs, there were severe political limits to furthering that approach especially when the existing level of living standards was already low. Indirect measures to limit the expansion of urban population proved to be more acceptable in the 1960s and 1970s. With reference to Equation 2 (see page 53), these measures focus on reducing the values of 'e', 'u', and 's'.

Restraints on the Freedom of Labour and Personal Mobility

Earlier attempts in the mid-1950s to restrain rural–urban population mobility were predicated on the concerns of urban unemployment. As urban food grain shortages intensified in the early 1960s, they became the prime factor for establishing a restraint system on the urban population size for the ensuing two decades. As the system evolved over time, planners also used it to limit transfer of peasants to urban areas based on a more general consideration of the concomitant increase in overall consumption (Zhang 1987).

Direct administrative controls on personal mobility formed the cornerstone of urbanization-restricting policies. Central to these controls was the household registration (*hukou*) system, which was restored under communist rule to serve, initially, the purposes of residence registration, and, later, migration control and food rationing (Zhang, Q. 1989). From its full implementation in 1958, the household registration regulations have required every citizen to obtain clearance from the public security bureau before changing residences. A formal, permanent residential change from rural to urban required the conversion of registration status from 'agricultural' to 'non-agricultural' (the so-called '*nongzhuanfei*'). Such a conversion was seldom granted; it only happened when a peasant 'entered' the state sector through one of the few channels of formal state labour or military recruitment, through state job assignments (especially for new college graduates), or as members of communes whose land had been requisitioned for urban purposes (*Hukou dengji tiaoli* 1958; Koshizawa 1988; Christiansen 1990). Even these entries were tightly controlled by the employment quotas specified in national and local economic plans (see Blecher 1988). The elimination of the urban labour market in 1958 by nationalization and collectivization also eradicated the possibility of any urban employment outside the state's control. Urban collective enterprises, though theoretically still outside the state sector, were also placed under close scrutiny of the government in the Maoist decades by the 'socialist transformation' campaign in the late 1950s.

Indeed, even marriage to an urban dweller, as a rule, did not entitle one to a permanent urban residence status (Whyte and Parish 1985; Zhang 1987). Kim (1990) reports that because of the system, some 4.6 million married men and women were separated from each another in 1980.[25] Essentially, a *de facto* internal passport system, similar to the 'passport system' in Russia under the Czar and Stalin (Zaslavsky and Yuri 1979; Smith 1989), was put in place.[26] The difficulty of rural–urban permanent migration for the average peasant was likened to 'climbing to heaven' (*nan yu shang qingtian*) (Gong 1989; Guo and Lin 1987).

Since the state practically controlled all the recruitment in, and job transfers to, the urban sector, few from the countryside were able to earn a living in urban centres without official sanction. Furthermore, the allocation of food rations and other consumer goods and social services were directly linked to household registration. In the pre-1980 period, the immense difficulty in obtaining staple foods outside the state-controlled food rationing channels was a major deterrent to unauthorized migration. With the aid of policing organizations, such as the local security bureaux and neighbourhood committees who often made unannounced house visits to families suspected of putting up illegal in-migrants, this whole array of measures formed a relatively effective web in prohibiting unsanctioned in-migration in the Maoist era. Though, as might be expected, the system was not totally watertight (Tang 1990). There were some who circumvented migration restrictions by using illicit means such as bribery.

The suppression of rural–urban mobility had far greater impact than just blocking unauthorized flows. At a broader level, it segmented society into largely isolated rural and urban sectors. The low rural outflows and the clear geographical rural–urban segmentation likewise simplified the statistician's task of differentiating rural and urban population under Mao. At the individual level, in Solinger's (1991) words, 'the *hukou* system absolutely determined not just where a person could live but along with that the person's entire life chances—his or her social rank, wage, welfare, food rations, and housing'. In sum, a person's fate.

Direct Resettlement of Urban Residents in the Countryside

Resettlement campaigns, collectively known as rustication in Western literature, ranged from coercive, direct removal of the urban unemployed to semi-voluntary 'sending-down' programmes aiming to 're-educate' intellectuals. These campaigns, though some were politically motivated, had the practical effect of cutting down the urban population size.

Initiated in the mid-1950s, the rural resettlement programme was expanded in the recession years of the early 1960s, during which more than 20 million urban residents were returned to the countryside for economic reasons (Chen 1961). Rustication was re-instituted during the Cultural Revolution decade (1966–76) under the *'shangshan xiaxiang'* and *'xiafang'* programmes. The former was designed originally to cope with the urban youth unemployment problem, which had been created by chaos in the urban economy and increases in the number of new entrants to the urban labour force resulting from the relatively high urban rates of natural increase in the 1950s. The average number of entrants to the labour force was close to 3 million per year in the late 1960s (Fang and Zhao 1982). In the 1970s, however, the programme was used more as a political tool for 're-educating' urban youths. The *xiafang* campaign, sharing similar objectives, was directed at intellectuals and cadres. Altogether, during the Cultural Revolution decade, an estimated 30 million urban residents were rusticated (Chan 1988a). The target groups of these campaigns shifted somewhat in different periods: new in-migrants (in the early 1960s), newly graduated youths (1966–9), and intellectuals and cadres (during the Cultural Revolution). Resettlement with permanent stripping of one's urban household registration status was also applied to 'bad elements' (ex-landlords, ex-capitalists, ousted officials,

Table 3.6 Sectoral Composition of Employment and
Urbanization, 1952–1990

Year	Percentage of Employment				Per cent Urban	Ratios	
	Agricu.	Industrial	Services	Non-agr.			
	A	I	S	N = I+S	U	U/I	U/N
1952	83.5	7.4	9.1	16.5	12.5	1.69	0.76
1957	81.2	8.9	9.9	18.8	15.4	1.73	0.82
1960	65.7	15.7	18.6	34.3	19.7	1.25	0.57
1965	81.5	8.3	10.2	18.5	18.0	2.17	0.97
1970	80.7	10.1	9.2	19.3	17.4	1.72	0.90
1975	77.1	13.3	9.6	22.9	17.3	1.30	0.76
1980	68.7	18.3	13.0	31.3	19.4	1.06	0.62
1985	62.4	20.9	16.7	37.6	23.7	1.13	0.63
1990	60.0	21.4	18.6	40.0	26.4	1.23	0.66

Source: State Statistical Bureau (1991a)

and other politically 'alien' groups) in the cities as a form of
punishment.

Limiting the Expansion of the Service Sector

Expansion of the service sector (commerce, financial services, and
personal services) was halted during the Maoist era from 1955.
This served not only to reduce the per capita urban expenditure,
but also helped to keep down the expansion of the non-industrial
population. Statistics in Tables 3.5 and 3.6 underscore the relative decline of the service sector in the Maoist era. They clearly
show that, contrary to most market economies, where the service
sector has expanded in both absolute and relative terms over time
with industrialization (Chenery and Syrquin 1975), China's 'urban
service' employment size (retail, catering, and services) decreased
in absolute terms between 1957 and 1978, despite substantial urban
population growth. Also, as a percentage of total employment,
the tertiary sector stagnated, hovering around 9–10 per cent during the Maoist era (with the exception of the Great Leap Forward
years), in the face of rapid industrialization[27] (Table 3.6). The
deliberate neglect and suppression of commerce and finance also

considerably eroded the base of the modern urban economy and limited the functions of cities.

Increasing the Proportion of the Employed in the Urban Population

Rawski (1979) estimates the urban labour participation rate in 1957 at 41.5 per cent. This rate increased to about 75 per cent by 1982 (State Council and SSB 1985), mainly due to a higher female labour participation rate. While only a small percentage of working-age women was in the labour force in the mid-1950s, the proportion had grown to over 50 per cent in the 1980s. Applying the international work-force age threshold of fifteen, China's urban female labour participation rate was 67 per cent in 1982, exceeding that of many market economies where female labour participation was considered to be high[28] (Chan 1990).

The size of the non-working population has also been minimized by rigorous urban family planning campaigns since the early 1960s. Following a period of relatively high urban fertility during the 'post-war baby boom' of the 1950s, China began to promote family planning in the urban areas in the early 1960s and, later, in the countryside (Banister 1987). The result—no doubt aided greatly by the drastic rise in women's labour participation and the deteriorating urban housing conditions—is significant. The total urban fertility rate declined from about 5–6 in the mid-1950s and the early 1960s to an impressive level of about 1.5 in the mid-1970s and onward (Chen 1983). The combined result of low fertility and increased labour participation considerably reduced the dependency ratio in urban families. The ratio of non-working persons to working persons fell from 3.29 in 1957 to 2.06 in 1978 and 1.71 in 1983 (SSB 1986a).

Increasing 'Non-urban' Industrial Production

Another means of breaking the connection between industrial employment growth and urban population growth is to locate as many as possible of the industrial labour force outside urban areas or to classify them as 'non-urban'. Rural industrialization has served well this goal and has been encouraged actively by the state because, while contributing to industrial output, rural industrial labour does not incur extra expenditure on urban infrastructures and services. Even with that saving in costs, rural industry under Mao was kept to certain less profitable sectors (Naughton

1992a). After an unsuccessful attempt during the Great Leap Forward, the rural industrialization (commune- and brigade-run industry) programme was resumed in the late 1960s to support agriculture and expanded speedily in the 1970s. While the exact size of the commune- and brigade-run industry sector may vary with the use of different statistical coverage, there is little doubt that the growth in the decade from the late 1960s was phenomenal. According to the State Statistical Bureau (1990b), employment in the commune- and brigade-run industry sector had reached 17 million by 1978, or about 28 per cent of China's total industrial work-force.

Although many of the commune-run industrial enterprises were actually located in small towns and cities and were not 'rural' *per se*, many brigade-run industrial enterprises were in 'rural' townships and can be considered as rural industry. In any case, all employees in the commune- and brigade-run industry sector were classified in the Maoist era as 'agricultural' in the national income accounting and were refused urban benefit entitlements (Chan and Tsui 1992; SSB 1988a). This, not surprisingly, created more fertile soil for misinterpreting China's rural development. Popular among the agricultural population, the rural industrialization programme was also favoured by the government for it did not increase the *de jure* urban population. This was the so-called '*jidi xiaohua*' (*in situ* occupational conversion) policy, which was preferred over migration to urban centres by the government (Guo and Liu 1990). It also formed the basis for the post-Mao policy of letting 'peasants leave the land but not the villages'.

Despite rapid rural industrialization, most industrial expansion was still in the urban state sector mainly because of the state's monopolistic control over industry. Urban industrial employment in the period 1970–9 grew at a relatively high rate of 5.5 per cent per year (SSB 1987b, p. 15). Not all the new urban jobs, especially unpopular ones like those in construction, could be filled by the urban labour supply as new urban graduates were being sent off to the countryside and the female labour participation rate was already at a high level. To solve this labour supply problem without increasing costs too much, 'temporary' or 'contract labourers' were brought in from the countryside.

Established in December 1957 when the mechanism of restricting rural–urban migration was also implemented, the temporary labour system was a way for urban enterprises to meet occasional or seasonal labour demands under the ban on formal urban in-migration (State Council 1957, 1962, 1965). While there were strin-gent employment quota and wage budget constraints imposed on formal urban labour recruitment from the countryside, the hiring of temporary workers was not subjected to such restrictions (State Council 1965). Given this, and the urban labour supply condi-tions, urban managers often turned to the temporary labour sys-tem for their permanent as well as seasonal labour needs. As a side note, given the 'soft' budget nature of temporary recruitment, urban managers tended to hoard more temporary workers. The practice also led to managerial manipulations for personal gain. Temporary employment was often a major back-door route to later formal employment (see State Council 1982a).

However, to prevent the unplanned, 'spontaneous' migration of labourers that resulted in 'blind flows' unwanted by the govern-ment, urban enterprises had to engage temporary labour through collective contracts with rural co-operatives. This ensured that rural outflows had formal government approval. Most important-ly, temporary workers were not entitled to full urban resident sta-tus and many of its accompanying benefits (such as housing, full medical coverage, job security, and, in some cases, subsidized food grain) (Blecher 1988). In essence, the temporary labour system is one that exploits cheap migrant labour, and has by no means been unique to China. But, because of a *de facto* internal migration system, rural, domestic migrant labourers have been more sys-tematically—and thoroughly—exploited than elsewhere. In stat-istical terms, though many of the 'temporary workers' might have stayed in the urban areas for years, they have been officially clas-sified and treated as 'agricultural' population (thus included in the Agricultural Population of Cities and Towns) and are not recog-nized as *de jure* urban population (the Non-agricultural Population of Cities and Towns). Some 'temporary' labourers commuted to work in the urban areas from nearby counties on a weekly or monthly basis (Blecher 1988; Zheng *et al.* 1985).

The popularity of this system in the 1970s has been documented at the local level, for instance, by Blecher (1983), who cites that three-quarters of recruits in the industrial labour force between 1964 and 1978 in Shulu County, Hebei, were contract workers. At the national level, the State Statistical Bureau (1987b, p. 35) reports that the size of state sector 'outside-plan' workers, most of whom were 'temporary labourers', had burgeoned from 1.7 million in

1973 to 9 million in 1978. Figures derived from Table 2.1 also show that the expansion of this category of urban 'agricultural' population, both 'temporary' workers and commune- and brigade-run industries workers included, was fuelling China's urban growth through migration since the mid-1960s. The Agricultural Population of Cities and Towns grew at an average annual rate of 4 per cent between 1965 and 1978 while the Non-agricultural Population of Cities and Towns rose at 0.9 per cent per year, barely above its natural growth rate. By 1978 the Agricultural Population of Cities and Towns had risen to about 48 million, or 28 per cent of the Total Population of Cities and Towns (computed from Table 2.1). From the 1970s, with the increasing prevalence of this type of urban 'agricultural' dweller, the Chinese urban populace was segmented into two classes: the privileged permanent non-agricultural householders, and the second-class 'temporary' agri-cultural householders. The social and economic consequences of this segmentation were far more profound, as have been vividly and powerfully portrayed by Guo and Liu (1990), than its analysed impact on urbanization presented here.

Industrial and Urban Growth: An Evaluation

Given that increasing the industrial output per urban resident (Q/UP) over time was the main objective of the Chinese plan-ners, it is possible, based on the existing data, to make an assess-ment of the extent to which this objective was met and to estimate the relative contributions of various factors to the observed result in different periods.

The rapidly widening gap between the growth rates of Q (net material product of industry) and UP (based on the Total Population of Cities and Towns) in Table 3.7 suggests a high degree of suc-cess in fulfilling the above objective, which is not surprising given the strength of the Maoist centralized state (Wang 1993). A close to seven-fold increase in the Q/UP ratio between 1952 and 1980 was recorded (Table 3.7, Column 14). The drastic increase in China contrasts with the modest ones in most developing market economies.[29] Effecting such a large increase in the Q/UP ratio within a short time was possible in the Chinese case because of the rural–urban segmentation policy premised on severe re-striction of individual freedoms of migration. One of the most

Table 3.7 Relative Contributions of Various Factors to the Increase in the Q/UP Ratio, 1952–1990

Year	Q	Li	Ln	s	e	u	1/s	1/e	1/u	TPCT	Q/Li	Li/UP	Q/UP
1	2	3	4	5	6	7	8	9	10	11	12	13	14
1952	11.50	1,528	3,413	2.234	3.29	0.676	0.448	0.304	1.478	7,163	0.008	0.213	0.002
1957	28.12	2,115	4,471	2.114			0.473			9,949	0.013	0.213	0.003
1960	62.26	4,059	8,884	2.189			0.457			13,073	0.015	0.310	0.005
1965	54.94	2,376	5,298	2.230	3.40	0.724	0.448	0.294	1.381	13,045	0.023	0.182	0.004
1970	99.25	3,479	6,618	1.902			0.526			14,424	0.029	0.241	0.007
1975	149.19	5,075	8,708	1.716			0.583			16,030	0.029	0.317	0.009
1980	231.46	7,736	13,244	1.712	1.87	0.773	0.584	0.535	1.294	19,140	0.030	0.404	0.012
1982	249.56	8,377	14,442	1.724	1.83	0.813	0.580	0.546	1.230	21,480	0.030	0.390	0.012
1990	613.01	12,158	22,691	1.866	1.77	0.752	0.536	0.565	1.330	30,191	0.050	0.403	0.020
Index (1965 = 1)													
1952	0.209	0.643	0.644	1.002	0.968	0.934	0.998	1.033	1.071	0.549	0.325	1.171	0.381
1957	0.512	0.890	0.844	0.948			1.055			0.763	0.575	1.167	0.671
1960	1.133	1.708	1.677	0.982			1.019			1.002	0.663	1.705	1.131
1965	1.000	1.000	1.000	1.000	1.000	1.000	1.000	1.000	1.000	1.000	1.000	1.000	1.000
1970	1.807	1.464	1.249	0.853			1.172			1.106	1.234	1.324	1.634
1975	2.716	2.136	1.644	0.770			1.300			1.229	1.271	1.738	2.210
1980	4.213	3.256	2.500	0.768	0.550	1.067	1.302	1.818	0.937	1.467	1.294	2.219	2.871
1982	4.542	3.526	2.726	0.773	0.538	1.122	1.293	1.858	0.891	1.647	1.288	2.141	2.759
1990	11.158	5.117	4.283	0.837	0.521	1.038	1.195	1.921	0.963	2.314	2.181	2.211	4.821

	Average Annual Growth Rate (%)									
1952–60	21.11	12.21	11.96				7.52	8.90	4.69	13.59
Contribution of Each Component (%)							65.5	34.5		100.0
Average Annual Growth Rate (%)										
1965–80	9.59	7.87	6.11	−1.76	−3.99	0.43	2.56	1.72	5.31	7.03
Contribution of Each Component (%)	25.1	56.7	−6.2	1.76	3.99	−0.43	75.6	24.4		100.0
Average Annual Growth Rate (%)										
1952–80	10.01	5.41	4.52					4.60	2.13	6.73
Contribution of Each Component (%)							68.4	31.6		100.0
Average Annual Growth Rate (%)										
1980–90	12.17	5.65	6.73	1.08	−0.69	−0.35	5.70	6.52	−0.05	6.48
Contribution of Each Component (%)	−16.7	10.6	5.3	−1.08	0.69	0.35	100.7	−0.7		100.0

Notes: Q = industrial output (net material product) in RMB¥billion, 1952 constant prices)
   Li = industrial employment (in 10,000)
   Ls = service employment (in 10,000)
   s = the service employment multipler (=Ln/Li)
   e = the non-working population multipler (estimates computed from State Statistical Bureau's data)
   u = the degree of urbanization of non-agricultural employment (derived)
   UP = urban population (Total Population of Cities and Towns)

Sources: State Statistical Bureau (1982, 1986a, 1987b, 1991a)

deleterious effects was a sluggish farm economy in the 1970s over-
burdened with increasing population.

Temporally, there were also significant variations in the Q/UP
ratio. It rose rapidly during the 1950s, averaging about 14 per cent
per year and then settled back to only 7 per cent per year during the period 1965–80. The relative contribution of the change
in industrial labour–output ratio, r(Q/Li), and the change in the
'urban multiplier', r(Li/UP), to the change in output per urban
resident, r(Q/UP), can also be evaluated by employing the following equation derived from previous formulae (see page 53):[30]

$$r(Q/UP) = r(Q/Li) + r(Li/UP) \tag{3}$$

As shown in the table, during the 1950s, increase in the Q/UP
ratio was mainly brought about by the rise in the Q/Li ratio
(65 per cent), expected because of the low initial productivity in
the early years and of a 'recovery' nature of growth. The rise in
the Li/UP ratio during the same period was not as rapid, contributing only 35 per cent to the increase in the Q/UP ratio. The
period 1965–80, however, exhibits a different pattern. Not only
was the rise in the Q/UP ratio significantly reduced, but the portion accounted for by the change in Q/Li was also smaller. Only
24 per cent of the increase in the Q/UP ratio was attributable to
the increase in the Q/Li ratio, due to the slow growth in the crude
industrial labour productivity examined before. This is different
from the observed patterns in some European socialist countries,
where the rise of the Q/Li ratio is the main contributor to the
rise in the Q/UP ratio in the second phase of industrialization
(see Ofer 1976). In China, the change in the 'urban multiplier',
made possible by the various measures examined earlier, was the
major factor responsible for the rise in Q/UP in the period 1965–80.
The change in the Li/UP ratio accounted for 75 per cent of the
increase in the Q/UP ratio during that period.

Existing data also permit an estimation of the relative contribution of each of the sub-components of the urban multiplier: 's',
'u', and 'e'. Of the 76 per cent contributed by the drop in
the value of the urban multiplier, the decline in 'e', the non-working population multiplier, played a major role (57 per cent), followed by the drop in 's', the service employment multiplier (25 per
cent). These positive contributions to the increase in the Q/UP
are offset to some extent by the increasing degree of urbanization of non-agricultural employment, 'u', mainly by use of

'temporary workers'. However, as pointed out, the growth of the urban population in the 1960s and 1970s was predominantly in the Agricultural Population of Cities and Towns category. This group, though physically in urban areas, was not entitled to many urban benefits provided by the state. In summary, China in the post-1965 Maoist period successfully raised the Q/UP ratio mainly by increasing the labour participation rates, especially of females, and by reducing the average urban family size.

These shifts are also reflected at the level of individual cities. Figure 3.2 presents the changing population composition of Changzhou, a regional industrial centre of 3 million in 1980 in Jiangsu and also a 'model city' in China. A significant drop in the percentage of the non-working population since 1953, especially between 1961 and 1980, is evident. The proportion of service employment also stagnated despite a rapid rise in the percentage of industrial employment between 1953 and 1980. These shifts in the urban population structure are typical of many large and medium cities in this period (Wu 1981; Ma 1981; Investigation and Research Group on Optimal Size of Cities 1986).

Owing to the attempts, both at the central and local levels, to raise industrial growth rates and slow down urban growth rates, urbanization lagged behind industrialization in China. This is just the opposite to the familiar phenomenon of 'over-urbanization' in many developing market economies, first observed by Hauser (1957) and Hoselitz (1957). Chinese 'under-urbanization'[31] can also be demonstrated by contrasting its urbanization level with a sample of comparable market economies, which can be taken to represent the approximate 'norm' under conditions of no active policy intervention.

Figure 3.3 establishes the statistical relationship between the urban percentage (UL) and the percentage of output in industry (GIL) based on a sample of twenty-nine market economies[32] having per capita GNP below US$2,000 in 1980. The plot reveals a manifestly huge deviation of China's position from the 'norm' constructed from market economies. China's UL (19 per cent) in 1979 was far below the 'expected' UL (53 per cent) as predicted from the existing lowest estimate of China's GIL (40 per cent) (World Bank 1983a). China's deviation computed from the regression is statistically significant at the level of 0.01. To further illustrate, China's UL/GIL ratio in 1980 was only half that of India, a country with a comparable per capita gross national product and size

Figure 3.2 Changzhou: Population Structure, 1953–1980

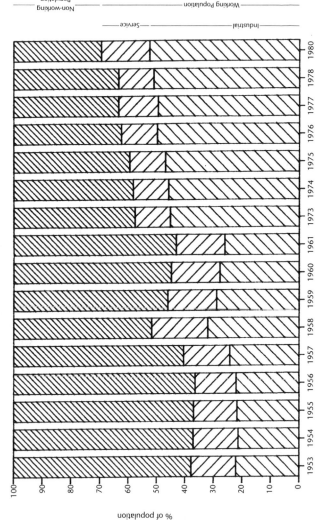

Source: Investigation and Research Group on Optimal Size of Cities (1986).

Figure 3.3 Industrialization and Urbanization: Low- and Middle-income Countries

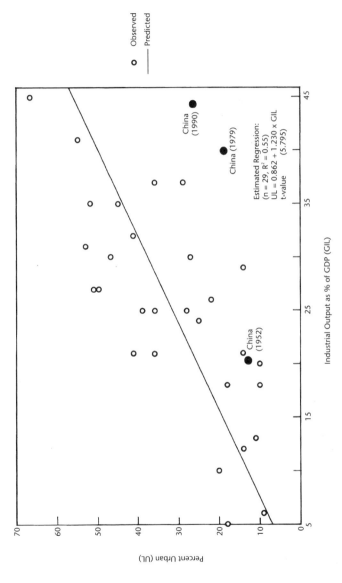

Observed   ○
Predicted —

Percent Urban (UL)

Estimated Regression:
(n = 29, R² = 0.55)
UL = 0.862 + 1.230 x GIL
t-value   (5.795)

China (1990)
China (1979)
China (1952)

Industrial Output as % of GDP (GIL)

Source: World Bank (1983b), State Statistical Bureau (1991a).

Figure 3.4 Percentages of Industrial Employment and Urban Population: China, 1952–1990

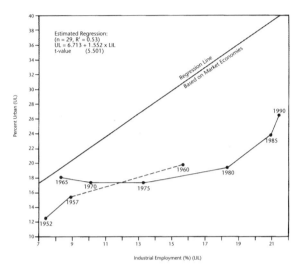

Sources: Regression estimates are based on 1980 data of 29 low- and middle-income countries (World Bank 1983b). Figures for China are from Table 3.6.

(calculated from the World Bank [1983a, 1983b]). The finding about China being under-urbanized in the Maoist era is also supported by Perkins (1990) and Gu (1991), who independently adopted a similar approach, and by Ran and Berry (1989) using Tolley's model based on urban–rural productivity differentials.[33] China's substantially lower urban percentage was probably due partly to its historical legacy, namely its limited urbanization and the lack of urban autonomy before 1949 (Weber 1951). But, it is argued here that government policy was a far more important factor. It is true that China's actual urban percentage in 1952 was lower than the level predicted by the regression, even based on a high estimate of GIL (20 per cent), but the deviation was substantially smaller[34] (Figure 3.3). There was an obvious widening of the deviation between 1952 and 1979 (accurate GIL figures for the interim years are not available). A plot based on the UL and industrial employment percentage (as a per cent of nation's total) reveals more detailed movements of China's position over time (Figure 3.4). There is a clear trend of China moving away from the norm between 1965 and 1980.

Conclusion

This chapter has outlined the major principles governing urbanization under classical socialism and has developed a framework, using a set of multipliers, to understand the mechanisms and logic of controlling urban growth. It was argued that the special set of socialist anti-urbanization policies owed their origins largely to the central imperative to industrialize the country quickly and, to a lesser extent, the 'hoarding' behaviors of industrial managers at the local level. The hostility toward urban development may have been more readily accepted because of the limited urbanization and lack of urban autonomy in pre-1949 China. A re-examination of the macro-economic aspects of China's development strategy and economic system in the pre-1979 socialist period reveals that an industrialization-biased Soviet approach, instead of one geared to rural development, was followed closely. The logic in shaping sectoral and urban–rural relationships common to socialist countries is shown to be relevant to understanding and analysing China's urbanization policics and growth patterns under Mao. Essentially, to induce the terms of trade favourable to the urban-industrial sector, the government replaced the market by a planned system with centrally dictated prices prejudicial to agriculture. The other concomitantly necessary mechanism was to restrict outflows of population from the rural sector. Such an approach provided the necessary welfare services to the urban population, securing political security in the cities, where almost all state-organized manufacturing activities were located. At the same time, the rural labourers, who were largely in agricultural activities, were ignored, producing a highly segmented economy of urban (state) and rural (non-state) sectors, and rigid social stratification of peasants and non-peasants in the Maoist era. A *de facto* internal passport system was established to enforce this sectoral, as well as geographical, segmentation in employment and population. Ironically, while many age-old, symbolically feudalistic, brick or stone city walls over the country were taken down soon after the founding the People's Republic, many new, but invisible, ones were erected under Mao to preserve or re-create a rigid rural–urban dualism.

Joint maximization of industrialization and minimization of costs of urbanization was a paramount concern under the Maoist system. Measures that helped 'economize' on urbanization throughout the pre-1978 period were suppression of the expansion of urban services and personal consumption, intensification of use of urban facilities and housing, and adoption of a capital-intensive approach to industrial development. As financial resources became scarcer and urban facilities more over-burdened in the 1960s and 1970s, a tight control of rural–urban labour and population mobility, fuller employment of the existing urban working-age population, promotion of rural industrialization, and increased use of low-cost 'temporary' workers were adopted. In contrast to the previous interpretation of China's urbanization policies, most of these measures contained an arguably strong Liptonian 'urban-bias'. They reinforced the wall between town and country.

Though the system of control was not totally watertight, there was a significant drop in the urban growth rate in the period of 1960–77. Measured by the rapid growth in the Q/UP ratio since 1949, China was highly effective in simultaneously fostering rapid industrial growth and slowing urban growth during the Maoist era. Because of the smaller 'urban multiplier' effect with respect to its industrial output or employment, China by the 1970s was relatively 'under-urbanized' compared to its level of industrialization or to other developing countries at similar stages. This is just the reverse to the phenomenon of 'over-urbanization' in many Third World market economies, where 'industrialization-biased' policies—but without migration controls—tend to produce 'excessive' in-migration to cities and chronic urban unemployment.

Notes

1. See a similar approach espoused by Kornai (1992).
2. Here I refer to the period where a rapid transition from a predominantly agrarian economy to an industrial one occurs. This period is characterized by a significant spurt in the rate of productive investment (to over 15 per cent of national output) and covers at least the first couple of decades of socialist industrialization.
3. As Kuznets (1965) pointed out, an authority determined to prevent urbanization could prohibit agglomeration of plants and firms within a small area, and could require construction of housing for the workers

of a single plant that would assure low density per square mile. 'Proto-industrialization' in eighteenth-century Europe is another form of indus-trialization with only limited urbanization (see de Vries 1984).
4. This is akin to the migration multiplier concept used in migration research (e.g. Arnold *et al*. 1989).
5. However, whether Soviet agriculture actually succeeded in providing massive savings for the industrialization process during the period 1928–37 is a subject of debate (see Millar 1970; Nove 1970; Ellman 1975).
6. The importance of infrastructure in accounting for the difference in costs of urban and rural development is explained in Lewis (1978) and Gugler (1982).
7. For an examination of this transition in the European socialist coun-tries, see Fallenbuchl (1970).
8. For a detailed treatment of this issue in China, see Chan (1989), who has also examined the relationship between the difficulty in raising the marketed share of grain output and the transfer of labour from the rural sector.
9. See Spulber (1963), Wheelwright and McFarlane (1970), Eckstein (1977), Amin (1981), and Van Ness and Raichur (1983). The argument was largely based on Mao's rhetoric (1956, 1961–2), especially his criti-cism of the Soviet approaches and his stress on non-material incentives; the Sino-Soviet ideological split; and selective official pronouncements which were more supportive of agriculture in the immediate aftermath of the Great Leap Forward.
10. Zhang Zhuoyuan's (1981, p. 93) remarks on the 'scissors gap' between industry and agriculture is most telling:

Things became so ridiculous that, at one time, the more grain output we demand-ed, the lower the grain prices became. Growing staple crops was not only unprofitable, but peasants actually lose money. [Under this situation], as the last resort to mobil-ize the peasants to grow staples, we had to discredit the idea of putting econom-ics first. Isn't this a joke played on the objective law of economics? (my translation)

11. Otherwise, as one observer makes it clear, faced with unfavourable conditions (low farm purchase prices dictated by the state), peasants will invariably 'vote with their feet' and leave the countryside (Shrestha 1987).
12. These figures are broadly consistent with most other sources. 'Industry' includes manufacturing, mining, and construction. Measurement of cap-ital is subjected to a high degree of error. These figures are meant only to indicate the general trends. For a detailed treatment of this issue, refer to World Bank (1983a, 1985) and Chen *et al*. (1988).
13. A shift to 'intensive' growth was observed in the USSR and some European socialist countries in the 1960s in the second phase of indus-trialization (Wilczynski 1972).
14. See Chen (1961) and Chan (1989) for an examination of this problem.

15. It has also been argued that the demand for labour may increase, rather than decrease, in the initial stage of agricultural modernization under certain conditions (Freedman 1982; Whitney 1980).

16. One can also argue that rural–urban transfer reduces population on the land and increases rural labour productivity. However, whether such a transfer will jeopardize the overall food output condition in a closed economy depends on the initial level of food surplus and the marginal labour productivity of rural labour in the countryside (see Chan [1989]).

17. This refers to $[Q(I) / L(I)] / [Q(A) / L(A)]$, where Q is output and L is labour.

18. In 1958, the Party decided to double steel production from 5.35 million tons in 1957 to 10.7 million tons in 1958 (Xue 1980; He and Wang 1983). Actual steel output more than tripled between 1957 and 1960 (SSB 1984a). Table 3.3 also shows that industrial employment and capital stock almost doubled during the same period.

19. For example, the Chinese planners' optimism led them to set extremely high grain output targets for 1958, ranging from 375 to 500 million tons, though the production actually turned out to be only about 200 million (Ashton *et al.* 1984). The level of state grain procurement for 1959 was raised drastically to 40 per cent of the total output (He and Wang 1983).

20. It has been argued that the terms of trade between industry and agriculture moved in favour of agriculture under Maoist policy (see Nolan and White 1984; Wu 1987; Bhalla 1990). The argument is based on a narrowing price differential between industrial and agricultural products using official price indexes. However, given the existence of various kinds of formal and informal rationing and the limited coverage of products on which these indexes are based, the prices are not valid indicators of the true exchange relationships. For a detailed treatment refer to Lardy (1983).

21. Given no or less-effective control on rural–urban migration and family planning programmes, cities in many Third World countries contain more unemployed and non-working people. This tends to depress their per capita income.

22. A recent measure by the Municipality of Guangzhou reveals the perceived per capita 'lifetime' costs of urban infrastructure in a large city borne by the state. Under a new policy to attract foreign funds to finance urban housing construction, the municipality has decided to allow relatives of buyers of homes in Guangzhou paid in foreign currencies to move to the city. These new in-migrants are charged RMB¥10,000 – 15,000 (US$ 2,500–3,500) per head (in foreign currencies) for the 'urban infrastructure costs' (*Wen Wei Po* 1988a).

23. A survey of two large cities in China in the early 1980s indicates that urban employees spent on average up to 4–5 hours on household work daily (Liu 1984). Preparing for meals took up much of this time. Low

pay and inadequate catering facilities meant most eat all meals at home. Few homes had refrigerators and there were few processed or semi-processed foods in the shops, so people spent a lot of time on grocery shopping. Laundry was also time-consuming because access to a washing machine was rare.

24. This is made clear in two stipulations by the Ministry of Internal Security in 1964 and 1977 cited by Zhang (1987).

25. This despite that fact that from mid-1970s onward, some exceptions were made to spouses of scientific personnel, workers in the Third Front region, and miners as an enticement policy (Zhang 1988).

26. Travelling within the country, however, has never been banned by law. The law requires that anyone who stays three or more days outside of his or her original place of residence report to the local household registration authority. Those who stay three months or more must receive official approval (*Hukou dengji tiaoli* 1958).

27. The World Bank (1985a) has investigated the extent of the so-called 'concealed services' in accounting for the small size of China's service sector and concluded that this problem in China 'is in fact only slightly greater than in other counties' (p. 3). In any case, with some adjustments for the above factor, the World Bank estimated that China's share of the labour force in transport and services in 1981 was relatively low, at 12.4 per cent, substantially lower than India's 16.5 per cent and was far below the predicted value of 21 per cent (p. 25). The World Bank figure also comes close to those in Table 3.6.

28. The 1980-round figures for Sweden, Canada, the USA, and Hong Kong were 60.5 per cent, 51.6 per cent, 52.1 per cent, and 49.5 per cent, respectively. For detailed information, see Sorrentino (1983), Bodrova and Anker (1985), Hong Kong Census and Statistics Department (1983), and Taylor (1986).

29. For instance, there was only a 2.2 fold increase in the Q/UP ratio in India between 1950 and 1979. In comparable terms, the industrial output per urban resident in China in 1979 was US$527, about two times that of India (US$246). The non-agricultural output value per urban resident in 1979 was about US$870 in China, compared to US$585 in India (computed from Mills and Becker [1986], World Bank [1982, 1983a] and Sichuan University [1982]).

30. Algebraically, r(Q/UP), the relative growth rate of Q/UP, can be decomposed into two components:

$$r(Q/UP) = r(Q/Li) + r(Li/UP)$$

because, by definition,

$$Q/UP = Q/Li \times Li/UP$$

Raising r(Q/UP) would mean increasing r(Q/Li) and/or r(Li/UP). Since Li/UP is the reciprocal of the urban multiplier, UM (= UP/Li = s × u × e), measures to increase Q/UP can be grouped as: raising the industrial output–labour ratio, and/or suppressing the value of the urban multiplier. More specifically, it follows from the above that:

$$r(Q/UP) = r(Q/Li) + r(1/s) + r(1/u) + r(1/e)$$

31. The Chinese case of 'under-urbanization' or 'de-urbanization' was previously observed by a number of scholars, such as Koshizawa (1978), Martinotti (1980), and Chang (1983), based on, however, largely misconceived urban population statistics and misinterpretation of China's development strategy.

32. Excluding countries for which information is incomplete, and countries with a population size less than 3 million, or area less than 100 square kilometres, countries with over 50 per cent of the industrial output accounted for by mining, and 'socialist' countries (e.g. Zimbabwe).

33. See a critique of Ran and Berry's paper by Ronna and Sjoberg (1993). This author, however, takes the view that problems with Ran and Berry's paper lie in the accuracy of statistics and not in the conceptual framework.

34. Figures produced by Perkins (1975) give a GIL of only 11 per cent for the modern industrial sector and 17.2 per cent if transportation and mining are included. Lower GIL figures would yield even smaller deviations of China's positions from the norm.

4 Urbanization Policies in the Post-Mao Era

To achieve industrialization at the highest possible speed, the government in the Maoist era adopted a policy exploitative of the rural sector. Such an approach necessitated strict migration controls to keep the rural population on the farms, as it was only natural that, without controls, millions of peasants would flee from the improvised countryside to cities. These measures, combined with a system of coercion and fear of sanction, heightened by Mao's insistence on the necessity of continuing 'class struggle' to fight against any deviant behaviour, worked relatively well to induce compliance with the state's objectives and bring down urban demographic expansion. The deep Maoist faith in the central command system and antipathy towards consumption were also seen in the rapid erosion of the commercial and financial roles of urban centres, both large and small. Outside state channels, private, spontaneous exchange of goods and the movement of people between the rural and urban sectors was heavily censored. The urban and rural economies operated more or less in isolation, with the exception of state-organized inter-sectoral flows of resources largely to the benefit of the urban-industrial sector. This segmentation was also duplicated spatially: an invisible wall separated the urban and rural populations.

The policy of isolated urban–rural development bottled up millions of surplus rural labourers in the countryside, but the urban sector still found itself faced with a host of serious problems in the late 1970s. These arose because of the past neglect of services and infrastructural development. Among the most obvious were too many people crowded in too few quarters, and too few shops with too many empty shelves. The problems became increasingly intolerable as the transition to the post-Mao era between 1976 and 1979 gave the public more opportunity to voice their grievances. One of the major causes of public discontent in the immediate aftermath of Mao's death was the two-decade-long policy of sacrificing consumption (including consumer goods, housing, and services). This had not only severely alienated the government from the people, but had also caused serious damage to the Chinese economy and made the task of modernizing the country extremely difficult. It became clear to the post-Mao leaders, as in the post-Stalin era in many Eastern European countries, that some reform

at least of the orthodox or classical socialist system must be insti-
gated to regain popularity before it was too late.

While the Marxist straitjacket has never been abandoned, post-
Mao reformers have shown a fair degree of pragmatism and flexibility in handling the economy and urban–rural relations. Three
elements were central to the post-Mao economic reform process.
These were the decollectivization of agriculture in favour of a
return to family farming; the 'open door' policy of promoting clos-
er economic ties with the outside world; and the attempt to replace
the classical system of vertically organized plans and bureaucratic commands with a mixed system of plans and markets (Perkins
1991). Along with new urbanization policies, policies used in the
1950s were revamped in the Post-Mao era. They were later institutionalized and became an integral part of the system under Deng
Xiaoping.

As described in Chapter Two, a new phase of relatively massive rural outflows and rapid urbanization was ushered in. Not
only have there been more rural–urban exchanges, but, morpho-
logically, Chinese coastal cities and towns today look more like
Asian boom cities with the familiar vibrancy of bustling private
businesses and street vendors, and problems ranging from pollu-
tion to prostitution. This represents a great change from the evid-
ently regulated and bleak urban scene of the Maoist era. But has
post-Mao policy broken with the past and embarked on a different path to urbanization, as suggested by Kwok (1987) and Lau
(1987) or is it merely a moderation of a fundamentally unchanged
legacy? To revisit the central issue—'What model now?'[1]—this
chapter explains and evaluates the impetuses for change and
mechanisms of urbanization in the 1980s.

New Impetuses for Change

In the face of strong pressures for urban in-migration, the stated
official policies of controlling urban in-migration and fostering the
growth of small settlements have remained largely unchanged.
However the floodgates began to gradually open, more as a by-
product of various policy changes than as an expected design
result. When China reopened its doors to the world in the early
post-Mao years, most Chinese people were dismayed by the glar-
ing disparities in living standards, especially in material terms, not

only between China and the West, but also between China and almost all of its East Asian neighbours. The problem became more acute as the economic development strategy adopted by Hua Guo-feng in 1977 and 1978, in another round of modernization drives following conventional practices, pushed the state's investment in material production to even higher levels.[2] At the same time, a more relaxed political atmosphere, the introduction of some mar-ket reforms, a rising per capita income, and a more realistic (in contrast to previously defensive and propagandist) official atti-tude towards economic problems also lowered the public's toler-ance of the existing dismal living conditions. Reformers after the transition under Hua realized that continuing suppression of con-sumption would be unpopular and the need for improvement in living standards could only be ignored at the regime's peril. Public demands for changes, coupled with new problems in the 1980s and the leadership's determination to raise living standards, cul-minated in a number of significant, mostly unplanned, changes. These took place in the wake of the momentous meeting of the Third Plenum of the Eleventh Party Congress in December 1978, where Deng Xiaoping's more pragmatic approach and open-door policy were outlined.

Pressures for Improvement in Urban Areas

While many urban problems that surfaced in the reform period had existed long before 1978, the return of millions of previous-ly rusticated urban youths and sent-down or exiled cadres and intellectuals in 1978 and 1979 was a catalyst for heightening pub-lic concern about them. A major and immediate problem was urban unemployment. At one point in 1978, the official urban unemployment rate was as high as 6 per cent, and, in absolute terms, as many as 6 million. This was startling to a country that had previously claimed success in permanently eradicating unem-ployment and was also a source of unrest because the urban pop-ulation was so used to full employment. It was too large a problem to be handled by the state sector alone, especially when the macro-economic policy continued to direct investment to heavy indus-tries with limited employment capability (refer to Table 3.2). The continued heavy reliance on state-run industry as the major source of government revenues also precluded any possibility of divert-ing massive state investment from the industrial sector, at least not before a fundamental overhaul of the economic and fiscal systems (Wong 1991; Naughton 1992a).

So in 1979 the government, admitting the limitations of the state-planned sector, began to revive urban collectives on a trial-and-error basis (Tang and Ma 1985). They were owned and run by local governments and committees. Reversing the previous demotion policy, the new approach focused on expanding the labour-intensive service sector and small urban enterprises outside the state sector. The shift in emphasis represented the government's accession to popular urban demand for more shops and more goods to buy, and a recognition of the useful contribution of locally initiated and run service companies to the national economy. Along with the reopening of free markets for agricultural produce in the late 1970s, these changes signalled a revised official view of the tertiary sector, the growth of which was soon destined to generate a noticeable urbanizing effect.

The other aspect of the urban employment expansion programme was the encouragement of individuals and groups of urban residents to open small businesses of their own, a taboo in Maoist doctrine. In a government regulation promulgated in 1981, a self-employed, individual enterprise (*getihu*) was permitted to freely hire up to two employees and five apprentices from the urban non-agricultural population (State Council 1981). Two years later, individual enterprises in towns were granted the freedom to hire from the agricultural population (State Council 1983a), culminating in the formal recognition of more established, company-type private enterprises in the late 1980s. The job creation programme also had profound implications for urbanization as it re-established a nascent urban labour market, an important starting point for more sustainable labour transfers from the countryside in the years to come.

At the same time, to muffle the widespread complaints about the low quality and limited variety of foodstuffs available in state grocery stores, the government moved quickly to reopen the long-suppressed free markets (*ziyou shichang*) for agricultural produce, beginning in 1977 in towns and suburbs outside cities. These free markets were direct sales outlets largely operated by peasants, who were encouraged to produce items, such as vegetables and poultry, in short supply in urban state-run stores. In the early post-Mao years these commodities came mostly from peasants' private plots. Reopening the markets was thus meant also to raise productivity in the farm sector by giving greater incentives for peasants to work on their private plots. In late 1978 another major step was taken when these markets were permitted to be reinstituted in some twenty large cities (*Renmin ribao* 1979; Skinner 1985). The farmers' markets, popular among urban dwellers, proved to be very successful in their ability to provide a wide range of fresh, high-quality produce never found in state-run outlets (Sit 1984). Chinese urban consumers must have been especially pleased by the drastic reduction in the unproductive time spent in queuing up for daily groceries.

The popularity of urban free markets soon sent their number soaring from a handful in 1976 to about 3,000 in 1980, and 13,106 ten years later (Table 4.1). In 1986 the nationwide sales of pork in free markets equalled one-fourth of sales by state-owned stores, while sales of poultry products outstripped state sales by sixty-five million kilograms (*Beijing Review* 1987). On average, each city is now served by some forty free markets, many of which are at the urban fringe because of the availability of sites and the ease of transporting goods (Taubman and Widmer 1987). The farmers' market sector has become an indispensable part of the current urban retail economy. In urbanization terms, the significance of permitting peasants to sell their products was both symbolic and real in breaking down the previous policy of sectoral and spatial segmentation. Migrant peasants, as vendors and peddlers—in fact, as small independent businessmen—have regained the legitimate and recognized status in the urban market-place they lost after the 'socialist transformation' in the 1950s. This new policy exposed many enterprising peasants to a new life experience, which was sure to have a long-term migration multiplier effect. The new urban status secured by peasant peddlers in the late 1970s re-opened a major sluice of temporary and, eventually, permanent migration to urban centres.

The other major change was in the urban housing sector. Again, urban housing shortages pre-dated 1978 but they were accentuated by the returning rusticated youths, many of whom were still unmarried but at that stage of their lives when they might be expected to start a family. As another material incentive for workers' productivity and to make up for the previous accumulated deficiency in housing development, the allocated investment in most urban housing in 1979 rose to 14.8 per cent of the total state capital investment from only 7.8 per cent in 1978 (Kuo 1989). As

Table 4.1 The Non-state Sector, 1978–1990

	1978	1980	1985	1989	1990	1978–90
A. Industrial Gross Output Value (%)					point	Change in percentage
State Enterprises	77.0	76.0	64.9	56.1	54.6	–22.4
Non-State Enterprises	23.0	24.0	35.1	43.9	45.4	+22.4
Collectives	23.0	23.5	32.1	35.7	35.6	+12.6
Individual Enterprises	–	–	1.9	4.8	5.4	+3.5
Others	–	0.5	1.2	3.4	4.4	+3.9
B. Retail Sales (%)						
State Enterprises	54.6	51.4	40.4	39.1	39.6	–15.0
Non-State Enterprises	45.4	48.6	59.6	60.9	60.4	+15.0
Collectives	43.3	44.6	37.2	33.2	37.7	–5.6
Joint Ventures	–	–	0.3	0.4	0.5	+0.2
Individual Enterprises	0.1	0.7	15.3	18.6	18.9	–18.8
Sales by Peasants to Urban Residents	2.0	3.2	6.8	8.6	9.3	+7.3
C. Free Markets (No.)						Annual Growth Rate
						(%)
Urban	na	2,919	8,013	13,111	13,106	+13.3
Rural	33,302	37,890	53,324	59,019	59,473	+5.0
D. Non-agricultural Employment (1,000)						
Urban ownerships						
State Enterprises	57,930	64,210	82,070	93,140	96,650	4.4
Collectives	19,890	23,770	32,730	34,570	35,190	4.9
Individual Enterprises	120	800	4,480	6,450	6,700	39.8
Others	–	–	440	1,310	1,630	
Rural Ownerships						
TVE (including rural private enterprises)	31,500	35,020	67,140	84,980	86,740	8.8
Non-state Subtotal	51,510	59,590	104,790	127,310	130,260	8.0
Percentage of total (%)	47.1	48.1	56.1	57.8	57.4	
Non-agricultural Total	109,440	123,800	186,860	220,450	226,910	6.3

Notes: TVE = Township and Village Enterprises
Sources: State Statistical Bureau (1985a, p. 477; 1987b, p. 10; 1990a, p. 115; 1990b, p. 13; 1991a, pp. 26, 97, 108, and 605).

Table 3.2 has shown, the proportion of state investment in hous-ing in the first half of the 1980s (21 per cent) was four times the average for the period 1966–75. In absolute terms the growth was even more phenomenal. In the second half of the 1980s, the proportion was lowered to 13 per cent, but still comparatively high by past records. Similarly, there were significant increases in the 1980s in investment in urban public utilities, commerce, and services, about two- to three-fold over the Maoist levels (Kuo 1989). Even with this impressive improvement in the 1980s, the level of urban infrastructure and service provision today remains low by international standards.

The open discussion of an urban housing 'problem' added fuel to a wider debate in the late 1970s about the fundamental purpose of socialist production. Using the metaphor of maintaining a balance between 'flesh' (production) and 'skeleton' (infrastructure), critics of the previous policy were able to gain an upper hand in the debate. What they favoured was a substantial cutback in the rate of investment to facilitate an increase in personal consumption and living standards (Lardy 1989). Investments in urban public utilities and services were considered important not only to the livelihood of the people, but also to the expansion of the national economy. The debate broadened the previously narrow view of treating cities as merely centres of production (*Renmin ribao* 1980b) and initiated an economic approach by the government more responsive to consumption demand and conducive to urbanization. In practical terms, the urban construction boom engendered initially by the housing crisis and later by foreign investment in hotel building acted as another centripetal force, intensifying many potential migrants' attraction to the 'city lights'.

In summary, what were started as mainly *ad hoc* measures to deal with the problem of urban unemployment and the inadequacy of the state-controlled retail and housing sectors set in motion changes that greatly expanded the non-industrial aspect of urban functions. Many cities have now regained their previous roles as centres of commerce, consumption, and cultural activity. These newly augmented urban functions and capacities formed the basis from which opportunities for peasant migrant labourers were generated.

A Reassessment of the Role of the City in Development

New urban functions also favoured a more positive perception about urban development among Chinese planners and academics in the early post Mao era. In this period, as housing, services, unemployment, and infrastructural problems became major concerns of urban dwellers, municipal governments were given a greater role in dealing with these social and economic affairs. As

cities rapidly expanded their non-industrial functions, there was
also an increased need to invest in infrastructural construction
and to co-ordinate these tasks at the local level. These tasks were
not covered by the contemporaneous planning framework dominated by 'vertical' industrial ministries. Thus it was significant that
city planning bureaucracies were reinstituted, after their elimination in the late 1950s. Two major national meetings were held in
1978 and 1980 among city mayors and planners to discuss setting
up a system of planning structures and legislation (Xu 1983).[3]

More fundamental changes came as a consequence of post-
Maoist reform aimed at developing a market sector, an open economy, and a more decentralized system of economic management
to improve efficiency. The stress on productivity and modern technology, along with the expansion of non-industrial urban functions, tended to favour cities and towns with locational advantages,
such as Shanghai, Tianjin, and Guangzhou (Pannell 1987). At the
same time, these new demands also exposed their gross infrastructural inadequacies. Urban development policy began to assert
itself and was not simply subordinated to industrialization policy.
The late 1970s saw the acceptance of the view that urbanization
should be treated as an inevitable process of modern development, instead of a product of rural–urban antithesis under capitalism. A low level of urbanization was seen as a symptom of
under-development. By 1980, the focus, as revealed at a National
Conference on Urban Planning Work, had already shifted to finding
out how to go about developing the urban sector, from the earlier debates on whether or not China should have more urban
development (Zhao 1988).

Though the 1980 Conference continued to reiterate the earlier
urban settlement policy of controlling the growth of large cities
and developing smaller urban places, many real changes have since
taken place, giving cities, especially those in the more developed
regions, a greater role in China's spatial economy. To remedy the
weak co-ordination of the previous rigid vertical, 'branch' approach
of central planning, 'horizontal' integration at local regional levels was promoted (*Renmin ribao* 1980a). The gravitation to large
urban centres was enhanced by market-oriented reform and the
open-door policy, which placed a premium on technology and savings generated by urban agglomeration economies[4] and their historical and commercial linkages with the outside world.

In policy terms, one of the most noteworthy steps has been the emphasis on building larger regional planning and administrative regions based on cities through a renewed stress on the *shiguanxian* programme (putting counties in the neighbouring regions under municipal administration). The programme was first introduced in the late 1950s in some large cities mainly to overcome vegetable supply problems (Fung 1980). The renewed programme in the 1980s gave cities greater control over largely agricultural resources, but also later, peasant labour in the neighbouring rural counties, so that the development of these counties could be geared to the needs of the city. From its inception in the late 1950s to 1981, altogether 173 counties, accounting for 7 per cent of the total number, were put under the administration of fifty-six, mostly large-sized provincial-level and prefectural-level cities (Chan 1985). The number of counties covered by this scheme had, by the end of 1984, risen to 541, or 25 per cent of the total number of counties. At that time, more than half (165 cities) of all the 286 cities administered some counties (Chan 1985). Since then the *shiguanxian* programme continued to expand, and by early 1988, the number of counties under urban administration had risen to 689, representing 35 per cent of all the counties (Ministry of Internal Affairs 1990). Another form of *shiguanxian*, not captured by the above figures, is the reclassification of counties into county-level cities, as described in Chapter Two.

At a broader level, the restoration of the '*zhongxin chengshi*' (key or centre city[5]) concept in the early 1980s cleared the way for large metropolises to expand further their influences and to reinforce their status in the Chinese spatial economy, in association with the drive to attract foreign trade and investment ('Disanci . . .' 1985). Being traditional regional economic centres, these big cities were viewed as the sinews of industrialization. Among the ways they gained that strength was by absorbing and disseminating new technology from home and abroad. In a report to the National People's Congress in 1982, Zhao Ziyang, for example, said that the development of these key cities was to help drive the economic growth of the regions and eventually the whole nation, especially in the area of technical transformation and the upgrading of industrial capacity (Zhao 1982). Similar to the *shiguanxian* programme, larger regional economic blocs based on these key cities, but transcending existing municipal and provincial boundaries, started forming in 1981. A list published in 1988 identifies twenty-three supra-provincial regional blocs (Yang 1988).

The most well-known is the Shanghai Economic Region, which is a supra-provincial region comprising Shanghai and five provinces (*Wen Wei Po* 1986). These regional blocs are loose, *ad hoc* organizations and do not form part of the regular planning-administrative system. A few of them have ceased to work and most of those remaining have functioned up to this stage largely as regional information clearing houses.

A real boost to the development of large cities has come from the expansion of economic planning powers given to coastal regions and most large cities under China's open-door economic policy (Yeung and Hu 1992). These measures included, initially, the designation of four Special Economic Zones (Shenzhen, Zhuhai, Shantou, and Xiamen) in 1979. Then, in the mid-1980s, the designation of Zhujiang (Pearl River) Delta, south Fujian, and Changjiang Delta as 'open areas', and fourteen coastal cities as 'open cities' for foreign investors (Figure 4.1) (*Economic Reporter* 1984). Hainan Island and Pudong in 1988 and 1990 respectively joined this broad category of 'open economic zones', which by early 1993 had included thousands of 'development zones' in many parts of China (*IMF Survey* 1993; *South China Morning Post* 1993). The open-door policy granted these areas and cities more financial autonomy and greater power in conducting foreign trade and attracting investment. A specific result of the policy of allowing open coastal zones to offer more favourable terms to attract foreign investors has been the bulldozing of hundreds of hectares of farmland in peri-urban regions to make room for foreign-related developments (such as the export-processing zones known as 'technological development districts' [*jishu kaifaqu*], towering joint-venture hotels and offices and high-rise apartments for Hong Kong compatriots). All this has had a massive urbanizing effect on the peri-urban fringe areas (Li and Chu 1987).

Another important reform that also gave large cities more economic autonomy was the designation of so-called 'separately listed cities' in the economic planning system (*jihua danlie chengshi*). These cities have been given an economic decision power equal to that of a provincial unit in the central planning system. Since 1983 ten cities have been granted this special status (Figure 4.1), and, reportedly, most of them benefited from this policy in generating higher rates of economic growth (*Wen Wei Po* 1987a; *Sing Tao Daily* 1988).

While predominantly regional in focus and favouring the coastal

Figure 4.1 Special Economic Zones and Open Cities

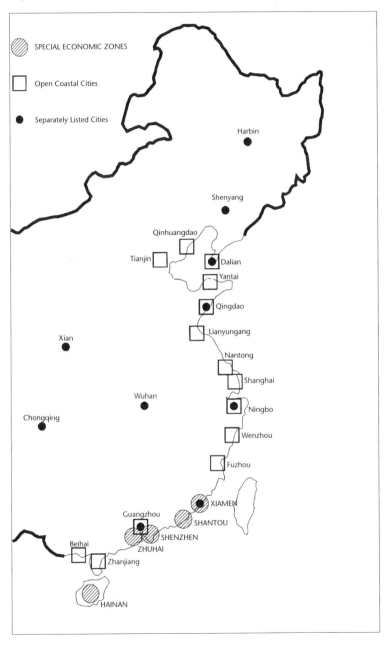

areas, these changes have significant implications for China's urban development. With large cities having a greater degree of autonomy and influence in the surrounding regions, urban development is no longer simply subordinated to central controls. The introduction of market forces and the opening to the outside world have fostered the rapid expansion of a market-oriented coastal economy, mostly outside the planned sector. The loosening of central controls has given local officials many opportunities for pursuing local (*vis-à-vis* central) and, at times, personal interests. At the same time, the institutionalization of the so-called 'double-tier' system of planned and market economies has also generated competitive pressures on urban enterprises to become efficient, thus making low-cost rural labour attractive to managers of urban enterprises under all kinds of ownership (Byrd 1991). In a nutshell, post-Mao reforms have fostered more connected urban and rural economic development, with an increasing focus on urban-related industrial production. Newly generated urban activities have turned many cities along the coast into great magnets. This approach can be described, in Chinese socialist parlance, as 'the urban sector as the leading sector and the rural sector as the foundation', although it is also true that greater pressures for change in the Chinese economy came from the rural economic forces unleashed by successful agricultural reform and not from the cities, which are still floundering about in the urban enterprise reform even in the 1990s.

The Problem of Rural Labour Surplus

Under the new household responsibility system introduced in the countryside in 1978, there have been great incentives to economize on labour use. These have been the main cause of the dramatic reduction in labour per sown unit area of crops. Taylor (1988) reports that in the early 1980s, in terms of average standard labour days per hectare used, figures for virtually every crop dropped sharply between 1978 and 1985. Labour used for wheat, for example, dropped by 53 per cent and soya beans by 48 per cent. While estimates of the precise size of surplus labour released by the growth in worker productivity vary according to the methods and assumptions adopted, there is little doubt that the labour surplus was sizeable. Taylor and Banister's (1991) recent estimate suggests that one-third of the labour force (about 100 million) in the agricultural sector in 1987 could be considered redundant.

The rapid rise in rural productivity after the momentous rural reforms beginning in late 1978 demonstrated clearly that alternative jobs outside the traditional domain of grain production had to be generated for the increasing surplus labour in the countryside. The government's first response was to encourage peasants to diversify their pursuits by moving into high-value cash crops and rural industry and services. Due to the shortage of suitable land and the relatively limited alternative agricultural employment opportunities in the rural sector, the only viable option in the longer run was to shift to non-agricultural pursuits and induce a long-overdue restructuring of rural employment. The heavy population burden on farm land and rapidly expanding rural commerce have produced tremendous pressures for urbanization. In the past, they were kept largely at bay by the whole array of measures described in the previous chapter. However, these pressures have become irresistible as the city lights burn brighter than ever and the peasants have been freed by the dismantling of their communes. The privatization of farming has created a different rural political economy marked by a significant decrease in state control and coercion, and a simultaneous increase of productive resources in the hands of peasants. The challenge posed to the Chinese government is gigantic. They must discover where to find jobs for this huge but also less controllable displaced rural labour force and, in relation to that, decide whether rural migrants should be allowed to go to urban centres.

Economic Development and Urbanization in the Reform Era

Despite the various changes initiated in the early post-Mao period, the leadership has been no less driven by the desire to rapidly develop a strong and modern industrial economy than was its predecessor. This is seen in the ambitious plans unveiled at the beginning of 1983 to quadruple China's industrial and agricultural output by the year 2000. In terms of state capital investment, China has continued to cling to an industrially biased approach, allocating most of the state capital investment to industry, especially heavy industry, and aiming at high economic growth rates (see Table 3.2 and Kueh 1989). This has limited the government's ability to invest heavily in the more labour-intensive light industry and non-material production sectors.

However, the leadership also understood that an improvement in urban consumption was urgently needed to regain its popularity. At the same time, there was a swelling surplus rural labour force that needed to be moved out of agricultural production in both the short and long runs. How to resolve the conflicts between greater demands for a shift from the agricultural sector and the limited funds available for urban infrastructures? Which road should China follow? These concerns have triggered a heated debate on rural development and urbanization strategy. While a substantial amount of the debate has been on the urban size issue of settlement development policy (e.g. Kirkby 1985; Zhou 1990; Wu 1992), the burden or cost migrants impose on cities remains the real issue. How can China solve its rural surplus labour problem and increase its industrial output without incurring the substantial social costs associated with urbanization?

In the initial post-Mao era, the government responded to the rural unemployment problem by continuing the Maoist rural industrialization programme, which, as explained before, fitted neatly the dual objectives of transferring labour out of the farm sector without effecting a residential change at the same time, or, in short, 'industrial growth without urbanization'. Premised on the perception that it would be disastrous if all underemployed rural labourers moved to urban areas, even if this happened over a longer period, the position adopted was that the surplus rural work-force transfered out of farming was to be kept as close to home as possible. Enthusiastically portrayed as the 'Chinese road to urbanization' by many scholars in China (e.g. Yao and Wu 1982), the so-called '*litu bulixiang*' (leave the land but not the village) programme by expanding the township and village enterprises sector (examined below) continued to receive government support in the early 1980s. Most important of all, around 1979–81 rural enterprises were allowed to enter the more profitable industrial sectors producing consumer goods, which were previously reserved for state-owned enterprises. This created the basis for the momentous growth of the township and village enterprises in the 1980s (Wong 1988; Naughton 1992a).

While the township and village enterprises programme was popular among many peasants, it helped little to release the mounting pressures for improving urban tertiary services and consumption. It was clear to the government that an expanded service sector was much needed. However, the overriding priority of industrial growth had left only limited room, if not just in financial terms, for the government to improve commerce, services, and consumption. This constraint forced the reform leaders to break from classical socialist practice to let a genuine non-state sector exist side by side with the state sector in the city, an exercise long ago tried by reformers in post-Stalin Eastern Europe. Under the principle of the market sector supplementing the planned sector, post-Mao reforms have helped invigorate the non-state sector through so-called 'commercialization' (Tang and Jenkins 1990). In the last decade, the share of the non-state sector in urban-based industries and retail sales has increased steadily in both absolute and relative terms (Table 4.1). Today the non-state sector has doubled its share of total industrial output from 23 per cent in 1978 to 45.4 per cent in 1990. Similarly, it accounts for 60 per cent of all retail sales. More impressive changes are seen in the price structure: by 1991 the proportions of consumer goods and industrial producer goods under state-controlled prices had shrunk to only 21 per cent and 30 per cent, respectively (*World Journal* 1992g).

While state-sector employment grew at a relatively high average speed of 4.4 per cent per year in 1978–90, non-state sector employment expanded at close to twice that rate, at 8 per cent per year. Such a high expansion rate in the non-agricultural sector, based on the officially recorded figures, created on average about 10 million jobs a year (slightly less than half in the township and village enterprises sector). To this, one must also add a huge, though unknown, number of jobs created by the growing hidden economy, a large portion of which is in urban and peri-urban areas (Huang 1992).[6]

There was little doubt that not all the new urban jobs in the non-township and village enterprises sector could be filled by the existing urban labour force, the new supply of which shrunk as a result of the depressed urban fertility rates of the 1970s and which was constrained by the already very high urban female labour participation rate. As supply of urban labour became scarce, urban graduates naturally avoided low-skilled and low-paid service and industrial jobs in both non-state and state enterprises. Rural labour had to brought in to cope with the shortage. Even within the 'urban' (excluding township and village enterprises) sector, new recruitment from peasant labourers totalled about 16 million, or 16 per cent of all the 'urban' recruitment, in the period between 1978 and 1990 (Table 4.2). On top of this number, another 55 million

CITIES WITH INVISIBLE WALLS

Table 4.2 Annual Urban Recruitment, 1978–1990 (in 1,000s)

| | By Type of Ownership | | | | | | |
Year	State	Collective	Individual	Other*	Total	From Rural Areas	As % of total
1978	3,920	1,524			5,444	1,484	27.3
1979	5,675	3,181	170		9,026	708	7.8
1980	5,722	2,780	498		9,000	1,274	14.2
1981	5,210	2,671	319		8,200	920	11.2
1982	4,093	2,223	334		6,650	660	9.9
1983	3,737	1,706	840		6,283	682	10.9
1984	4,156	1,973	1,086		7,215	1,230	17.0
1985	4,991	2,038	1,107		8,136	1,502	18.5
1986	5,363	2,238	330		7,931	1,665	21.0
1987	4,994	2,140	857		7,991	1,668	20.9
1988	4,922	2,632	889		8,443	1,599	18.9
1989	3,673	1,915	370	24	6,198	1,220	19.7
1990	4,750	2,350	400	35	7,850	1,180	15.0
1978–90	61,206	29,371	7,200	59	98,367	15,792	16.1
% of total	62.2	29.9	7.3	0.1	100	16.1	

Note: * included under state enterprises before 1989
Source: State Statistical Bureau (1983a, p. 146; 1991a, p. 116)

jobs were generated in 1978–90 in the township and village enterprise sector (Table 4.1), which were almost totally filled by peasant labour. Most of these peasant workers became *de facto* urban residents as a result of these job changes.

As before, these peasant workers have provided many useful services, especially by filling gaps left by the state sector workers in urban construction, manufacturing, and petty commerce. Also, these new entrants have imposed only small additional direct expenses on urban budgets since they have not been eligible for urban economic and social benefits such as housing and medical care. Seeing that peasant migrants fill low-skilled positions shunned by urban youths and provide fresher and better quality foodstuffs, the post-Mao government has allowed the urban in-migration trend to continue. Consequently, the connection between rising urbanization costs borne by the state and expanding urban population growth has been increasingly broken off.

There were other changes that contributed to the increases in the rate of rural–urban migration. The success of containing urbanization had previously been contingent upon the strict regulation of food grain delivery through location-specific rationing and a control system close to a police state, but since the late 1970s such regulation and control have been more difficult to sustain. Bumper harvests in the early 1980s flooded Chinese markets with all kinds of food, whilst the omnipotent image of the Party was shattered when it began to admit that the Cultural Revolution, orchestrated by the 'great helmsman', was a human disaster. This caused a significant erosion of the Party's control, at least psychologically and ideologically, over the populace. But perhaps the greatest boost to rural–urban flows was agricultural decollectivization in 1979–83, which substantially diminished the general administrative and political capacities of rural collectives and their ability to regulate the mobility of peasants (Mallee 1988).

Following the framework used in Chapter Three, one can also assess the performance of the Q/UP (industrial output per urban resident) ratio in the 1980s by reference to Table 3.7. In this table, it is shown that the Q/UP ratio rose by 6.5 per cent per year, about the same as the average for the period 1952–80. It is also clear that productivity-oriented economic reform has succeeded in raising at least the crude industrial labour–output ratio (Q/Li), which shows an annual average growth of about 6.5 per cent. More significantly, among the two common factors considered before, the increase in the Q/Li ratio was the sole factor accounting fully for the increase in the Q/UP. The other factor, the change in the Li/UP ratio (the so-called 'urban multiplier'), remained more or less the same over the 1980s and did not contribute to the rise in the Q/UP ratio.

Looking down one level at the sub-components of the 'urban multiplier', there was a small drop in the non-working population multiplier ('e') and the degree of urbanization of non-agricultural employment ('u'). Hence, their changes contributed to a small extent to the rise in Q/UP. But their small contributions were offset more or less wholly by an increase in the service employment multiplier ('s'). In other words, the major mechanism, 'e', which was central to achieving 'industrialization without much urbanization' during the period 1965–80, was only marginally important in the 1980s. By contrast, the expansion of the service sector in the post-Mao era indicates a reversal of the previous practice of suppressing the 'non-productive' service industry.

At a more general level, the rise in the Q/Li ratio being the main (the sole) contributor to the rise in the Q/UP ratio contrasts with the previous Maoist pattern in the period 1965–80, but resembles similar patterns in some East European socialist countries in their second phase of industrialization, such as the USSR (1951–9), Poland (1960–70), and Romania (1960–70) (see also Ofer 1976). In post-Mao China, efforts to control urbanization costs have been directed chiefly at prohibiting the extension of urban benefits to the majority of new migrants through the discriminatory system based on household registration described previously. The successful control of the expansion of urban population through depressing the various urban multipliers had by the 1980s become harder as the multipliers were probably already close to their limits.

Categories of Urban In-migration

Based on the above analysis, the remaining part of the chapter examines the various channels for urban in-migration, with particular reference to work-related migration. Data from the 1990 Census compiled in Table 4.3 reveals that work-related rural–urban migrants accounted for a little less than half of all the rural–urban migrants during the period between 1985 and 1990. As far as urbanization is concerned, job-related migration is far more important than other types of migration as it often supports current or future non-work-related migration. To the majority of the migrants who are not employed (for example dependents), the financial resources generated by the jobs of other family members provide the wherewithal of their urban living. There are, of course, other groups of migrants whose movement is not related to employment. The only significant group is made up of those who come to study or receive training in urban centres, and they accounted for about one-eighth of all the rural–urban migrants in the 1985–90 period.

While expanded job opportunities in the urban areas have been the basis for high rural–urban transfers since the beginning of the reform era, the increasing availability of other 'ingredients' necessary for *de facto* migration has been equally important. Food grain and other foodstuffs have become readily obtainable without ration coupons in free markets, as have grain coupons themselves, and they are often affordable to those who have an urban job (Huang 1992). Finding permanent housing in cities is still a big problem, but temporary and semi-permanent housing—ranging

Table 4.3 Rural–Urban Migration, 1985–1990: Reasons for Migration (%)

	To Cities	To Towns
Work-related		
Work transfers	4.2	12.2
Job assignments after graduation	3.7	3.2
Wugong jingshang (seeking employment in industry and running businesses)	40.4	30.8
Subtotal	48.3	46.2
Non-work related		
Studies and training	12.9	14.4
Seeking support from relatives and friends	12.9	10.9
Retirement and resignations from job	0.3	0.5
Migration with families	9.7	17.7
Marriages	9.0	4.8
Others	6.9	5.4
Subtotal	51.7	53.8
Total	100.0	100.0

Source: compiled from 1990 Population Census by Yunyan Yang

from low-class guest-houses and shared rental apartments to squatter huts and village houses at urban fringes—is increasingly available at market rates outside the state-sector for those who can afford it. Other migrant workers often simply make do for the night at railway stations or in makeshift quarters at the construction sites and factories they work in. In short, the very basic items necessary for an urban living (including forged identity cards) have become available in the market or black market due to the increasing commercialization of the various economic sectors and the emergence of an informal, at times hidden, economy (Huang 1992).

What has evolved then since the early 1980s is a greater official acceptance of urban in-migrants on their own initiatives, mostly outside the conventional channels of entry to state sector employment and without conversion of household registration status. As a result of this change, two categories of urban in-migrants, one with formal urban household registration status and one without, co-exist (Gu 1991). At the heart of this duality lies the state and

Table 4.4 Formal and Informal Rural–Urban Migration

Characteristics	Formal	Informal
Change in household registration	from agricultural/rural to non-agricultural/urban	no change
Entitlement to state-supplied food grain	full	from nil to temporary entitlements
Legal urban resident status	full status	illegal or temporary
The socio-economic sector the migrant moves to	state sector	mostly to non-state sector also as temporary workers in state enterprises
Mechanism of effecting migration	transfers in accordance with state economic plans (mostly non-competitive)	'spontaneous' based on personal contacts and market information
Stability of moves	relatively stable	mostly unstable
Labour characteristics of principal migrants		
Skill level	mostly skilled workers	mostly unskilled or low-skilled labour
Employment type	mostly permanent jobs in state enterprises	temporary or semi-permanent jobs in non-state enterprises; or self-employment

Source: compiled from Gu (1991)

non-state socio-economic structure of socialist China. It is mirrored in the peasant and non-peasant segmentation of the populace,[7] organized along the most fundamental watershed of contemporary Chinese society, the household registration system[8] (Guo and Liu 1990; Chan and Tsui 1992). It is along this line that we will categorize the migration flows in the 1980s. Borrowing the 'formal/informal sectors' or 'upper/lower circuits' terminology from the development literature (e.g. Santos 1979), we may categorize migration involving a formal change to full urban household registration status as 'formal' and migration without as 'informal'. The two exhibit very different functional features, broadly similar to the nature of formal and informal socio-economic sectoral categorization in many other developing countries.

As summarized in Table 4.4, the major difference between formal

and informal migration occurs in the entitlement to full urban resident benefits, consisting of both an urban non-agricultural household registration status and an entitlement to commodity food
grain. Other socio-economic aspects also differ: with informal
migration, the principal migrant is mostly drawn to temporary or
unstable, unskilled or low-skilled jobs in the urban economy, while
formal migration often results from recruitment of the principal
migrant to skilled and permanent jobs in state-run enterprises.
More importantly, the former type is 'spontaneous', largely based
on migrants' own initiatives, while the latter is heavily regulated
by government plans. The urban residency status of a majority of
informal migrants is legally only 'temporary' for those who have
informed the authorities; for those who have not, it is technically illegal (see below). In contrast, the urban residency status of
formal migrants is permanent. That is why Chinese official usage
refers to informal migration as 'population movement' (*renkou
liudong*) and formal migration as 'migration' (*qianyi*). Migrants
in the former category are accordingly termed '*liudong renkou*'
(floating population).

Formal Urban In-migration

Formal urban in-migration involves conversion to full urban status, and the channels through which it occurs have remained
unchanged. The most common are assignment for college graduates, state labour recruitment and job transfers, demobilization,
and persons displaced by urban annexations. But persons seeking support from their immediate family members, and persons
previously rusticated can also apply to (re)enter urban places. One
estimate (see Chapter Two) suggests that the number of new conversions to urban non-agricultural household registration status
(*nongzhuanfei*) in the period 1980–9, excluding those changes due
to natural population growth, was roughly half the net gains in
the urban population due to migration in the same period. This
number appears larger than one would expect given the repeat-
ed issuing of official directives to tightly control these channels.
Two[9] developments documented below contributed to a situation
in the second half of the 1980s described as being 'out of control'
by one report in *Guangming ribao* (1989).

First, there was an effort to improve conditions for intellectuals and state cadres, a large number of whom had long suffered

from family separation under the previous rigid assignment policy and tight *hukou* restrictions. It included granting them a special 'family reunion' allowance, which allowed their spouses, children
under fifteen, and parents who could not earn a living, to move
to the cities with urban *hukou* status (Department of Personnel
1991, p. 53). It was first granted to senior professionals and cadres
in 1980. Then it was extended in 1982 to returned intellectuals
from overseas and in 1984 to a considerably larger population of
state employees down to middle-ranking professionals and cadres.
Workers and technicians in 'harsh' regions (*jianku diqu*) like the
Third Front region also benefited from the special allowance
(Department of Personnel 1992, p. 55; *Zhejiang ribao* 1985), as
did dependents of military officers who were stationed in frontier
regions, islands, and deserts. The latter was more as an enticement to work in these unpopular regions than a remedy for any
particular problem of family separation. Under the scheme officers'
dependents (mostly wives and children) were allowed to convert
to urban *hukou* where they were living (Department of Personnel
1992, pp. 321–8).

Second, as part of a programme to decentralize government
duties in an effort to better co-ordinate information flows and
decision-making within the different bureaucracies, local authorities down to the township level were given greater powers in
approving *nongzhuanfei*.[10] They were allowed to set up, for example, their own eligibility criteria of those who were going to benefit
from the 'family reunion' policy. Apparently, many local authorities and officials, especially after 1984, intensively exploited the
opportunities to pursue local interests, which were often at odds
with the central ones (*Guangming ribao* 1989). Meanwhile, there
was rapid urban physical aggrandizement, resulting in huge increases in the non-agricultural population category in 1984 and 1985
in particular, a familiar situation of chaos and 'slack' once power
is decentralized in China.[11] At the same time, inadequate fiscal
resources have forced many local governments to succumb to tap-
ping local funds by imposing a variety of legal and illegal levies
on enterprises and population (Wong 1991). With increased autonomy in deciding local household registration conversions, selling
urban residency rights has also become a popular means to raise
funds for construction and other purposes. The approach adopted
has been similar in nature to those investment immigration programmes used by countries like Canada. In Guangdong, starting

from 1988, a new measure designed to attract funds from over-seas Chinese to finance urban housing programmes has allowed those who bought certain types of property in the cities or towns using hard foreign currency to move in one of their relatives, who would also be granted an urban household registration status. In addition, these new migrants were required to pay a large sum (in Guangzhou, this amounts to RMB¥10,000–15,000 per head) for urban infrastructure costs (*Wen Wei Po* 1988a, 1991; *Ming Pao* 1988). In recent years, newspapers in Hong Kong have been full of advertisements selling this type of apartment with the special privilege of household registration conversion for relatives in main-land China.

Other places far from Hong Kong, however, have targeted newly rich peasants. For example, Botou in Hebei Province has allowed peasants to move to the city provided they invested at least RMB¥10,000 in commerce or industry and pay an urban infra-structural fee (*peitou fei*) (Li 1990). Similar enticements ranging from temporary to full urban residency rights, at different price tags, were tried out in many places to attract capital from the peasants (see *Wen Wei Po* 1987b; Wang and Fang 1990). In the early 1990s, especially in 1992, one could purchase an urban house-hold registration in many county-level cities and towns in Jiangsu and Henan. Reportedly, despite the hefty price tag, averaging about RMB¥8,000 to 15,000 per person, there were no shortage of buyers (*The Nineties* 1992b). In Taixing, one small city in Jiangsu, the local government was able to raise RMB¥20 million plus with-in a short time by selling 3,000 urban household registrations. This kind of practice has recently been criticized by the Ministry of Public Security as illegal (*World Journal* 1992b).

Decisions regarding who could benefit from the new family reunion allowance often involved officials' subjective assessments or discretionary powers. For this reason the system was widely open to misuses and abuses. With more power in the hands of local officials in a more compartmentalized administrative struc-ture controlled by different ministries, illegal household conver-sions, mostly involving favouritism or briberies, were rampant in the 1980s.[12] This grave situation prompted the State Council to take action to tighten up and recentralize the system in late 1989. A precise annual quota of *hukou* conversions was set for each province by the State Planning Commission and county-level gov-ernments were stripped of their powers to implement conversions

(Ministry of Personnel 1991, pp. 330–7). Judging from the 1990 non-agricultural population figures reported in Table 2.1, which indicates a drop from the 1989 figures, it appears that these measures, along with the austerity policy, have had some dampening, if only temporary, effect on the expansion of non-agricultural population.

Informal Urban In-migration

Informal migration refers to population shifts involving no conversion to full urban status. As such, it does not impose direct and permanent costs on the state—though some indirect or temporary state outlays are unavoidable (such as those resulting from use of roads and other non-exclusionary urban infrastructures). Table 4.3 suggests that formal migration, in the form of 'work transfers' and 'assignments' carried out by the state sector, was only a minor component (16 per cent and 33 per cent to cities and towns, respectively) in work-related rural–urban migration in the second half of the 1980s. By contrast, the category of *wugong jingshang* (seeking employment in industry and running businesses) was the single most important component (84 per cent and 67 per cent to cities and towns, respectively) of work-related migration and overall rural–urban migration. The category of *wugong jing shang* includes a small but unknown amount of migration generated by permanent recruitment in the state sector, but a large part of it is informal migration associated mostly with the development of the non-state sector, including the informal urban economy. The predominance of informal migration in rural–urban flows in the 1980s represents a drastic change from the Maoist era when it was kept to a very limited level.[13] Many other studies (e.g. Goldstein and Goldstein 1991) have also underscored the enormous popularity of this type of migration in the post-Mao urban scene.

Though the impulse for informal migration comes from the booming economy, two sets of state regulations have been particularly crucial in easing this type of migration. Many of the measures contained within the regulations were first carried out in some provinces prior to their formal enactment by the relevant central ministries (Solinger 1985; Lee 1992; Chan 1992a). The first set of regulations pertains to the creation of a new permanent urban household category. In 1984 a circular issued by the State

Council formally permitted peasants meeting employment and housing requirements to settle (*luohu*) in undesignated towns (*jizhen*) under the name of 'households with self-supplied grains' (*zili koulianghu*) (*Renmin ribao* 1984c). The new provision required that the peasants be employed or self-employed in these towns for a significant period (in some cases, three years) and have secured accommodation. In practice, in some locales, the 'accommodation' requirement was simply a matter of furnishing an address of an existing town resident who was willing to co-operate with the applicant. As the name suggests, these households were not eligible for state-supplied low-price grains and edible oils, but they could purchase food grains and oils from the state at higher prices ('negotiated prices'). The new provision was important in that it offered permanent residence security to these people, thus inducing or requiring them to abandon their often half-hearted agricultural pursuits, which were detrimental to the farm economy. Though officially classified as non-agricultural population, this new category was often not treated on a par with existing non-agricultural householders. In some reported cases, local officials treated them as agricultural population when it came to deciding their eligibility to social benefits (Zhu *et al.* 1991). In other locales, the group was excluded from the non-agricultural registers, or treated as a special category of its own (Chan, J. 1990). In terms of functional and labour characteristics, these 'households with self-supplied grains' were also more similar to the informal than formal migrant category described in this study. Although the State Council's circular referred to undesignated towns (*jizhen*), in practice, this special type of household was accepted in many designated towns, including some cities in Guangdong (*Nanfang ribao* 1984). Zhu *et al.* (1991) reports that about 5 million people were granted these new household registrations between 1984 and 1988.

The second set of regulations governs temporary residence in urban areas. At least as early as 1983, regulations allowing non-native personnel 'temporary residence permits' were formally introduced in Wuhan (Solinger 1985). Similar nationwide regulations were later stipulated by the Ministry of Public Security in 1985 (*Renmin ribao* 1985). These set up procedures for unorganized migrant workers in urban centres to register for 'temporary residence permits' (*jizhu zheng* and *zhanzhu zheng*), thereby providing them with some form of legal cover under the household registration regulations. The new stipulation differs from the previous ones in that 'spontaneous' migration to jobs in urban centres is tacitly allowed (Solinger 1985). The concern of these regulations appeared to have shifted to public order (in other words, prevention of crimes) from blocking urbanward migration.[14] At the same time, this stipulation also empowers the authorities to regulate flows of this temporary population through the issuance of residence permits. In the early years, getting a temporary residence permit for a migrant who had already found an urban job was probably not more than a matter of formality. As migrants flooded cities—in 'waves of blind flows' as described by the Chinese media— during the second half of the 1980s, these permits became increasingly harder to obtain. In the boom town of Shenzhen, for instance, a temporary residence permit could cost as high as RMB¥30,000 on the black market in 1992 (*The Nineties* 1992a).

While informal migration to urban centres in the Maoist era was confined to a small stream of 'temporary workers' whose movement was organized between communes and state enter-prises, the deluge in the 1980s came from a great variety of sources. Four broad categories of migration based on different employ-ment channels are identified in Table 4.5. These range from daily movements of small vendors, not involving any change in house-hold registration status and entitlement to commodity grains, to the more permanent moves such as those of contract workers in state enterprises, involving some temporary entitlement to urban benefits. No matter how temporary these flows were, they have added to the *de facto* size of the daytime urban population.

Free Markets

The free markets for agricultural produce were a major reason why petty traders from the country came to the urban areas. As explained before, greater use of private plots by rural households to grow non-grain crops and rear animals was silently allowed as early as in 1977. Encouraged to sell things to the markets after negotiated contract requirements were met, farmers took goods from private plots to be exchanged in rural markets. These activ-ities were later endorsed in the rural diversification policy put forward by the Third Plenum of the Eleventh Party Congress in December 1978. Previous restrictions on rural marketing, such as bans on trading of draught animals, and long-distance trade, were all lifted in the early 1980s, and, as Skinner (1985) observes, as

Table 4.5 Employment Channels of Informal Rural–Urban Migration in the Post-Mao Era

Channel	Location	Change in household classification	Change in commodity grain entitlement
1. Small vendors	all urban centres	no	no
2. Nannies	mainly in large cities	no	no
3. Employment in Non-state Sector			
in TVE	mostly in towns	} may apply for change to *zili kouliang hu*	} *zili kouliang hu* are eligible for 'negotiated priced' grains and oils provided by the state
in private enterprises	all urban centres		
in urban collectives	all urban centres		
4. Contract workers mostly in cities in state enterprises	all urban centres		temporary entitlements to commodity grains and oils

Notes: TVE = Township and village enterprises

of 1984 trade in China's rural markets was less restricted than at any time since 1953.

As markets needed to be relatively centrally located to serve their customers, many of them were placed in existing towns of varying sizes, both designated and undesignated. In fact, as Yan *et al.* (1964) and Skinner (1964–5) long ago observed, many towns traditionally functioned largely as marketing centres for the surrounding rural hinterland. This urban economic base was almost totally wiped out during the Cultural Revolution decade (1966–76) owing to the suppression of rural marketing. As rural commerce returned to these towns in the early post-Mao years, so did their economic prosperity and population growth (Fei 1984). Indeed, the growth since 1978 in rural commerce has been phenomenal. The number of rural markets steadily rose from 33,302 in 1978 to 43,500 in 1983. It further surged to 53,324 in 1985 and stabilized at about 59,500 in the early 1990s (Table 4.1; SSB 1991a, p. 605). The pattern of the sales volume of free markets mirrored their growing number. There was also an expansion of the line of commodities sold in these markets. An increasing proportion of sales was contributed by industrial products, creating a far more important role for these markets in the urban retail system (*Jingji ribao* 1984).

Most of the peasant vendors commute daily from the nearby villages to farmers' markets in urban and peri-urban areas. This requires no change in their agricultural household registration or entitlement to commodity grain. They do not actually constitute additional permanent urban population though they are a part of the *de facto* day-time urban population. The indirect urbanization effects generated by these rural markets, however, cannot be underestimated. Not only have many of the initial trading farmers undergone occupational changes, becoming part-time or full-time traders (especially after 1983 when long-distance trading was permitted) and stayed in cities as 'floating population', but these markets have also generated congregations of other businesses, like restaurants and hotels. These businesses become an important basis for the urban expansion of existing centres and the town-forming process of smaller settlements. Designated towns and cities have been enlarged in size. Thousands of newly designated towns since 1984 owed their origins to the rapid growth in rural commerce, as well as the township and village enterprises, in these marketplaces.

Another important step toward more urbanization was made when permission was granted in 1979 to hold free markets within municipal boundaries. Not only do a huge number of peasants enter urban areas on a daily basis, but more importantly, they are exposed to the attractions of urban life and its opportunities. This is crucial to the gradual process of rural–urban transformation of the Chinese peasant population.

Employment of Nannies

If the middle class in many major Asian metropolises today cannot operate the way they are accustomed to without maids from the Philippines or Thailand, it is hardly surprising that there is a strong demand for *baomu* or domestic helpers in many large Chinese cities among double-worker families. With a similar pattern of growing urban prosperity and shifts to smaller nuclear families in cities, many double-worker families are desperate for helpers to look after their children and take up domestic chores. While hiring maids was not uncommon among high-ranking officials' families during the Maoist era, the practice only became popular among families of urban intellectuals and workers with the tolerance of the government in the 1980s, who wanted to improve urban living conditions and create jobs for the rural unemployed.

One estimate suggests that, for example, 5 per cent of the families in Beijing in 1986 would have liked to hire domestic help, this translates into a demand for about 80,000 domestic helpers (Liu *et al.* 1988). With low-skilled labour generally in short supply in cities, there is a strong market for young rural women who happen to have the willingness and connections. In Beijing, the municipal government initially responded by asking the Women's Federation to form a household help placement company, the famous March Eighth Domestic Service Co., to organize country women, mostly from Anhui (which has a long tradition of exporting domestic helpers) for the nanny jobs in the city.

As the demand for nannies continues to outstrip what can be provided by the government-regulated placement companies, there has developed an unregulated market in many cities. Despite the government's attempts to close down the market, it has continued to thrive. Maids hired from the unregulated market often have difficulties in getting temporary residence permits, and technically speaking, have no legal right to live in cities under the current rules governing urban residency. However, in practice, the authorities frequently turn a blind eye to the situation. The legality of nannies coming to the city on their own remains a grey area of policy. Nationwide statistics on the size of the nanny population probably do not exist, but studies in Beijing suggest that in 1986 the number of nannies was more than 50,000, of whom only 12,000 were handled by the various government-sanctioned placement companies (Liu *et al.* 1988).

The nanny market is another important part of the burgeoning urban labour market and is a major urbanization cause. Typically, a nanny job is the first urban job within the reach of many country women who have few marketable urban skills and are unfamiliar with urban settings. It is common that once they have learned more about the job market and found their way around the city, they are likely to hop to another job with better pay or prestige, usually in private enterprises (Beijing Municipal Government 1989). The job of working as a nanny is a crucial first step in the gradual process of rural–urban transition for these women.

Employment in the Urban Non-state Sector (Collective and Private Enterprises)

The marketization policy of the 1980s contributed to the growing numbers of non-state-owned enterprises in cities and towns. There are two major types: the township and village enterprises, and the urban collective and private enterprises. The township and village enterprises include all those run and owned by rural organizations and individual peasants. Most of these enterprises are in the manufacturing sector (Wong 1988; Zweig 1991). These enterprises are often termed 'rural enterprises', but a large proportion of them are not in the countryside but in designated towns and market towns. Urban collective enterprises, found mostly in designated cities and towns, are those owned and managed by local authorities, urban neighbourhoods, and groups of urban residents. Increasingly moving out of the direct control of the government in the reform period, these are largely small enterprises concentrating on low-skill services such as repair shops, restaurants, and retail outlets (see Tang and Ma 1985). Added to these are private enterprises, which are run and owned by individuals or foreign nationals, or jointly by them. The boundary between the collective and private ownerships has been increasingly blurred in recent years as many private individuals register their businesses as collectives, the so-called 'fake collectives', to avoid higher taxes and other unfavourable terms levied on private businesses (*Wen Wei Po* 1990b). The distinction between 'urban' and 'rural' private and collective enterprises is not easy to make as the forms of ownership of these businesses have become more diverse and they have tended to converge in the same profitable trades, behaving similarly in the market-place.

Favoured by the government's low tax policy and an open policy that emphasized the competitiveness of the labour-intensive sectors, rural enterprises in the 1980s were a rapidly burgeoning segment of the economy (Zhang 1991), as illustrated by Table 4.1. Employment in these enterprises does not engender any change to one's original household registration classification or grain supply status. As in the pre-reform period, peasant workers in these enterprises maintain their formal rural household registration status (the official term used in the early 1980s was '*yinong yigong*' or peasant-workers). This is the so-called *litu bulixiang* policy: peasants move out of agriculture but continue to stay in their villages and with their formal rural affiliations. It is still an avowed, or at least preferred, official policy, as Premier Li Peng stated as recently as April 1989 (*Wen Wei Po* 1989d), though in practice the emphasis has been on maintaining the rural migrants' *hukou* affiliations rather than keeping them physically from the urban areas. Critics in China have persistently pointed out the many disadvantages of trying to keep rural people where they are (e.g. Guo and Liu 1990). Chinese journals in the last few years have been full of articles discussing the merits of allowing rural surplus workers to migrate to larger cities despite the burden they might impose (Taylor 1988; Meng and Bai 1988).

A real boost to the development of the township and village enterprises came in about 1983–4 when the government saw an urgent need to diversify employment not just within the rural sector but also outside it, as the large amount of surplus rural labour became apparent. Administrative restrictions against rural enterprise's entry in to more profitable industries, except the cigarette industry, were lifted in 1984 (Wong 1988). Generally, more administrative support and greatly increased funds were made available to the township and village enterprises. In relation to population movement, in 1983 the State Council formally approved peasants setting up private businesses (under the name of 'co-operative enterprises') in *jizhen* (undesignated towns) while retaining their rural household registrations (State Council 1983b). Another State

Council regulation promulgated in February 1984 permitted peasants, with self-provided food grain, to set up individual industrial and commerce enterprises in *jizhen* (State Council 1984a). This
support was reiterated in the Party's 1985 No.1 Document. Following
further liberalizations endorsed by regulations on *zili kouliang hu*
in 1984 and 'temporary residence' in urban areas in 1985, new
regulations in 1987 and 1988 put all individual enterprises (*getihu*) and private enterprises (*siying qiye*) by rural and urban householders under the governance of the same regulations (State
Council 1987b, 1988). Township and village enterprises have grown
most rapidly in the suburban zones outside the urban administrative areas of major industrial cities, such as in Guangdong and
Jiangsu Provinces. The bulk of the newly set-up joint ventures
specializing in exports, including rural enterprises, are also concentrated in these zones (Wu and Xu 1990). The rural enterprises are intricately linked to the urban production in nearby cities:
as there is greater availability of inexpensive land, but weak
government surveillance and controls, these peri-urban zones have
become the favourite places for urban factories to expand their
production (Li and Chu 1987; Perkins 1990; Naughton 1992b).

Table 4.1 shows employment in the township and village enterprises in non-agricultural sectors more than doubled in the 1980s,
from 35 million in 1980 to close to 87 million in 1990. Though
these figures cannot capture the township and village enterprises
in the 'hidden economy', it is clear that at least 50 million farm
labourers had been absorbed into this non-agricultural sector
between 1978 and 1990. A major cause of the phenomenal growth
of township and village enterprises in the second half of the 1980s
was the rapid expansion of the privately owned (co-operative and
individual) rural enterprises, whose share rose from about one-
quarter of the total township and village enterprises employment
in 1984 to about half in 1988 (Zweig 1991).

The growth of the township and village enterprises has generated a powerful momentum for urbanization, especially in coastal
regions. The expansion of those already in designated urban areas
has certainly contributed to rural–urban migration. Equally important, in the suburban rural zones outside major cities, industrialization generated by these enterprises has been the prime force
urbanizing the areas and their residents, as exemplified by what
has happened in the Zhujiang Delta (Xu and Li 1990; Hu 1991;
Guldin 1992). Many of these enterprises, in combination with the

rapidly expanding rural markets, have been crucial in turning thousands of previous small settlements into newly designated towns by generating the required threshold of non-agricultural resident population and activities. The expected continuing growth of the township and village enterprises still in 'rural' areas—villages and market towns (*jizhen*)—will no doubt contribute to their urban designations in future. The recent decision by the authorities of the Shenzhen Special Economic Zone to grant urban status to all the zone's remaining 241 villages, the majority of whose working population are in the township and village enterprises associated with export processing, represents an example in this direction (*World Journal* 1992e). The township and village enterprises in the peri-urban regions have also substantially raised the incomes of their residents relative to urban incomes, thereby reducing the dangers of massive outflows to cities (Lee 1991).

On the 'urban' ownership side, when collective enterprises, mostly in the service industries, were first promoted in the late 1970s, they were not meant for rural in-migrants but for the large numbers of returning rusticated youths. As another way of opening up employment opportunities for these youths, self-employment or individual enterprises (*getihu*), which for more than two decades were either demoted or nationalized, were allowed again in 1978, at least in places like Guangzhou (Liu 1981). In the 1981 and 1982 regulations enacted to deal with the new circumstances, it was explicitly stated that these enterprises were only open to those with non-agricultural household registration status, implying that peasants were not eligible (State Council 1981, 1982a). However, as the urban non-state economy further expanded, imports of extra hands from outside the urban sector became necessary and attractive to urban private enterprises, particularly in the face of escalated competition. In a supplementary stipulation to the previous regulations regarding urban individual enterprises, the State Council in 1983 approved hiring of rural householders by enterprises in small towns (State Council 1983a). Even before this hiring was made legal by the enactment of the regulations regarding temporary urban residence in 1983–5, such employment occurred on a noticeable scale in the early 1980s in many towns and some cities (Solinger 1985). The formal legalization of these 'temporary' workers in many places from 1983 led to a surge in official urban recruitment (excluding the township and village enterprises) figures from the countryside around the mid-1980s (Table 4.2).

Furthermore, in the second half of the 1980s, as China continued marketizing its economy, larger private enterprises (*siying qiye*), defined as those hiring eight or more workers, were formally allowed to operate (State Council 1988). At the same time, small and large private enterprises were given a free hand to hire whomever they deemed appropriate, without reference to the employee's household status (State Council 1987b; 1988).

Employment figures in Table 4.1 show that the urban collective sector has grown steadily at about 5 per cent per year since 1978, while the urban individual enterprises sector has risen on average 39.8 per cent per year, beginning from 120,000 in 1978. The size of the urban private economy is even larger if one includes *siying qiye* and many unregistered enterprises (Ogaard 1990; Huang 1992). Other factors, such as private enterprises registering as collectives, have also contributed to undercounting (*Wen Wei Po* 1990b; Ogaard 1990). In any case, it is certain that this budding sector grew rapidly, at least until 1988. The most recent report suggests that both urban and rural private (including individual) enterprises were making a strong comeback in 1992 following Deng's new marketization moves (e.g. *World Journal* 1992a). Reflecting their rapid expansion in the 1980s, provincial associations of private enterprises started forming in 1984 and a national organization was founded in 1986 (Hu *et al.* 1988). Systematic information at the national level as to what proportion of workers in these enterprises are from the countryside does not exist; a survey of Beijing's urban private enterprises conducted in 1987 suggests that out of the 15,206 workers (excluding 41,480 self-employed) hired by these enterprises, three-quarters of them came from the countryside (Beijing Municipal Government 1989).

'Contract' and 'Temporary' Workers in State Enterprises

Another major employment route for peasants moving into urban areas has been the expanding opportunities created for 'contract workers' and 'temporary workers' in urban state enterprises in a number of sectors. As explained in Chapter Three, contract and temporary workers were used by urban managers to fill strenuous manual and low-skilled jobs, as well as to cut down indirect costs (social costs) of industrial labour in the face of greater fiscal pressures. As new urban labour supplies became increasingly scarce in the 1980s, many low-skilled and physically demanding industrial jobs in the construction, textiles, chemical, and sanitation industries ran into great difficulties finding willing urban youth to fill their vacancies. Urban graduates were turning their backs on these jobs in favour of more fashionable and rewarding jobs in tourism and foreign trade (Chen 1990).[15]

These unfilled vacancies, on the other hand, opened up many opportunities for rural migrants. With greater pressures to cut costs, state enterprises in those trades have often turned more to rural labour as their source of front-line workers. Indeed, a regulation promulgated by the State Council in 1984 demanded state-run construction enterprises hire only rural labourers 'contract workers' for their construction work or contract their work out to 'rural construction teams' organized by peasants (State Council 1984b). As in other countries, the 'temporary' label was more a legitimizing device used by enterprises to cut indirect labour costs (namely, welfare benefits) than an indicator of the stability of worker status of these labourers. Some of the 'temporary' labour contracts signed were as long as 20 years (Ban and Xie 1986). As of the end of 1985, rural labourers hired by state construction enterprises numbered about 420,000, or 31 per cent of the permanent work-force in the sector (Ban and Xie 1986). Another piece of information collected by the authorities administering the township and village enterprises indicates that in 1988, rural construction teams employed altogether 13 million labourers, of whom 4.8 million were working in the urban areas (Huang 1992).

The practice has in no way been limited merely to the construction sector. In Hangzhou, for example, peasant 'contract workers' in state-owned enterprises numbered 123,000 in 1987, accounting for 36.7 per cent of the total employment in construction, textiles, engineering, and transportation (Wu and Zheng 1986). Similar situations are found in many other major cities. Today, contracted 'temporary' workers have become the backbone of the work-force in these industries in China. Hiring of rural labourers by state enterprises must still formally be through collective contracts with agricultural co-operatives, which in turn must be approved by higher authorities. However, it appears that with a decollectivized rural economy, this requirement has been difficult to implement, and many state enterprises have simply ignored it (see e.g. *Wen Wei Po* 1988b).

Others

The above explains the mostly 'legal', though often informal, urban employment channels through which non-urban residents can earn a living. There are, of course, illegal channels that generate the necessary resources to support an urban living for many other migrants. These would include many 'crimes', ranging from prostitution, illicit trading of foreign currencies and state-controlled commodities, to drug trafficking and robbery. These are detailed in Huang's (1992) account of China's 'hidden economy', a large part of which is in the urban and peri-urban regions. The expansion in the size of the floating population in major cities has in the official literature been associated with the surge of urban crimes in the 1980s (Solinger 1991). Li and Hu (1991), for example, cite that in 1988–9, of the arrests in Shanghai, Wuhan, Chongqing, Guangzhou, and Shenyang, 33 to 77 per cent were floating population, compared to only a few per cent in the late 1970s.[16] The negative impact of floaters on urban law and order has been a greater concern of the authorities since the mid-1980s.

Chinese law has never forbidden its citizens to travel within the country, including to cities. The Chinese household registration regulations allow individuals to stay in places different from where they have registered their households up to three months, as long as the stays are registered with the local public security bureau. The restriction on mobility is more directed against 'migration' (*quanyi*) than travel. However, in many instances, it is almost impossible to distinguish a 'migrant' from a 'traveller'. Hence control of the former category in the past was essentially done through the administrative controls of urban hiring, of daily supplies such as food grain, allocation of housing, and access to medical and education facilities, with the threat of prosecution and the backing of a relatively effective urban neighborhood policing mechanism, staffed largely by the unpaid labour of retirees and the elderly.

However, since the early 1980s the rapid growth of the urban sector has created millions of jobs that can only be filled by rural migrant labour. At the same time, marketization has also made available outside the state-controlled channels all the necessary ingredients for effecting migration in most urban centres, beginning with food grains and foodstuffs, then housing, and even education (private schools). In addition, commercialization has also corrupted some officials and cadres, opening many back doors to formal and informal migration. The effectiveness of the neighbourhood watch mechanism meanwhile has been significantly eroded as elderly men and women find more gainful alternatives to spending their time. The residence control system has also been weakened by the fact that the police are simply too busy to deal with the relatively trivial issues of unreported stays (over three months) and overstays, as more serious, disruptive urban crimes have commanded their attention.

Greater mobility of the population has also made society less transparent and more difficult to monitor (Mallee 1988). It has not been uncommon in recent years for migrants, who are unemployed or employed in small businesses, not to report or register their stay, even though technically they were breaking the law and could have faced deportation. In an attempt to clear out unemployed migrants during the retrenchment years of 1988 and 1989, many cities required that temporary residence permits be given to only those who had obtained a 'work permit' (*laodong xukezheng*), which could only be applied for by urban employers on behalf of the prospective employees (*Wen Wei Po* 1989c, 1990a). These measures are akin in nature and in procedure to those used widely by other countries in dealing with foreign migrant labourers. The new restriction appears to have some modest, if only temporary, curbing effect on the waves of 'blind flows' in 1989 and 1990.

The description above suggests that Chinese peasants in the late 1980s were by and large free to travel to the urban centre, a situation similar to the first half of the 1950s. Whether they could make it to the city and manage to stay was another question, hinging more on whether they had the resources to support themselves than whether they had an official permit to stay. Many women evading birth control in their home towns or counties have exploited the new freedom by taking refuge in other localities, including many cities, creating big headaches for central family planners, who are eager to keep births under control but who generally do not have an effective mechanism to implement their objective at the local level. These evaders' mobility has led them to be characterized as 'guerrillas of above-quota births,' an army too elusive to catch and fight against.[17] All in all, urban employment remains the primary source of sustaining an urban living for a migrant family. The expanding unregulated market for rural labour has made urban living within reach of many able-bodied peasants. Even those who have not secured a means of living can also come to urban areas and try their luck. Although the Chinese media tends to denigrate these movements as 'blind flows', most of them are probably fairly rational in nature, as Harris and

Todaro (1970) have hypothesized in a more general Third World context.

On the other hand, witnessing periodic sweeps on unwanted and unemployed migrants in some big cities such as Guangzhou, Shenzhen, and Beijing in 1988 and 1989, many peasant migrants have been careful enough not to relinquish totally ties with their home villages. Most of them have been reluctant to give up the plots of land allocated to them under the production responsibility system, preferring to let family members hold them as a form of income insurance in the event of a policy shift. This type of behaviour has adversely affected farm yields in coastal regions and areas bordering large- and medium-sized cities (Taylor 1988). In sum, the uncertainty over the long-term urban residency status of 'informal' migrants, the intermittent campaigns to clear out unwelcome migrants, and a generally improved farm sector and expanded non-agricultural opportunities in the countryside have acted as deterrents to excessive, uncontrolled urban inflows. To many enterprising migrants, staying unemployed in unfamiliar cities is not necessarily preferred to trying out new non-agricultural pursuits near their home villages, such as hauling and selling goods or working in the informal economy in the peri-urban region. As a result, despite lax migration restrictions in the 1980s and probably blown-up media images of waves of 'blind flows' in major metropolises, Chinese cities appeared to be still functioning and coping with the extra burden of influxes fairly well (Christiansen 1992). Most agree that despite higher levels of unemployment, major cities have not been crippled by the army of jobless migrants, certainly not on a scale comparable to some other Third World metropolises like Mexico City and Bombay. Existing urban residents, though naturally unhappy with more cramped buses and less safe urban living, appear to be tolerant of these inflows as they themselves have benefitted from the many useful and inexpensive services directly and indirectly brought by migrants.

Concluding Remarks

The post-Mao era has been an important period of transition in China's urban history. Chinese society began the reform era with the legacies of strong state coercion and controls, and a heavily planned economy, and by the early 1990s had gained greater wealth and economic freedoms, and less state controls. The economy in the 1980s was marked by increasingly market-driven bottom-up initiatives and a much expanded non-state sector. There was also the emergence of a more mobile and diverse society in which state controls appeared to be increasingly less potent. Two important changes in the post-Mao period have had the greatest impacts on urbanization. The first was the reform of agriculture, which, on the one hand, has boosted rural incomes and helped narrow the urban–rural gap, thereby reducing pressures for rural out-migration. On the other, it has made tens of millions of rural labourers redundant because of the dramatic rise in productivity. Labourers at the same time were freed by the dismantling of communes, thus producing an even greater centripetal force from the countryside. The other major change has been the willingness of the post-Mao government to give up its monopoly over urban-industrial production and let a non-state sector—functioning on market mechanisms—'supplement' the state sector. Reforms in commerce, growth of the township and village enterprises sector, and increased commercialization of many aspects of the urban sector have replaced the former urban employment system, heavily dependent on and controlled by the state sector, with a multi-sector system composed of state, collective, private, and foreign enterprises, and self-employed peddlers. More generally, these developments have led to a truly two-tier system, with a non-state sector driven largely by entrepreneurial instincts and operating with greater hiring freedoms.

With the phenomenal expansion of the non-agricultural economy and more decentralized economic management, importation of rural migrant labour became an obvious solution to the urban labour shortages, as the existing urban labour pool was depleted and rural hands were more economical to hire. The expanded employment opportunities in the non-state enterprises especially led to the prevalence and popularity of 'informal' migrant labourers in the post-Mao era. These people were neither entitled to permanent residence (with the minor exception of *zili kouliang hu*) nor the regular urban social benefits; they were largely absorbed into temporary and semi-permanent low-skilled jobs in the urban and peri-urban economy. Chinese reform socialism has created, structurally, a sizeable, 'second class' of urban citizens without permanent urban household registration status. This informal segment of urban labour and population is an extension of the rural segment, which was largely bottled up in the countryside under Mao (Figure 4.2). While the co-existence of two classes of people side by side in the urban areas will definitely sensitize public awareness to system injustices and may cause conflicts, as some have worried (Blecher 1988), the opening of the city gate to peasants represents a big step towards breaking down the rural/urban, and agricultural/non-agricultural segmentation and in narrowing sectoral disparities. Today, most urban and rural dwellers live better than a decade ago, but urban life, though still largely protected, is less privileged and, at times, more stressful. The living standards of the rural population, especially in the coastal regions, have risen more quickly than in remote regions because of the increased opportunities in the coastal regions. In these regions in some peri-urban areas the stark division between city and countryside has begun to break down.

However, it is too early to conclude that post-Mao leaders have abandoned previous urban-biased practices. Quite the contrary, many Maoist political and economic legacies have continued to play an important role. Politically, China continues to function under a relatively authoritarian, one-party system. On the economic front, huge amounts of state investment carry on being poured into heavy industry instead of agriculture and other sectors (like transportation and education) that desperately need help. As far as urbanization is concerned, the Maoist policy of restricting urban in-migration to control urbanization costs is a continuing theme.

Today the government's apprehension over excessive urban migration, while diminished, has not disappeared. More urban inflows, both formal and informal, have been permitted, but considerations about the fiscal impact of migration are still paramount in the post-Mao planners' minds. With the exception of its more humane policy toward the family reunions of intellectuals and cadres, the state has continued to exercise a relatively tight grip on formal rural–urban migration to the urban state sector, though this has been from time to time frustrated by local government initiatives under a more decentralized polity. Urban residency continues to be treated as a privilege not a right, only granted to families who have skills or money to contribute to the country's modernization. The most recent migrants, who have been brought in from the countryside to work in unpopular jobs in cities and towns, continue to be denied the privilege of permanent residency. The status of 'temporary' workers with reference to the state

Figure 4.2 Urban and Rural, and Agricultural and Non-Agricultural Population Based on Household Registration Status

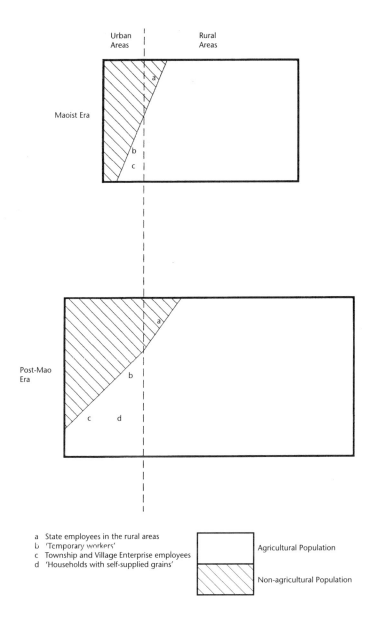

a State employees in the rural areas
b 'Temporary workers'
c Township and Village Enterprise employees
d 'Households with self-supplied grains'

supply system remains largely the same as in the Maoist era; so
is the discrimination against them. The need to strictly control
rural–urban flows has, however, been less compelling as the government has found ways to privatize the social costs of migration
through informal migration to the non-state economy. The booming, mostly informal, economy in the peri-urban regions outside
metropolises has also in many ways reduced the dangers of excessive outflows from neighbouring villages.

Because of these changes, urbanization in the 1980s had at least
kept pace with industrialization based on the indicators used in
Chapter Three. Industrial employment and urban population grew
at about the same average rate of 5–6 per cent per year during
the 1980s (Table 3.7). An inspection of China's UL (urban percentage) and GIL (industrial output percentage) in 1979 and 1990
relative to the 'norm' established by a regression line based on
twenty-nine market economies (Figure 3.4) reveals that the gap
between China and the norm has remained more or less constant
since 1979, suggesting a close synchronization of the industrialization and urbanization process during the 1980s. More complete
time-series information about urban percentage and industrial
employment percentage presented in Figure 3.5 also reveals that
the previous trend of divergence from the norm was arrested in
the 1980s. Instead, the figure indicates some signs of a small convergence between China and the market norm occurring in the
1980s. In many ways, China's major urban centres in the 1990s
look increasingly like their East Asian counterparts in other countries one or two decades ago.

To sum up, rural–urban migration in China has brought many
benefits, as well as costs, to the urban economy. It is argued that
the post-Mao migration policies represent an attempt to address
the cheap labour versus increased social expenditure dilemma generated by migration. While more migration has been allowed, the
approach adopted by the government in the 1980s to control
urbanization costs focused more on the prevention of granting
urban status and benefits to new migrants than on a strict ban on
their entry to the city. In contrast with the Maoist era, the *de facto*
internal passport system was employed not to prevent peasants
flowing into the cities but to deny them urban benefits. The post-
Mao objective of shedding urbanization costs is hardly different
from that under Mao, however. In many ways, the post-Mao state
has been able—through some degree of 'privatization' of urbanization—to shift most of the indirect social costs it previously bore

(or was expected to bear) to the non-state sector and/or to the migrants themselves. Many governments in market economies have long been acquainted with this approach especially in dealing with foreign migrant labourers. China, on the other hand, has also succeeded in applying this discrimination to internal migrants precisely because of the existence of a *de facto* internal passport system. Wenzhou's recent plan to implement a 'green card' system, bearing exactly the same name as the US system, to regulate migratory flows (*World Journal* 1992c) is a clear indication of the precise character and function of the current Chinese strategy.

Finally, to return to the question posed at the beginning of this chapter—What model now?—I would argue that Maoist efforts to economize on urbanization costs are still dominant in the post-Mao era. The policy of restricting the growth of urban population has taken a different, certainly more humane and accommodating face, but with a scarcely changed nature. The Maoist policy was one of isolated rural–urban development with the privileged and state-controlled urban sector largely sealed off to rural migrants. The post-Mao emphasis on efficiency and rural–urban interaction has created a new set of state–society relations, weakening many migration barriers to cities. There has been a lot of urban in-migration inside and outside the state sector, but largely in the 'informal' category. For those who have money to invest or even 'buy' an urban household registration or have skills to offer, entry to the urban 'formal' sector in the 1980s was less difficult than it was in the 1970s. For many other migrants from the rural areas, the Maoist policy of discriminating against them has remained relatively intact in the post-Mao era. The increase in the spatial and occupational mobility of the 'peasantry' in the 1980s represents moderations to a fundamentally unchanged Maoist legacy derived from the classical system.

Notes

1. This is the title of a volume of collected conference papers dealing mostly with urbanization in the 1980s presented in Hong Kong in 1987 (Kwok *et al.* 1990).

2. In two Chinese writers' words, 'During 1977 and 1978 . . . we were still following a leftist line featuring "high targets and high accumulation" but "low efficiency and low consumption"' (Fang and Zhao 1982, p. 127). In 1978 the rate of accumulation was 36.5 per cent, higher than the averages of the 1971–5 and 1966–70 periods.

3. A bureau of city planning was set up in 1977 within the State Council. The bureau was expanded in early 1982 to become a full-status ministry, then named as the Ministry of Rural and Urban Construction and Environmental Protection.

4. As one official commentary puts it, large cities possessed 'high technology', 'strong material base', and 'modern management expertise', all of which were essential but scarce resources for China's modernization (*Renmin ribao* 1981). This new thinking is encapsuled in the then-Premier Zhao Ziyang's statement on the Sixth Five-year Plan delivered in 1982: 'Production and circulation should be unified, centering on the more economically developed cities so as to carry along the surrounding rural areas and gradually from city-based economic regions of different sizes and types' (Zhao 1982).

5. Chen and Chen (1984) report that there were fifteen key cities in China. They were Beijing, Shanghai, Tianjin, Shenyang, Harbin, Changchun, Dalian, Xian, Lanzhou, Qingdao, Hangzhou, Wuxi, Wuhan, Chongqing, and Guangzhou.

6. As an indication of the size of the hidden economy, according to Huang (1992), about 20 per cent of all industrial products in the market in 1991 came from 'unknown' sources.

7. In many respects, this duality also coincides with the division of industry and agriculture, large and small enterprises, and 'modern' and 'traditional' sectors (Perkins and Yusuf 1984).

8. The role of the system has declined since economic reform was introduced. In the pre-reform period an urban household registration status generally implied access to all urban benefits. The situation has become more complex in the post-Mao period. A non-agricultural household registration status alone does not automatically entitle one to all urban benefits. Generally, the registration status determines one's eligibility for urban education and employment, while the commodity grain entitlement decides one's qualifications for subsidized food and other commodities supplied by the state.

9. Possibly three, if the creation of a transitional category of 'households with self-supplied grains' is included. Considering the functional characteristics, this category of migration is a borderline group between formal and informal migration, and leans more toward the informal category.

10. It appears that the responsibility of providing food grains for the non-agricultural population in their jurisdictions also lies with local governments.

11. See Table 2.1 for the huge increases in the non-agricultural population category in 1984 and 1985 and Wang (1993) for the central–local relations in the post-1949 period.

12. Tales of illegal conversions to non-agricultural household registration status made by officials are many. See *Nanfang ribao* (1988) and *Renmin ribao* (1984a, 1984b) for detailed descriptions of some cases in Guangdong, Shangdong, and Anhui. The August 1993 issue of *The Nineties* also carries a detailed report of corruption cases, many of which involved illegal conversions of household registration status granted by officials.

13. Though early-period statistics strictly comparable to those included in Table 4.3 are not available, a rough estimation suggests that the category called *wugong jingshang* accounted for less than 5 per cent of all net rural–urban migration in the period 1949–86 and less than 10 per cent of all work-related migration in the same period (based on information in Ma and Wang [1988], and Goldstein and Goldstein [1991]). These percentages would be even smaller in the pre-reform period.

14. A thorough examination of previous urban employment policy in the 1950s is made by Howe (1971).

15. Sectors popular among new urban graduates were the textile industry in the 1950s, the chemical industry in the 1960s, the electronics industry in the 1970s, and the tourism industry and foreign trade in the 1980s (Li and Hu 1991).

16. One is also reminded by Solinger (1991, p. 20) that migrants 'are more likely to attract police suspicion and arbitrary treatment than are natives, are concentrated in the demographic group (young, male) most apt to commit crimes and so have disproportionately high criminal rates, and are understandably desperate, given their meagre incomes and negligible prospects'.

17. Local family planning officers, eager to maintain births within prescribed quotas, were often willing to let pregnant women go to other jurisdictions, outside their responsibility.

5 Conclusion

This book has sought to fill a major gap in our understanding of Chinese urbanization by providing a descriptive-explanatory account of urban population growth since 1949 based on a synthesis of empirical details and broader urbanization and development literature, especially on Soviet-type economies. Following a review of China's post-1949 urbanization literature in Chapter One, which served to expose the limitations of previous studies, Chapter Two provided the empirical, as well as statistical, background necessary for the ensuing analysis and interpretations. Despite some earlier attempts, the urban population definition problem continued to seriously plague the study of China's recent urban growth as new problems emerged under different conditions. Using an urban concept based on smaller jurisdictions first adopted in the 1990 Census, that chapter constructed a series of urban population and net rural–urban migration figures that enabled a meaningful study of the urbanization and migration trends since 1949.

The urban population data presented suggests very rapid urban growth and rural–urban migration in the 1950s, contrasting with large net urban outflows in the early 1960s. This was followed by a period of stagnant urbanization, as a result of low rates of urban natural population growth and net in-migration during the latter half of the 1960s and most of the 1970s. A large increase in the absolute size of net urban in-migration was noted in the post-1978 period, though the average annual rate per unit of urban population during this period was still below the mean rate for the period under the First Five-year Plan.

Chapter Three re-examined the explanations for the significant deceleration in urban growth during the Maoist period after the initial spurt in the 1950s, and proposed a new framework of socialist 'under-urbanization' developed from a nuanced understanding of the sectoral population implications of industrial growth dynamics under socialism. Specifically, it was argued that central planners' preference for industrializing the country quickly under classical socialism resulted in the need for inducing terms of trade favouring the urban-industrial sector. This imperative, combined, to a lesser extent, with the hoarding behaviour of industrial managers at the micro-level, had led to a series of policy measures to restrict the outflows of rural population and the expansion of urban population and consumption. Typical of economies under classical socialism, these measures to 'economize' on urbanization without decelerating rapid industrialization adopted in China included tight administrative measures forbidding rural–urban labour and population mobility—amounting to migration restrictions by passports, fuller utilization of the existing urban working-age population, suppression of the expansion of urban service employment and personal consumption in general, promotion of rural industrialization, and increased use of urban 'temporary' workers.

At a broader level, the Maoist urbanization policy was largely a product of China's dualistic economy. This produced a rigid, somewhat static, rural–urban segmentation of population in sectoral and geographical terms. Cities and, to a large extent, towns have been protected by numerous newly erected walls composed of administrative measures against in-migration. Disguised in the then revolutionary rhetoric of equality and urban proletariat–peasant brotherhood, these walls were not visible to most. While urban–rural dualism is symptomatic of societies in transition, it was probably stronger in Maoist China than in many other Third World countries in similar development stages, mainly because the former was both structural and state-policy initiated.

Applying a model based on population multipliers, this study has shown that China was highly effective in simultaneously fostering rapid industrial growth and slowing down urban growth in the Maoist era. Much of the disparity in the two processes was achieved by a significant increase in the urban, especially female, labour participation rate, the rapid decline in urban fertility, and the increasing use of urban 'temporary' workers. Because of the smaller 'urban multiplier' effect with respect to its industrial output or employment, China by the 1970s was relatively 'under-urbanized' compared to its level of industrialization or to other developing countries at similar stages. This is just the reverse to the phenomenon of inexorable urban growth amidst modest industrial job expansion—the so-called 'over-urbanization'—in many Third World market economies, where excessive in-migration to cities and chronic urban unemployment coexist.

Chapter Four turned to an examination of the urbanization process in the post-Mao period since 1979. While there is still a clear continuity in the state investment allocation in favour of heavy industry and in control over 'formal' urban in-migration with changes to household registration status, the rapid expansion of the fledgling, largely market-oriented, economy of non-state enterprises has gradually altered the Chinese urban employment and demographic scenes. Pressures generated from the accumulated problems of the Maoist era have prompted many important reforms since the late 1970s. The breakup of the commune system not only made disguised rural unemployment apparent, but also let loose millions of rural labourers. At the same time, hectic urban construction, vibrant township and urban collective enterprises and mushrooming private business seemed to create an endless demand for low-cost migrant labour. The former urban employment system, more or less exclusively dependent on the state sector, was also gradually replaced by a more competitive multi-layered system composed of state, collective, private, and foreign enterprises, with greater hiring freedoms.

These factors have led to increasing legitimization of largely self-initiated informal migration to the city. Most of these migrants are entitled to neither permanent residency nor the regular urban social benefits, thus obviating the state's responsibility for providing subsidized food and social facilities. A large portion of the migrant workers are absorbed into less formalized jobs, mostly of a temporary or semi-permanent nature, demanding relatively low skill levels. Despite the government's more accommodating attitude towards urban growth, considerations about the fiscal impact of migration are still paramount in the post-Mao planners' minds. The central government continues to impose tight control over formal rural–urban migration, except those involving reunions of family members of urban intellectuals and cadres living in different locales. The avowed policy of controlling formal urban in-migration was, however, frustrated by the actions of local governments who were increasingly interested in pursuing their own priorities, which did not necessarily coincide with those of the central government. Sales of urban residency rights, through which formal urban in-migration is induced, have been a popular route used by local authorities to raise funds to supplement their coffers.

A more significant change is the greater popularity of informal migration, which has become a hallmark of post-Mao urbanization. The expanding and increasingly market-oriented economy has turned more to rural sources for low-cost labour. Refused official permanent urban status (and thus entitlement to subsidized food and social facilities), most migrant labourers remain in the somewhat awkward categories of 'temporary population' and 'floating population', regardless of their length of stay in the urban areas. Through this kind of differential treatment of urban residents, the post-Mao government has succeeded in dealing with the escalating demand for labour without being encumbered with a significantly larger fiscal responsibility. While the rural and urban segmentation based on household registration classification was enforced under Mao in both sectoral and geographical terms, the system has continued in the post-Mao era to discriminate against rural householders, even though the geographical divide is now mostly broken down. Rural householders have been freed from the shackles of the collectives and have new opportunities in the burgeoning urban and peri-urban labour market. As the wall between rural and urban sectors has become semi-porous, the physical boundary between them has become increasingly unclear in many fast-growing regions, which have been aptly described as the *desa kota* regions. As Christiansen (1992) puts it, 'the mechanisms of rural–urban divide have become more flexible and selective in many ways, but still remains in force'. Today, a sizeable urban underclass without permanent resident registration status live side by side, or surround, a privileged population of urban house-holders under the mixed economic system of plans and market.

In retrospect, one can argue that modern urban transition began under socialism in China in the 1950s as the country moved into the fast industrialization gear. However, the process was halted for nearly two decades from 1960. Urbanization momentum began to pick up again only in the late 1970s (Figure 2.3). Table 5.1 and Figure 5.1 highlight the major features of urbanization in the two different eras. Because the priority given to industry in the two eras remained unchanged, industry maintained high output growth rates throughout the post-1949 period, with the exception of the recession years of the early 1960s. Industrial employment growth was also high, but the urban growth rate was a long way behind. Figure 5.1 underlines the divergence of growth rates between industry and urban population. Over the four decades, industrial employment rose by about seven times, while urban population increased only by about three times. The discrepancy in growth rates was particularly obvious during 1965–78 when various

Table 5.1 A Comparison of Characteristics Associated with Urbanization in Different Eras in Post-1949 China

	Maoist Era		Reform Era
	1st phase 1952–60	2nd phase 1961–78	1979–90
Sectoral Features			
Industrial labour growth	very high (12.2%)	modest to high (3.0%, 1961–78; 8.3%, 1965–78)	high (4.0%)
Urban growth rate	very high (7.5%)	low to modest (1.5%, 1961–78: 2.1%, 1965–78)	high (4.7%)
Components of urban growth:			
Natural increase	30%	100%	25%
Net migration	70% (both planned and unplanned)	negative contribution	75% (both planned and unplanned)
Measures used to economize on urbanization costs (M = major; m = minor; n = not used)			
Increasing industrial labour-output ratio	M	m	M
Restricting urban inflows	m	M	m
Rural resettlement	n	M	n
High labour participation rate	m	M	m
Suppressing urban consumption (incl. intensification of use of existing infrastructure)	M	M	n
Rural industrialization	(attempted but failed)	M	M
Reducing urban fertility	n	M	M
Refusing urban benefits to new migrants	m	M	M

measures to economize on urban population growth were effectively implemented.

A recurrent theme of China's development in the last four decades, dictated by the needs of the chosen industrialization strategy, was controlling the costs of urbanization through rural–urban segmentation. These costs were incurred because of the necessity

Figure 5.1 Industrial Growth and Urban Growth, 1952–1990

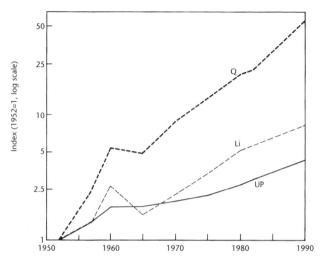

Notes: Li: industrial employment
Q: industrial output
UP: urban population
Source: Table 3.7

of providing basic welfare to please urban workers in the high-priority industrial sector. Actual measures used to achieve this objective, summarized in Table 5.1, varied, however, over time in response to the dynamics in different periods. The household registration system, acting in effect as an internal passport system, played a central role in keeping down the costs of urban welfare services. As a restrictive device, the Chinese internal passport system functioned to limit entry to the urban sector in the Maoist era and to refuse welfare services to rural residents in both the Maoist and post-Mao eras. In essence, under Mao, an invisible wall kept out the peasantry and protected the urban population. In effect, the history of walled cities did not end with the demise of imperial China. Many of the allegedly unique features of Chinese development, such as rural development programmes (sending down urban-educated youths, and the preponderance of rural industrialization), relatively high women's status in cities (which was undoubtedly enhanced greatly by high female labour participation rates), and cities free of squatters and crime, are all closely related to the Maoist rural–urban segmentation policy.

To be more precise, in the 1950s, measures to restrict urban inflows were generally not strictly enforced as, during this early phase of development, 'extensive' industrial growth required massive infusions of labour, which had to be drawn from the countryside. Also, the costs of urban growth were kept low as existing urban housing and infrastructures were more intensively used through sharing and rationing, without much investment. However, the unexpected famine in the late 1950s and early 1960s and the threat of larger urban consumption costs (as intensification of use of the urban infrastructure could not be indefinitely stretched) prompted the government to adopt drastic measures to keep the urban population within a manageable size. These included rural resettlement campaigns and stringent administrative measures to check migratory flows to cities and towns. This 'closed-city' approach cut off many of the traditional linkages between the rural and urban sectors, segregating spatially the peasant and non-peasant populations during the 1960s and 1970s and creating a relatively static, feudalistic-type society only interrupted by occasional large-scale movements triggered by famines and political upheavals. In the post-Mao era, the government has turned, with new emphasis on competitiveness in the economy, more to containing urbanization costs by refusing state-subsidized urban benefits to many urban newcomers.

To sum up, this book has offered a new interpretation of allegedly unique Maoist urbanization policies by relating them to the systemic characteristics of classical socialism. The typical 'pro-rural' explanation that dominated the literature for a long time has been refuted. Although, as stated at the outset, the framework put forward in this book will not be able to explain every facet of China's urbanization under socialism, the set of components identified is definitely an important, if not the most important, dimension of the Chinese urbanization process. It is quite clear that many of the Chinese features identified in this study are common to socialist economies under similar conditions (see e.g. Kansky 1976; Ofer 1976; Demko and Roland 1977; Chan 1990; Sjoberg 1992). Seen in this way, the utility of the present work goes beyond the parochial confines of Chinese urbanization. As one recent review of urbanization under central planning points out (Ronnas and Sjoberg, 1993, note 2), the type of framework used here has contributed to a more sophisticated general conception of urbanization in the centrally planned economy. In many ways this book can be read as a case study of socialist urbanization, an important and broad topic that has neither been fully understood nor adequately theorized in the literature. More integrative work transcending the relatively compartmentalized focuses of traditional area specialists, notably Soviet and East European Studies, and Sinology is a priority task in broadening our understanding of the complex urbanization process under socialism.

More generally, the book has also contributed to the literature on urbanization and development. While the focus so far has primarily been on 'under-urbanization' in centrally planned economies, it will not take too many more steps to see that the general principles developed here are relevant to the understanding of the urbanization process in many Third World countries. As explained in earlier chapters, industrial growth in many developing market economies tends to generate even faster urban population growth, resulting in what has largely been deemed dysfunctional 'over-urbanization'. The observations drawn from the present study of 'under-urbanization' in China is instructive of the nature of the urbanization and migration process in a developing economy and many of the associated problems and policy dilemmas. Indeed, Chinese exploitation of internal migrants is comparable with the treatment of, particularly, foreign migrant labour in other countries.

Prospects for Future Urbanization

Having surveyed urban population growth in the last four decades, the more future-oriented reader may be interested in knowing the likely urbanization scenarios for China in the coming decades. Forecasts of China's future urban population size abound, as they are a favoured subject of some international organizations and have been encouraged by the Chinese government in its zeal to draw up grand plans for the year 2000, when the nation is timed to reach its goal of quadrupling the gross national product. These prognoses include primarily demographic projections such as those by Banister (1986), the United Nations (1987), and Zeng (1991), and other types of projections and plans proposed by geographers, planners, and economists, notably Wu (1982), Zhou (1982), the World Bank (1985b), and Gao (1990). The former type has treated population dynamics—especially migration—as an exogenous variable, and the latter has usually considered urban population as a function of other independent variables such as grain supplies, industrial employment, and national income.

While all these exercises may have served their objectives of making clear the impact of certain factors on China's future urban population size and, in some cases, the future urban demographic structure, most of them have rigidly adopted one of the two official urban definitions available at the time, the Non-agricultural Population of Cities and Towns and the urban administrative area-based Total Population of Cities and Towns, as their basis. Neither of these, as reviewed in Chapter Two, is satisfactory for a meaningful analysis. For instance, those adopting the urban administrative area-based Total Population of Cities and Towns (e.g. Banister 1987; Gao 1990; Zeng 1991) have begun with a much inflated urban population basis, while others choosing the Non-agricultural Population of Cities and Towns (e.g. Wu 1982; Zhou 1982; United Nations 1987) have found smaller ones; extrapolation based on either does not yield reasonable results. Owing to this discrepancy in the use of urban definition and, in some cases methodological problems,[1] the results of these exercises are not readily usable for the purpose here. Equally important, seen from the vantage point of the early 1990s, many of the earlier studies have produced unsatisfactory predictions of China's urbanization in the coming decades as they have failed to capture the precise nature of current Chinese urbanization, arising from a more dynamic economy since the mid-1980s.[2]

Undoubtedly, any crystal ball-gazing exercise is a risky business, and especially so for one that deals with China, which has trailed a zigzag political and economic path in the Maoist era. This is not the place for any sophisticated projection exercise, certainly not more so in technical terms than those reviewed above, for not only does it lie beyond the scope of the present study, but such an attempt is also probably quite futile in view of the recent volatility of Chinese economics and demographics. Nonetheless, having studied especially the changes in the 1980s and the various scenarios put forward, and the likely directions set forth by developments in China in 1992, one feels a little more confident in defining a few of the broad parameters within which China's urbanization process in the two coming decades may operate.

By the beginning of 1993 it was quite clear to outsiders that reforms in China had not stopped after the setbacks in the late

1980s. Deng Xiaoping's south China tour, in the spring of 1992, indicated that China was making greater strides toward marketizing the economy. The new effort to build 'market socialism', ratified at the Fourteenth Party Congress in the autumn of 1992, has now gained considerable support within the Communist Party and outside.[3] Essentially, the leadership has decided that the capitalist market should play a dominant, instead of a subsidiary, role—though few changes to the current one-party political system have been planned in the near future (*New York Times* 1992). This is a strategy that resembles broadly those adopted by China's more economically successful neighbours such as South Korea and Taiwan in the 1960s and 1970s. With the diminished role of the planned state sector, the new wave of economic reforms is expected to generate strong growth, borne out in 1992 by the robust economy's performance.

The prophesied economic boom, mostly in the industrial and service sectors, will continue to generate large rural–urban population shifts. The marketized economic engine is showing itself to be willing to bulldoze farm land in the peri-urban regions, particularly the mushrooming free-trade zones on the urban fringes, to make room for lucrative building and service industries (*World Journal* 1983b). This trend has certainly intensified since the spring of 1992 and appears to be irresistible (*World Journal* 1992f; 1993a). At the same time, continuing heavy population pressure in the rural sector will push even more off the land. The floating population problem was very much in evidence in the winter of 1992 in hot spots such as Guangdong (*South China Morning Post* 1992; *World Journal* 1992g). A large number of job-seeking labourers will be absorbed in the fast growing and increasingly marketized industrial and, especially, service sectors, which have many low-skilled jobs suited to labour from the countryside. These structural shifts in the countryside and in the peri-urban region are bound to generate high rates of urban population growth, largely by net migration and by designations of newly urbanized *desa kota* areas as urban districts and centres, especially the small ones. Seen in the light of Zelinsky's (1971) stylized 'mobility transition' framework, China will continue the second phase of high levels of rural–urban migration well into the early twenty-first century.

While there have been heightened concerns about the possibility of a total breakdown of the migration-restricting mechanisms and massive, uncontrollable population drifts to cities, a number of factors are likely to hold back the rural exodus. Though expectedly unpopular among peasants, the household registration system will probably endure, in a less significant manner, for another decade or more, functioning as a distribution system of economic and social goods to different segments of the population and perpetuating the dual system of urban in-migration. It is also a migration-restricting mechanism that the government may use from time to time to carry out periodic direct or indirect sweeps on illegal urban residents, those without proper registration papers, and to clear out excessive numbers of urban in-migrants when the situation threatens to get out of hand.

More fundamentally, while an urban labour market is gradually being re-established, the process of rebuilding a private urban housing market in larger urban centres will take a much longer time because of the complexity of property financing, pricing, land assembly, compliance with building and planning laws and so on. That would act as an impediment to large-scale permanent migration to major cities. Certainly, millions of farm labourers are going to leave the land, but most of them will be stopped midway by the swelling open and hidden economies of non-state sectors, mostly in small towns and in the coastal peri-urban regions. And in so far as the Party continues to dominate China's polity, urban social and demographic manageability should be maintained.

Having considered the direction China appears to be heading, it appears reasonable to accept a prediction of an average annual urban population growth rate of about 4 to 5 per cent for the 1990s and the first decade of the next century (Table 5.2). The rate (4 per cent) used in Scenario One roughly equals the average of the post-1949 period and that of the 1980s, and is used here to represent the medium forecast. Scenario Two uses 5 per cent, which is a high forecast under more marketization. Of course, one would expect the coastal regions and middle and lower Changjiang valleys to have higher rates than the rest of the country. Using assumptions about the overall population growth rates taken from Peng (1991) and Zeng (1991), and population targets recently pronounced by the Director of the State Family Planning Commission (*World Journal* 1992d), two urbanization scenarios for the coming two decades are detailed in Table 5.2. These scenarios suggest that China's urban percentage will be between 37 per cent and 39 per cent by the turn of the next century and will be hitting the 50 per cent mark around 2010. In other words, in

Table 5.2 Projections of China's Urbanization Levels in the Years 2000 and 2010

	Actual		Projected		
	Size (in Millions) 1990	Annual Average Growth Rate (%) 1990–2000	Size (in Millions) 2000	Annual Average Growth Rate (%) 2000–2010	Size (in Millions) 2010
National Population Totals	1143.3	1.4	1313.8	0.9	1437.0
Scenario One Urban Population	316.0	4.0	467.8	4.0	692.4
% of National Total	27.6		35.6		48.2
Scenario Two Urban Population	316.0	5.0	514.7	5.0	838.4
% of National Totals	27.6		39.2		58.3

Note: The urban population totals in 1990 include urban population from the 'floating population' category (See Chapter Two)

less than one generation's time, China will be transformed into a primarily urbanized society, in both demographic and occupational terms. The momentum of urban growth after passing the 50 per cent urban percentage point is bound to slow down as the urban population base becomes larger and the pool of prospective migrants shrinks in relative, if not absolute, terms.[4]

What is going to happen in China in the coming two decades is thus truly momentous—the urban percentage will almost double and the size of the urban population added will be about that of the current US urban population. The urban growth dynamism shown in Table 5.2 appears to be broadly parallel to what happened in Taiwan on a smaller scale in the two decades between the mid-1950s and mid-1970s, during which the island experienced an enviable and rapid transformation of the population from predominantly rural to urban, with an average annual rate of urban growth running between 5 and 8 per cent (Tsai 1990).[5] Unprecedented in Chinese history and perhaps in the modern world's history, the scale of construction and rapidity of human and societal adjustments required in the current transformation taking place on the Chinese mainland are truly awesome and at times painful, posing many challenges to the government. But if the experience of rapid economic structural change and urban transition in other East Asian societies, such as South Korea and Taiwan, offer any hints (see for example Lo and Salih 1987), there are grounds for believing that, given political stability and continuing economic liberalization, China will follow the pack of newly industrializing economies in East Asia and experience this rapid transition in the early decades of the next century.[6] Not only will these changes, as Perkins (1990) points out, have a profound effect on the way of life of most Chinese people and the way that Chinese society is organized, but the outcome of such a mammoth transformation will also create a totally different dimension in the future global political economy.

Notes

1. Zhou (1982) typifies many other similar studies produced by Chinese scholars based on mostly crude cross-nation studies of per capita gross national product and urban percentage. As pointed out by Kirkby (1985, pp. 202–3), most of them are 'based on dubious assumptions and extrapolations' and suffer from a 'mechanical transfer of foreign experience to China'.

2. For example, Wu's (1981) projection is based on China's supportable non-agricultural population, resting on grain production targets, a proposition that is no longer valid in view of the rapid rise in agricultural productivity in the 1980s following reform (see also Chan 1989). A detailed critique of this type of argument is made by Koshizawa (1988). The World Bank (1985) appears to base its study on an urban definition that is generally consistent with what is used in this study. However, the Bank's forecast is on the conservative side. The highest urbanization level forecasted for the year 2000 (under its BALANCE model) is only 30 per cent. China had already reached 27.6 per cent by the end of 1990.

3. A full report of the Fourteenth Party Congress can be found in the *Beijing Review* (1992).

4. Mathematical relations dictate that, keeping the rate of net rural outmigration constant, the higher the urban percentage of the population, the lower the net urban in-migration rate. See a detailed explanation in Harris (1970).

5. Tsai's figures show that Taiwan's urban percentage soared from 29 per cent in 1953 to 59 per cent in 1973. These figures are similar to those reported by others (for example Williams 1990).

6. Projections of phenomenal economic growth in China abound, for example *The Economist* (1992) and *Business Week* (1993). One detailed proposal on how a scenario of rapid urban transition is feasible in mainland China, including phasing, investments required, and industrial sectoral strategy, is examined by Gao (1990) in his doctoral dissertation presented to Beijing University.

Appendix 2.1

Most Recent Urban Designation Criteria Promulgated by the State Council

(a) *Designations of Towns*

1. All seats of county-level governments should be designated as towns.

2. A township with a total population of less than 20,000 and a non-agricultural population of more than 2,000 in the township government seat qualifies for town designation. A township is also eligible for town designation if its total population is more than 20,000 and the non-agricultural population in the township government seat is more than 10 per cent of the total township population.

3. Settlements in minority regions, remote and mountainous, and mining regions which are sparsely populated, small (river/sea) ports, tourist points, and border ports may also qualify for town designations when deemed essential even if the non-agricultural population is less than 2,000.

4. In areas where townships have been designated as towns, villages are to be put under the administration of towns. In market towns which have not yet reached the conditions for designations as towns, the administration is to be under the township government.

(Excerpt from Ministry of Internal Affairs 1984)

(b) *Designations of Cities*

1. A town with a non-agricultural population of at least 60,000 and an annual gross product (*guomin shengchan zongzhi*) of at least RMB¥200 million, and that has already become a regional economic centre, will qualify for designation as a city. Important towns in minority regions, remote regions, major industrial, mining or research bases, famous tourist areas, transportation nodes, and border ports, may also qualify for designations when deemed essential even if the sizes of the non-agricultural population and annual gross product have not yet reached the above specified minima.

2. A county meeting the following conditions is eligible for designation as a city: a total population of less than 500,000, a non-agricultural population of more than 100,000 in the town where

the seat of the county government is situated, less than 40 per cent of the resident population in that town is agricultural, and an annual gross product of at least RMB¥300 million. The county is to be re-classified as city; villages and towns formerly under the county's administration will be put under the city's administration.

Counties with a total population of more than 500,000, a non-agricultural population of more than 120,000 in the seat of the county government, and an annual gross product of more than RMB¥400 million are also eligible for designation as cities.

Counties with towns which are the seats of governments of autonomous prefectures (or leagues), though the non-agricultural populations of these towns are less than 100,000 and the annual gross product less than RMB¥300 million, are eligible for reclassification to cities when deemed essential.

3. A medium-sized city (one with urban districts) which has a non-agricultural population of more than 250,000 in the urban districts and an annual gross product of RMB¥100 million and which has become a regional political, economic, scientific and cultural centre, exerting influence on and attraction to its surroundings, may implement the system of 'city leading counties'. The number of counties to be put under its administration depends on the actual situation, mainly determined by the existing urban–rural economic connections and the economic power of the city.

(Excerpt from State Council 1986)

Appendix 2.2

1990 Census: Components of Urban Population
(Population in Millions)

| Urban Place | Number | Population Size | | | Urban Population | | |
		Total	Residents' Committees	Villagers' Committees	Coverage	Population Size	% of Nation's Pop. Totals
PPL Cities*	188	187.2	**121.8**	**65.4**	Urban Districts	**187.2**	**16.6**
CL Cities	268	95.7	**24.1**	71.6	Streets	**24.1**	**2.1**
Towns**	10945	318.5	**85.3**	233.2	Resident's Committees	**85.3**	**7.5**
Total	12391*	601.4	231.2	370.2		296.5	**26.2**

Notes: PPL = Provincial/Prefectural-level
CL = County-level

Figures in **bold** are those defined as 'urban' in the 1990 Census
* Including 990 towns within urban districts of PPL cities
** Excluding towns within PPL cities;

Population numbers may not add up to due to rounding.

Source: Computed from State Council (1991)

Appendix 2.3

Components of Urban Population Growth by Year, 1950–1990
(in millions)

| Year | Urban Population (end-yr) | As % of National Population | Urban Population Increase | | Urban Growth Rate % | Urban Population (mid-yr) | Urban Natural Increase | | Net Rural–Urban Migration | |
| | | | crude | adjusted | | | % | No. | % | No. |
i	UP_i I	urb_i II	API_i III	API_i IV	ar_i V	UPM_i VI	ur_i VII	NI_i VIII	$UIMR_i$ IX	NM_i X
1949	57.65	10.6								
1950	61.69	11.2	4.04	4.04	7.0	59.67	2.463	1.47	4.308	2.57
1951	66.32	11.8	4.63	4.63	7.5	64.01	2.592	1.66	4.642	2.97
1952	71.63	12.5	5.31	5.31	8.0	68.98	2.598	1.79	5.101	3.52
1953	78.26	13.3	6.63	6.63	9.3	77.26	2.980	2.30	5.601	4.33
1954	82.49	13.7	4.23	4.23	5.4	80.38	3.279	2.64	1.984	1.59
1955	82.85	13.5	0.36	3.36	4.1	82.67	2.954	2.44	1.111	0.92
1956	91.85	14.6	9.00	9.00	10.9	87.35	2.878	2.51	7.425	6.49
1957	99.49	15.4	7.64	7.64	8.3	95.67	3.387	3.24	4.599	4.40
1958	107.21	16.2	7.72	7.72	7.8	103.35	2.307	2.38	5.163	5.34
1959	123.71	18.2	16.50	16.50	15.4	115.46	1.711	1.98	12.580	14.52
1960	131.73	19.7	7.02	7.02	5.7	127.22	1.074	1.37	4.444	5.65
1961	127.07	19.3	-3.66	-3.66	-2.8	128.90	0.904	1.17	-3.743	-4.83
1962	116.59	17.3	-10.48	-10.48	-8.3	121.83	2.715	3.31	-11.317	-13.79
1963	116.46	16.8	-0.13	-0.13	-0.1	116.52	3.667	4.27	-3.779	-4.40
1964	129.50	18.4	13.04	0.15	0.1	130.46	2.538	3.31	-2.423	-3.16
1965	130.45	18.0	0.95	0.95	0.7	129.97	2.219	2.88	-1.488	-1.93

Appendix 2.3 (cont.)

	I	II	III	IV	V	VI	VII	VIII	IX	X
1966	133.13	17.9	2.68	2.68	2.1	131.79	1.706	2.25	0.328	0.43
1967	135.48	17.7	2.35	2.35	1.8	134.30	1.762	2.37	-0.013	-0.02
1968	138.38	17.6	2.90	2.90	2.1	136.93	1.891	2.59	0.227	0.31
1969	141.17	17.5	2.79	2.79	2.0	139.77	1.802	2.52	0.195	0.27
1970	144.24	17.4	3.07	3.07	2.2	142.70	1.783	2.54	0.368	0.53
1971	147.11	17.3	2.87	2.87	2.0	145.67	1.720	2.51	0.250	0.36
1972	149.35	17.1	2.24	2.24	1.5	148.23	1.540	2.28	-0.029	-0.04
1973	153.45	17.2	4.10	4.10	2.8	151.40	1.384	2.09	1.324	2.01
1974	155.95	17.2	2.50	2.50	1.6	154.70	1.066	1.65	0.550	0.85
1975	160.30	17.3	4.35	4.35	2.8	158.12	1.041	1.65	1.710	2.70
1976	163.41	17.4	3.11	3.11	1.9	161.85	0.757	1.22	1.165	1.89
1977	166.69	17.6	3.28	3.28	2.0	165.05	0.859	1.42	1.129	1.86
1978	172.45	17.9	5.76	5.76	3.5	169.57	0.905	1.53	2.492	4.23
1979	184.95	19.0	12.50	12.50	7.3	178.70	0.912	1.63	6.083	10.87
1980	191.40	19.4	6.45	6.45	3.5	188.17	0.924	1.74	2.504	4.71
1981	201.71	20.2	10.31	10.31	5.4	196.55	1.187	2.33	4.059	7.98
1982	214.80	21.1	13.10	13.10	6.5	208.25	1.327	2.76	4.964	10.34
1983	222.74	21.6	7.94	7.94	3.7	218.77	1.041	2.28	2.589	5.66
1984	240.17	23.0	17.43	17.43	7.8	231.46	0.947	2.19	6.583	15.24
1985	250.94	23.7	10.77	10.77	4.5	245.56	0.881	2.16	3.505	8.61
1986	263.66	24.5	12.72	12.72	5.1	257.30	1.226	3.16	3.717	9.56
1987	276.74	25.3	13.08	13.08	4.9	270.20	1.192	3.22	3.648	9.86
1988	286.61	25.8	9.87	9.87	3.6	281.68	1.159	3.27	2.345	6.60
1989	295.40	26.2	8.79	8.79	3.0	291.01	1.127	3.28	1.894	5.51
1990	301.91	26.4	6.51	6.51	2.2	296.51	1.095	3.25	1.101	3.26
1950–90			240.90	231.10	3.9			96.72		134.39

Notes and Sources:

I and II: SSB (1991a, p. 79).

III: $API_i = UP_i - UP_{i-1}$

IV: Pre–1982 adjustments are from Chan (1988a). No adjustments are made for the period 1982–90.

V: ar_i = adjusted $API_i/UP_{i-1} \times 100$.

VI: $UPM_i = (UP_i + UP_{i-1}) / 2$.

VII: ur_i for 1950–81 are from Chan (1988a). Those after 1981 are estimated based on the same principle used in Chan (1988a). Specifically:

Year	Natural Increase Rate (%)			Urban Population Weight		Urban Natural Increase Rate (%)
	Cities	Counties	Towns	Cities	Towns	
i	cr	rr	tr	cw	tw	ur
1982	1.296	1.497	1.397	0.695	0.305	1.327
1983	1.007	1.220	1.114	0.684	0.316	1.041
1984	0.914	1.117	1.016	0.672	0.328	0.947
1985	0.806	1.251	1.029	0.661	0.339	0.881
1986	1.164	1.520	1.342	0.650	0.350	1.226
1987	1.117	1.533	1.325	0.639	0.361	1.192
1988	1.071	1.546	1.308	0.627	0.373	1.159
1989	1.024	1.559	1.292	0.616	0.384	1.127
1990	0.977	1.572	1.275	0.605	0.395	1.095

cr and rr: From SSB (1991 a) except those of 1987, 1988, and 1990, which are derived by linear interpolation.

tr = (cr + rr)/2

cw and tw: figures for 1982 and 1990 are from census figures. Those in between are interpolated.

$ur = cr \times cw + tr \times tw$

VIII: $NI_i = UPM_i \times ur_i$

IX: $UIMR_i = NM_i / UPM_i \times 100$

X: NM_i = adjusted $API_i - NI_i$

Bibliography

Acta Geographica Sinica, 1984. 'Dili xuebao 1(1)–39(2) fenlei zongmu 1934–1984' (Index By Subject of *Acta Geographica Sinica* 1(1)–39(2), 1934–1984), *Dili xuebao* (*Acta Geographica Sinica*), 39(3), pp. 321–342.

Alexander, John W., 1957. 'The Basic–Nonbasic Concept of Urban Economic Functions', *Economic Geography*, 30(3), pp. 246–261.

All China Women's Federation and Shaanxi Provincial Women's Federation, 1991. *Zhongguo funu tongji ziliao* (*Statistics on Chinese Women*), Beijing: Zhongguo tongji chubanshe.

Amin, Samir, 1981. *The Future of Maoism*, New York: Monthly Review Press (translated by Norman Finkelstein).

Arnold, Fred *et al.*, 1989. 'Estimating the Immigration Multiplier', *International Migration Review*, 23(4), pp. 813–838.

Ashton, Basil *et al.*, 1984. 'Famine in China, 1958–61', *Population and Development Review*, 10(4), pp. 613–645.

Bai, Jianhua, 1986. 'Woguo chengxiang renkou de jige wenti' (Questions on China's Rural and Urban Populations), *Renkou yanjiu* (*Population Research*), 2, pp. 11–14.

Ban, Shuren and Xie, Chuntai, 1986. 'Fahuei youshi jingyibu shenhua yonggong zhidu de gaige' (Extending the Strength and Further Deepening the Reform of Recruitment System), *Jianzhu jingji* (*Construction Economics*), 9, pp. 2–4.

Banister, Judith, 1986. 'Urban–Rural Population Projections for China', Centre for International Research, US Bureau of the Census, *CIR Staff Paper* No. 15, Washington, DC: US Bureau of the Census.

Banister, Judith, 1987. *China's Changing Population*, Stanford: Stanford University Press.

Beijing Municipal Government, 1989. *Beijing chengzhen de siren gugong* (*Private Employment in Beijing City and Towns*), Beijing jingji xueyuan chubanshe.

Beijing Review, 1987. 'Coping With Effects of Rural Influx', February 16, pp. 28–29.

Beijing Review, 1992. October 26, pp. 10–33.

Beijing Revolutionary Committee, 1968. 'Directive On Assignments of Middle School Graduates', in Institute for the Study of Chinese Communist Problems (1973) *Important CCP Documents of the Great Proletarian Cultural Revolution*, Taipei: Shanghai Publishing Press, pp. 126–127.

Bernstein, Thomas P., 1977. *Up to the Mountains and Down to the Villages*, New Haven: Yale University Press.

Bhalla, A. S., 1990. 'Rural–Urban Disparities in India and China', *World Development*, 18(8), pp. 1097–1110.

Bideleux, Robert, 1985. *Communism and Development*, London: Methuen.

Blecher, Marc, 1983. 'Peasant Labour for Urban Industry: Temporary Contract Labour, Urban–Rural Balance and Class Relations in a Chinese County', *World Development*, 11(8), pp. 731–745.

Blecher, Marc, 1988. 'Rural Contract Labour in Urban Chinese Industry', in Gugler, Josef (ed.), 1988. *The Urbanization of the Third World*, New York: Oxford University Press, pp. 109–123.

Bodrova, Valentina and Anker, Richard, 1985. *Working Women in Socialist Countries: The Fertility Connection*, Geneva: International Labour Office.

Bornstein, Morris, 1985. 'The Soviet Centrally Planned Economy', in Morris Bornstein (ed.), *Comparative Economic Systems*, Homewood: Richard D. Irwin, Inc., pp. 188–219.

Brown, Lester R., 1976. 'The Limits to Growth of Third World Cities', *The Futurist*, 10(6), pp. 307–310.

Brown, Lester R., 1978. *The Twenty-Ninth Day*, New York: W. W. Norton & Company.

Buck, David D., 1981. 'Policies Favoring the Growth of Smaller Urban Places in the People's Republic of China, 1949–1979', in Ma, Laurence J. C. and Hanten, Edward W. (eds.), *Urban Development in Modern China*, Boulder: Westview Press, pp. 114–146.

Business Week 1993. May 17 (Special Report: 'China: The Making of An Economic Giant').

Byrd, William A., 1991. *The Market Mechanism and Economic Reforms in China*, Armonk: M. E. Sharpe.

Cell, Charles P., 1980. 'The Urban–Rural Contradiction in the Maoist Era: The Pattern of Deurbanization in China', *Comparative Urban Research*, 7(3), pp. 48–69.

Chan, June Sau Hung, 1990. *The Population Growth of Towns in Guangdong, 1980–88*, University of Hong Kong, Department of Geography, Unpublished BA Thesis.

Chan, Kam Wing, 1985. 'Urbanization Issues in China's Development', in Chen, Min-sun and Shyu, Lawrence N. (eds.), *China Insight*, Ottawa: CASA, pp. 185–214.

Chan, Kam Wing, 1986. Review of R. J. Kirkby's *Urbanization in China*, *Economic Geography*, 62(3), pp. 280–282.

Chan, Kam Wing, 1987. 'Further Information About China's Urban Population Statistics: Old and New', *The China Quarterly*, 109, pp. 104–109.

Chan, Kam Wing, 1988a. 'Rural–Urban Migration in China, 1950–1982: Estimates and Analysis', *Urban Geography*, 9(1), pp. 53–84.

Chan, Kam Wing, 1988b. *Urbanization in China, 1949–1982: Policies, Patterns, and Determinants*. Unpublished PhD Dissertation, University of Toronto.

Chan, Kam Wing, 1989. 'Determinants of Urbanization in Post-1949 China: Empirical Investigations', Paper presented at the International Conference on Internal Migration and Urbanization in China, Beijing, China, December 6–8, 1989.

Chan, Kam Wing (Chen, Jinyong), 1990. 'Shi fenxi shehuizhuyi guojia chengshihua de tedian' (An Analysis of the Features of Urbanization in Socialist Countries), *Zhongguo renkou kexue (Population Science of China)*, 21, pp. 6–12, and 53. An English translation appeared as Chen Jinyong, 1991. 'The Distinguishing Features of Urbanization in Socialist Countries', *Chinese Journal of Population Science*, 3(3), pp. 165–178.

Chan, Kam Wing, 1992a. 'Post-1949 Urbanization Trends and Policies: An Overview' in Guldin, Gregory (ed.), *Urbanizing China*, Westport: Greenwood Press, pp. 41–63.

Chan, Kam Wing, 1992b. 'Economic Growth Strategy and Urbanization Policies in China, 1949–82', *International Journal of Urban and Regional Research*, 16(2), pp. 275–305.

Chan, Kam Wing, 1994. 'Urbanization and Rural-urban Migration in China since 1982: A New Baseline', *Modern China*, 20(3), pp. 243–81.

Chan, Kam Wing and Tsui, Kai Yuen, 1992. ' "Agricultural" and "Non-agricultural" Population Statistics of the People's Republic of China: Definitions, Findings and Comparisons', Hong Kong: University of Hong Kong, Department of Geography and Geology, *Occasional Paper No. 1*.

Chan, Kam Wing and Xu, Xueqiang, 1985. 'Urban Population Growth and Urbanization in China Since 1949: Reconstructing a Baseline', *The China Quarterly*, 104, pp. 583–613.

Chan, Kam Wing and Yang, Yunyan, 1992. 'Inter-provincial Migration in China, 1949–90: Spatial and Temporal Dimensions', Paper presented at the 27th International Geographical Congress, August 9–14, Washington, DC.

Chang, Sen-dou, 1963. 'The Historical Trend of Chinese Urbanization', *Annals of the Association of American Geographers*, 53(2), pp. 109–143.

Chang, Sen-dou, 1976. 'The Changing System of Chinese Cities', *Annals of the Association of American Geographers*, 66(3), pp. 398–415.

Chang, Sen-dou, 1977. 'The Morphology of Walled Capitals', in Skinner, G. William (ed.), 1977. *The City in Late Imperial China*, Stanford: Stanford University Press, pp. 75–100.

Chang, Sen-dou, 1983. 'Urbanization and Economic Readjustment in China' in Leung, Chi-leung, and Chin, Steve S. K. (eds.), *China in Readjustment*, Hong Kong: Centre of Asian Studies, pp. 193–215.

Chao, Kang, 1986. *Man and Land in Chinese History*, Stanford: Stanford University Press.

Chen, Cheng Siang, 1973. 'Population Growth and Urbanization in China, 1953–1970', *Geographical Review*, 63(10), pp. 55–72.

Chen, Jiaqi, 1990. *Zhongguo nongmin de fenghua yu liaodong* (*The Differentiation and Mobility of the Chinese Peasantry*), Beijing: Nongcun duwu chubanshe.

Chen, Kaiguo, 1982. 'A Tentative Inquiry into the Scissors Gap in the Rate of Exchange between Industrial and Agricultural Products', *Social Sciences in China*, 3(2), pp. 55–74.

Chen, Kuan, *et al.*, 1988. 'New Estimates of Fixed Investment and Capital Stock for Chinese State Industry', *The China Quarterly*, 114, pp. 243–266.

Chen, Pi-chao, 1972. 'Overurbanisation, Rustication of Urban educated Youths, and Politics of Rural Transformation', *Comparative Politics*, April, pp. 361–386.

Chen, Shenli, 1983. 'Sishier nian (1940–1981 nian) lai funu de shengyu zhuangkuang' (Women's Fertility in Forty-two years [1940–1981]) in *Quanguo qianfen zhiyi renkou shengyolu chouyang diaocha fenxi* (*An Analysis of a National One-per-thousand Population Sample Survey in Birth Rate*), Special Issue of the *Renkou yu jingji* (*Population and Economy*), July, pp. 30–51.

Chen, Xin and Chen, Zhongda, 1984. 'Yituo zhongxin chengshi zushi jingji wangluo wenti de tantao' (Discussion on the Question of Forming Economic Networks Based on Centre Cities), *Shehui kexue zhangxian* (*Social Sciences Front*), 2, pp. 88–93.

Chen, Yun, 1954. 'Guanyu jihua shougou he jihua gongying' (On Planned Procurement and Supply) in *Chen Yun wenxuan 1949–1956 (Selected Articles of Chen Yun 1949–56)*, (1984), Beijing: Renmin chubanshe, pp. 254–263.

Chen, Yun, 1955. 'Jianchi he gaijin liangshi de tonggou tongxiao' (Insist and Improve the Unified Purchase and Distribution System of Grain) in *Chen Yun wenxuan 1949–56 (Selected Articles of Chen Yun 1949–56)*, (1984), Beijing: Renmin chubanshe, pp. 272–279.

Chen, Yun, 1961. 'Dongyuan chengshi renkou xiaxiang' (Mobilizing Urban Population to the Countryside' in *Chen Yun wenxuan 1956–1985 (Selected Articles of Chen Yun 1956–1985)*, (1986), Beijing: Renmin chubanshe, pp. 151–160. An English version appeared as 'An Important Work that Relates to the Overall Situation', in Lardy, Nicholas R. and Lieberthal, Kenneth (eds.), 1983. *Chen Yun's Strategy for China's Development: A Non-Maoist Alternative*, Armonk: M. E. Sharpe, pp. 144–154.

Chen, Yun, 1986. *Chen Yun wenxuan 1956–1985 (Selected Works of Chen Yun 1956–1985)*. Beijing: Renmin chubanshe.

Chenery, Hollis and Syrquin, Moises, 1975. *Patterns of Development, 1950–70*, London: Oxford University Press.

Cheng, Xuan, 1987. 'Problems of Urbanization under China's Traditional Economic System', in Kwok, *et al.* (eds.), 1990. *Chinese Urban Reform: What Model Now?* Armonk: M. E. Sharpe, pp. 65–77.

Chinese Academy of Social Sciences (CASS), 1986. *Zhongguo renkou nianjian, 1985 (Population Yearbook of China, 1985)*, Beijing: Zhongguo shehui kexue chubanshc.

Chinese Academy of Social Sciences (CASS), 1988. *Migration of 74 Cities & Towns: Sampling Survey Data (1986)*, Beijing: Zhongguo renkou kexue bianjibu.

Chinese Academy of Social Sciences (CASS), 1990. *Zhongguo renkou nianjian, 1990 (Population Yearbook of China, 1990)*, Beijing: Zhongguo shehui kexue chubanshe.

Chinese Academy of Social Sciences (CASS), 1991. *Zhongguo renkou nianjian, 1991 (Population Yearbook of China, 1991)*, Beijing: Zhongguo shehui kexue chubanshe.

Chiu, Tze Nang, 1980. 'Urbanization Processes and National Development', in Leung, C. K. and Ginsburg, Norton (eds.), *China: Urbanization and National Development*, Chicago: University of Chicago Press, pp. 89–107.

Christiansen, Flemming, 1990. 'Social Division and Peasant Mobility in Mainland China: the Implications of Hu-k'ou System', *Issues and Studies*, 26(4), pp. 78–91.

Christiansen, Flemming, 1992. 'Market Transition in China: The Case of the Jiangsu Labour Market, 1978–1990', *Modern China*, 18(1), pp. 72–95.

Clark, D. 1982. *Urban Geography*. London: Croom Helm.

Combined Research Group of Eight Cities, 1990. *Zhongguo dachengshi renkou yu shehui fazhan (Population and Social Development in Chinese Metropolises)*, Beijing: Zhongguo chengshi jingji shehui chubanshe.

Compton, Paul, 1976. 'Migration in Eastern Europe' in Salt, John and Clout, Hugh (eds.), *Migration in Post-War Europe*, London: Oxford University Press, pp. 168–215.

Constitution of the PRC, 1954. Hong Kong: University of Hong Kong Students' Union.

Constitution of the PRC, 1982. Hong Kong: Joint Publishing Co.

Cui, Gonghao and Wu, Jin, 1990. 'Zhongguo chengshi bianyuanqu kongjian jiegou tezheng jiqi fazhan' (The Salient Features of the Spatial Structure at Urban Fringes in China and Their Development), *Dili xuebao*, 45(4), pp. 399–410.

Davis, Kingsley, 1965. 'The Urbanization of the Human Population', *Scientific American*, 213(3), pp. 41–53.

Davis, Kingsley, 1966. 'The First Cities: How and Why Did they Arise?' in Kingsley Davis (ed.), *Cities: Their Origin, Growth and Human Impact*, San Francisco: Freeman and Co., pp. 9–17.

de Vries, Jan, 1984. *European Urbanization: 1500–1800*, London: Methuen and Co., Ltd.

Demko, George J. and Fuchs, Roland J., 1977. 'Commuting in the USSR and Eastern Europe: Causes, Characteristics and Consequences', *East European Quarterly*, 9, pp. 463–475.

Demko, George J. and Regulska, Joanna, 1987. 'Socialism and Its Impact on Urban Processes and the City', *Urban Geography*, 8(4), pp. 289–292.

Department of Personnel, 1991. *Liudong diaopei gongzuo zhinan (A Guide to Employment Mobility and Transfers)*, Beijing: Gaige chubanshe.

Ding, Jinhong, 1991. 'Lun Zhongguo renkou chengzhenhua shuiping yu jizhi' (A Discussion on China's Urbanization Level and Mechanisms), mimeo, East China Normal University.

'Disanci quanguo zhongxin chengshi jingji lilun taolun jiyao' (A Summary of Discussion at the Third National Conference on Economic Theories of Centre Cities), 1985. *Jingji tizhi gaige (Economic System Reforms)*, 4, pp. 48–51.

Douglass, Mike, 1988. 'Urbanization and Urban Policies in China', *Discussion Paper No. 10*, Department of Urban and Regional Planning, University of Hawaii.

Ebanks, G. Edward, and Cheng, Chaoze, 1990. 'China: A Unique Urbanization Model', *Asia-Pacific Population Journal*, 5(3), pp. 29–50.

Eckstein, Alexander, 1977. *China's Economic Revolution*, Cambridge: Cambridge University Press.

Economic Reporter (Hong Kong), 1984. 24, pp. 5–14.

The Economist, 1992. November 28 (Special Report: 'When China Wakes').

Editing Committee, 1989. *Zhongguo chengshi jianshe nianjian (China's Urban Construction Yearbook)*, Beijing: Zhongguo jianshe gongye chubanshe.

Ellman, M., 1975. 'Did the Agricultural Surplus Provide the Resources for the Increase in Investment in the USSR during the First Five Year Plan?', *The Economic Journal*, 85, pp. 844–864.

Fallenbuchl, Zbigniew M., 1970. 'The Communist Pattern of Industrialization', *Soviet Studies*, 21, pp. 458–484.

Fallenbuchl, Zbigniew M., 1977. 'Internal Migration and Economic Development Under Socialism: The Case of Poland', in Brown, A. A. and Neuberger, E. (eds.), *Internal Migration: A Comparative Perspective*, New York: Academic Press, pp. 305–327.

Fang, Lanrui and Zhao, Lukuan, 1982. *Zhongguo chengzhen de jiuye he gongzi (Employment and Wages in Urban China)*. Beijing: Renmin chubanshe.

Fang Lanrui and Jiang, Weiyu, 1987. 'Nongye shengyu laodongli zhuanyi moshi de bijiao yanjiu', (A Comparative Study of the Models for Transferring Agricultural Surplus Labour) *Zhongguo shehui kexue*, 5, pp. 43–52.

Fei, Xiaotong, 1984. 'Xiao chengzhen da wenti' (Small Towns, a Big Issue), *Liaowang (Outlook)*, January 16–30, No. 2–5.

Feng, Litian, 1988. 'Zhongguo chengxiang huafen biaozhun zhuanjia yan-taohui guanyu zhongguo chengxiang huafen biaozhun ji youguan wenti taolun yijianshu' (Experts Meeting's Suggestions on the Criteria of Classifying Urban and Rural Areas and Related Issues on China's Urban/Rural Classification Criteria), *Renkou yu jingji* (*Population and Economy*), 5, pp. 3–6.

Field, Robert M., 1986. 'The Performance of Industry during the Cultural Revolution: Second Thoughts', *The China Quarterly*, 108, pp. 625–642.

Forbes, Dean and Thrift, Nigel, 1987. 'Introduction', in Dean Forbes and Nigel Thrift (eds.), *The Socialist Third World*, Oxford: Basil Blackwell, pp. 1–26.

Freeman, Stephen, 1982. 'Human Labour as an Energy Source for Rice Production in the Developing World', *Agro-Ecosystems*, 8, pp. 125–136.

Friedmann, John and Douglass, Mike, 1978. 'Agropolitan Development: Toward a New Strategy for Regional Planning in Asia', in Lo, F. and Salih, K. (eds.), *Growth Poles Strategy and Regional Development Policy*, Oxford: Pergamon Press, pp. 163–192.

Frolic, B. Michael, 1976. 'Noncomparative Communism: Chinese and Soviet Urbanization', in Field, Mark G. (ed.), *Social Consequences of Modernization in Communist Societies*, Baltimore: Johns Hopkins University Press, pp. 149–161.

Fung, Ka-iu, 1980. 'Suburban Agricultural Land Use Since 1949', in Leung, C. K. and Ginsburg, Norton (eds.), *China: Urbanization and National Development*, Chicago: University of Chicago Press, pp. 156–184.

Fung, Ka-iu, 1981. 'The Spatial Development of Shanghai', in Howe, C. (ed.), *Shanghai: Revolution and Development in an Asia Metropolis*, Cambridge: Cambridge University Press, pp. 269–300.

Gao, Peiyi, 1990. 'Weilai zhongguo de chengshihua fazhan zhanlue' (Urban Development Strategy for Future China), *Jingji xuejia* (*The Economist*), 6, pp. 43–53.

Gao, Peiyi, 1991. *Zhongwei chengshihua bijiao yanjiu* (*A Comparative Study of Urbanization in China and Other Countries*), Tianjin: Nankai daxue chubanshe.

Gittings, John, 1968. *Survey of the Sino-Soviet Dispute*, London: Oxford University Press.

Gold, Thomas B., 1980. 'Back to the City: the Return of Shanghai's Educated Youth', *The China Quarterly*, 84, pp. 755–770.

Goldstein, Sidney, 1990. 'Urbanization in China, 1982–87', *Population and Development Review*, 16(4), pp. 673–701.

Goldstein, Sidney and Goldstein, Alice, 1991. 'Permanent and Temporary Migration Differentials in China', *Papers of the East–West Population Institute*, No. 117.

Gong, Xikui, 1989. 'Zhongguo xianxing huji zhidu toushi' (A Perspective on China's Current Household Registration System), *Shehui kexue* (*Social Sciences*), 2, pp. 32–36.

Government Administration Council, 1953. 'Implementing the Planned Purchase and Planned Supply of Grain' in State Council Legal System Bureau, 1987. *Zhonghua renmin gongheguo xianxing fagui huibian* (*Collection of Current Laws and Regulations in the People's Republic of China)*, Beijing: Renmin chubanshe, pp. 458–462.

Gray, Jack, 1972. 'The Chinese Model', in Nove, Alec, and Nuti, D. M. (eds.), *Socialist Economics*, New York: Penguin, pp. 491–510.

Gray, Jack, 1976. 'Stalin, Mao and the Future of China', *New Society*, April 1, pp. 9–11.

Gu, Shengzu, 1993. *Feinonghua ji chengzhenhua lilun yu shijian* (*The Theory and Practice of Non-agriculturalization and Urbanization*), Wuhan: Wuhan daxue chubanshe.

Gu, Shengzu, 1991. *Feinonghua yu chengzhenhua yanjiu* (*Research on Non-agriculturalization and Urbanization*), Hangzhou: Zhejiang renmin chubanshe.

Guangmin ribao, 1989. March 3, p. 2.

Gugler, Josef (ed.), 1988. *The Urbanization of the Third World*, New York: Oxford University Press.

Gugler, Josef, 1982. 'Overurbanization Reconsidered', *Economic Development and Cultural Change*, 31(1), pp. 173–189.

Guldin, Gregory (ed.), 1992. *Urbanizing China*, Westport: Greenwood Press.

Guldin, Gregory, 1992. 'Urbanizing the Countryside: Guangzhou, Hong Kong, and the Pearl River Delta', in Guldin, Gregory (ed.), *Urbanizing China*, Westport: Greenwood Press, pp. 157–184.

Guo, Shutian and Liu, Chunbin, 1990. *Xiheng de Zhongguo* (*An Unbalanced China*), Shijiazhuang: Hebei renmin chubanshe.

Gurley, John, 1970. 'Maoist Economic Development: The New Man in the New China', *The Center Magazine*, 3(3), pp. 25–33.

Gurley, John, 1976. *China's Economy and the Maoist Strategy*, New York: Monthly Review Press.

Gurley, John, 1979. 'Rural Development in China 1949–75, and the Lessons to be Learned from it', in Maxwell, Neville (ed.), *China's Road to Development*, Oxford: Pergamon Press, pp. 5–25.

Harris, Chauncy D., 1970. *Cities of the Soviet Union*, Association of American Geographers Monograph No. 5, Chicago: Rand McNally.

Harris, Chauncy D., 1971. 'Urbanization and Population Growth in the Soviet Union, 1959–1970', *The Geographical Review*, 61(1), pp. 102–124.

Harris, J. R. and Todaro, M. P., 1970. 'Migration, Unemployment and Development: A Two-sector Analysis', *American Economic Review*, 60, pp. 126–142.

Hauser, Philip M., 1957. 'Summary Report of the General Rapporteur', in Hauser, Philip (ed.) *Urbanization in Asia and Far East*, Calcutta: UNESCO.

He, Fuxin *et al.*, 1992. 'Guanyu chengxiang huafeng baiozhun he shizhen renkou tongji wenti' (On the Questions Related Urban–Rural Classification and Urban Population Statistics), *Tongji yanjiu (Statistical Research)*, 6, pp. 8–11.

He, Jianchang and Wang, Jiye (eds.), 1983. *Zhongguo jihua guanli wenti (Questions on China's Planning and Management)*, Beijing: Zhongguo shehui kexue chubanshe.

Henderson, John Vernon, 1986. *International Experience in Urbanization and its Relevance for China*, World Bank Staff Working Papers No. 758, Washington, DC: The World Bank.

Hong Kong Census and Statistics Department, 1983. *Hong Kong 1981 Census, Main Report, Vol. 1: Analysis*, Hong Kong: Government Printer.

Hoselitz, Bert F., 1957. 'Urbanization and Economic Growth in Asia', *Economic Development and Cultural Change*, 6(1), pp. 42–54.

Howe, Christopher, 1971. *Employment and Economic Growth in Urban China 1949–1957*, Cambridge: Cambridge University Press.

Hsu, Mei-ling, 1985. 'Growth and Control of Population in China: The Urban–Rural Contrast', *Annals of the Association of American Geographers*, 75(2), pp. 185–202.

Hu, Guohua, *et al.*, 1988. *Dosediao de Zhongguo geti jingyingzhe (China's Multi-faceted Individual Entrepreneurs)*, Beijing: Beijing jingji xueyuan chubanshe.

Hu, Huaying, 1991. 'Urbanization and Rural Development in China: The Case of Pearl River Delta', (in Chinese), presentation at the University of Hong Kong, November 11.

Hu, Kaihua and Chen, Wei, 1984. 'Woguo chengzhen renkou tongji de youguan wenti' (Questions Related to China's Urban Population Statistics), *Renkou yu jingji (Population and Economy)*, 3, pp. 39–42 and 24.

Hu, Xuwei, 1983. 'Dui woguo chengzhenhua shuiping de pouxi' (Analysis of the Urbanization Level in China), *Chengshi guihua (Urban Planning Review)*, 2, pp. 23–26.

Huang, Weiting, 1992. *Zhongguo de yinxing jingji (China's Hidden Economy)*, Beijing: Zhongguo shangye chubanshe.

Hukou dengji tiaoli (Household Registration Regulations) 1958. Reproduced in CASS (ed.), 1986. *Zhongguo renkou nianjian, 1985 (Population Yearbook of China, 1985)*, Beijing: Zhongguo shehui kexue chubanshe, pp. 83–85.

IMF Survey, 1993. April 19, pp. 114–117.

Investigation and Research Group on Optimal Size of Cities, 1986. *Yanjiu chengzhen heli guimo de lilun he fangfa* (*Theory and Methods of Study-ing the Optimal Size of Cities*), Nanjing: Nanjing daxue chubanshe. *Jingji ribao*, 1984. July 11, p. 2.

Johnson, Chalmers, 1982. 'What's Wrong With Chinese Political Studies?', *Asian Survey*, 22(10), pp. 919–933.

Kansky, Karel Joseph, 1976. *Urbanization Under Socialism: The Case of Czechoslovakia*, New York: Praeger Publishers.

Kim, Won Bae, 1990. 'Population Re-distribution Policy in China: A Review', *Regional Development Dialogue*, 11(1), pp. 159–187.

Kirkby, Richard J., 1977. 'China's Strategy for Development' in Jeffrey, Nick and Caldwell, Malcolm (eds.), *Planning and Urbanism in China*, Oxford: Pergamon Press, pp. 111–116.

Kirkby, Richard J., 1985. *Urbanization in China: Town and Country in a Developing Economy 1949–2000 A.D.*, New York: Columbia University Press.

Kojima, Reeitsu (ed.), 1978. *Chugoku no toshika to noson kensetsu* (*Urbanization and Rural Development in China*), Tokyo: Ryuskeishosha.

Kojima, Reeitsu, 1987. *Urbanization and Urban Problems in China*. Tokyo: Institute of Developing Economies.

Konrad, Gyorgy and Szelenyi, Ivan, 1977. 'Social Conflicts of Under-urbanization' in Harloe, Michael (ed.), *Captive Cities*, London: John Wiley & Sons, pp. 157–173.

Kornai, Janos, 1986. *Contradictions and Dilemmas: Studies on Socialist Economy and Society*, Cambridge, MA: MIT Press.

Kornai, Janos, 1992. *The Socialist System*, Princeton: Princeton University Press.

Koshizawa, Akira, 1978. 'China's Urban Planning: Toward Development without Urbanization', *The Developing Economies*, 16(1), pp. 3–33.

Koshizawa, Akira, 1988. 'Chengshihua jingcheng he chengshi jianshe de zhanwan', (Urbanization Process and the Prospects of Urban Development) in Japan–China Association on Economy and Trade, *Zhongguo jingji de zhongchangqi zhanwan* (*Medium and Long-Term Outlook for the Chinese Economy*), Beijing: Jingji chubanshe, pp. 176–225.

Kueh, Y. Y., 1989. 'The Maoist Legacy and China's New Industrialization Strategy', *China Quarterly*, 119, pp. 420–447.

Kuo, T. C. and Myers, Ramon, 1986. *Understanding Communist China*, Stanford: Hoover Institution.

Kuo, Wen H., 1989. 'Economic Reforms and Urban Development in China', *Pacific Affairs*, 62(2), pp. 188–203.

Kuznets, Simon, 1965. *Economic Growth and Structure Selected Essays*, New York: W. W. Norton & Company, Inc.

Kwok, R. Yin-Wang, 1982. 'The Role of Small Cities in Chinese Urban

Development', *International Journal of Urban and Regional Research*, 6(4), pp. 549–565.

Kwok, R. Yin Wang, 1987. 'Recent Urban Policy on Development in China: a Reversal of "Anti-Urbanism" ', *Town Planning Review*, 58(4), pp. 383–399.

Kwok, R. Yin-Wang, *et al.* (eds.) 1990. *Chinese Urban Reform: What Model Now?* Armonk: M. E. Sharpe.

Lalkaka, Dinyar, 1984. 'Urban Housing in China', *Habitat International*, 8(1), pp. 63–73.

Lardy, Nicholas, 1978. *Economic Growth and Distribution in China*, Cambridge: Cambridge University Press.

Lardy, Nicholas, 1983. *Agriculture in China's Modern Economic Development*, New York: Cambridge University Press.

Lardy, Nicholas, 1987. 'The Chinese Economy Under Stress, 1958–1965', in Twitchett, Dennis and Fairbank, John (eds.), *The Cambridge History of China*, Cambridge: Cambridge University Press, Vol. 14, pp. 543–590.

Lardy, Nicholas, 1989. 'Dilemmas in the Pattern of Resource Allocation in China, 1978–1985', in Nee, Victor and Stark, David (eds.), *Remarking the Economic Institutions of Socialism: China and Eastern Europe*, Stanford: Stanford University Press, pp. 278–305.

Lau, C. C., 1987. 'Urban China in Transition: the Impact of Economic Reforms', in Chai, Joseph C. H. and Leung, Chi-keung (eds.), *China's Economic Reforms*, Hong Kong: University of Hong Kong Centre of Asian Studies, pp. 108–129.

Lee, Yok-shiu, 1989. 'Small Towns and China's Urbanization Level', *The China Quarterly*, 120, pp. 771–786.

Lee, Yok-shiu, 1991. 'Rural Non-agricultural Development in an Extended Metropolitan Region: The Case of Southern Jiangsu', in Ginsburg, Norton, *et al.*, *The Extended Metropolis: Settlement Transition in Asia*, Honolulu: University of Hawaii Press, pp. 137–156.

Lee, Yok-shiu, 1992. 'Rural Transformation and Decentralized Urban Growth in China', in Guldin, Gregory (ed.), *Urbanizing China*, Westport: Greenwood Press, pp. 89–118.

Leung, C. K. and Ginsburg, Norton (eds.), 1980. *China: Urbanization and National Development*, Department of Geography Research Paper No. 196, Chicago: University of Chicago.

Leung, H. C. K., 1987. 'Avoiding Soviet Mistakes? A Critical Reassessment of the Maoist Model', University of Toronto, Unpublished manuscript.

Leung, H. C. K. and Chan, Kam Wing, 1986. 'Chinese Regional Development Policies: A Comparative Reassessment', Paper presented at the Annual Meeting of the Canadian Asian Studies Association, Winnipeg, Canada, June 4–6, 1986.

Lewis, Arthur, 1954. 'Economic Development with Unlimited Supplies of Labour', *The Manchester School*, 22(2), pp. 139–191.

Lewis, Arthur, 1958. 'Unlimited Labour: Further Notes', *The Manchester School*, 26(1), pp. 1–32.

Lewis, Arthur, 1978. *The Evolution of the International Economic Order*, Princeton: Princeton University Press.

Lewis, John Wilson, 1971. 'Introduction: Order and Modernization in the Chinese Cities', in Lewis, John Wilson (ed.), *The City in Communist China*, Stanford: Stanford University Press, pp. 1–26.

Li, Mengbai, 1991. 'Mobile Population and City Development in China: Effects and Solutions', Seminar presentation at the University of Hong Kong, Hong Kong, April 11.

Li, Mengbai and Hu, Yin, 1991. *Liudong renkou du dachengshi fazhan de yingxiang ji duice* (*Impact of Floating Population on the Development of Large Cities and Recommended Policy*), Beijing: Jingji ribao chubanshe.

Li, S. M. and Chu, D. K. Y., 1987. 'The Implications of System Reforms for Urban Land Uses and City Landscapes', in Chai, Joseph C. H. and Leung, Chi-keung (eds.), *China's Economic Reforms*, Hong Kong: University of Hong Kong Centre of Asian Studies, pp. 248–261.

Li, Wen Lang, 1987. 'Social Inequality and Recent Social Development in the Mainland', in Hungdah Chiu (ed.), *Survey of Recent Developments in China Mainland and Taiwan*, Baltimore: University of Maryland School of Law, pp. 99–113.

Li, Wen Lang, 1992. 'Migration, Urbanization, and Regional Development: Toward a State Theory of Urban Growth in Mainland China', *Issues & Studies*, 28(2), pp. 84–102.

Li, Yining, 1990. Seminar on China's agricultural economy given at University of Hong Kong, Centre of Asian Studies.

Linn, J. F., 1982. 'The Cost of Urbanization in Developing Countries', *Economic Development and Cultural Change*, 30(3), pp. 625–648.

Lipton, Michael, 1977. *Why Poor People Stay Poor*, London: Temple Smith.

Lipton, Michael, 1984. 'Urban Bias Revisited', *Journal of Development Studies*, 20(3), pp. 139–166.

Liu, Fangyu, 1984. *Xiaofei jingjixue gaikun* (*An Outline of Consumption Economics*), Guiyang: Guizhou renmin chubanshe.

Liu, Jialin, *et al.*, 1988. *Zhongguo laodong jidu gaige* (*Reform of Chinese Employment System*), Beijing: Jingji kexue chubanshe.

Liu, Lufeng, *et al.*, 1989. *Zhonghua renmin gongheguo yaoshilu* (*A Record of Important Events in the People's Republic of China, 1949–1989*), Jinan: Shangdong renmin chubanshe.

Liu, Shaoqi, *et al.*, 1949. *Xinminzhu zhuti chengshi zhengce* (*Urban Policy of New Democracy*), Hong Kong: Xinminzhu chubanshe.

Liu, Wanlong, 1981. 'Guangzhoushi fazhan geti gongshanghu de zuofa' (Measures to Expand Individual Industrial and Commercial Enterprises in Guangzhou City', in *Fazhan chengzhen geti jingji* (*Expanding Individual Enterprises in Cities and Towns*), Tongxian: Gongshang chubanshe, pp. 69 76.

Liu, Zheng, *et al.*, 1981. *China's Population: Problems & Prospects*, Beijing: New World Press.

Liu, Zheng, *et al.*, 1990. *Woguo yanhai diqu xiaochengzheng jingji fazhan he renkou qianyi* (*Economic Development in and Population Migration to Small Towns in Coastal Region in China*), Beijing: Zhongguo zhanwan chubanshe.

Lo, Fu-chen and Salih, Kamal, 1987. 'Structural Change and Spatial Transformation: Review of Urbanization in Asia, 1960–80', in Fuchs, Roland *et al.* (eds.) *Urbanization and Urban Policies in Pacific Asia*, Boulder and London: Westview, pp. 38–64.

Luo, Shouchu, 1987. 'Labor Mobility and Reform of the Labor System', *Social Sciences in China*, (Autumn), pp. 119–32.

Luo, Yu and Pannell, Clifton, 1991. 'The Changing Pattern of City and Industry in Post-Reform China', in Veeck, Gregory (ed.) *The Uneven Landscape: Geographical Studies in Post-Reform China*, pp. 29–52.

Ma, Hong (ed.), 1982. *Xiandai Zhongguo jingji shidian* (*Dictionary of Economic Events in Modern China*), Beijing: Zhongguo shehui kexue chubanshe.

Ma, Laurence, 1976. 'Anti-urbanism in China', *Proceedings*, Association of American Geographers, 8, pp. 114–118.

Ma, Laurence, 1977. 'Conterurbanization and Rural Development: the Strategy of *Hsia-Hsiang*', *Current Scene*, 15(8 & 9), pp. 1–12.

Ma, Laurence, 1980. *Cities and City Planning in the People's Republic of China: An Annotated Bibliography*, Washington, DC: US Government Printing Office.

Ma, Laurence and Cui, Gonghao, 1987. 'Administrative Changes and Urban Population in China', *Annals of the Association of American Geographers*, 77(3), pp. 373–395.

Ma, Laurence and Hanten, Edward (eds.), 1981. *Urban Development in Modern China*, Boulder: Westview Press.

Ma, Xia, 1987. 'Sanshiduo nian lai woguo de guonei renkou qianyi ji jinhou de zhanwan' (Internal Migration in China in the Past Thirty Years and its Future Prospects), *Jingji yu renkou* (*Population and Economy*), 2, pp. 3–9. An English translation is in *Chinese Geography and Environment*, 1988, 1(2), pp. 67–82.

Ma, Xia and Wang, Weizhi, 1988. 'Zhongguo chengzhen renkou qianyi yu chengzhenhua yanjiu' (A Study on China's Urban Population Migration and Urbanization), *Renkou yanjiu*, 2, pp. 1–7.

Mallee, Hein, 1988. 'Rural–Urban Migration Control in the People's Republic of China: Effects of the Recent Reform', *China Information*, 11(4), pp. 12–22.

Mann, Susan, 1984. 'Urbanization and Historical Change in China', *Modern China*, 10(1), pp. 70–113.

Mao, Zedong, 1949. 'Report to the Meeting of Second Session of the Eighth Central Committee of the CCP' in *Mao Zedong xuanji* (*Selected Works of Mao Zedong*), 4, Beijing: Renmin chubanshe, pp. 1314–1329.

Mao, Zedong, 1956. 'Lun shida guanxi' (On the Ten Great Relationships), in *Mao Zedong xuanji* (*Selected Works of Mao Zedong*), 5, (1977), Beijing: Renmin chubanshe, pp. 267–288.

Mao, Zedong, 1961–62. 'Sulian *Zhengzhi jingji xue* dushu biji' (Notes on Reading Soviet *Political Economy*), in *Mao Zedong sixian wansui* (*Long Live Mao Zedong Thought*), pp. 316–398.

Martinotti, Guido, 1980. 'Deurbanization and Villagization', *International Journal of Urban and Regional Research*, 4, pp. i–xiii.

Maxwell, Neville (ed.), 1979. *China's Road to Development*, Oxford: Pergamon Press.

McGee, T. G., 1991. 'The Emergence of *Desakota* Regions in Asia: Expanding a Hypothesis', in Ginsburg, Norton, *et al.*, *The Extended Metropolis: Settlement Transition in Asia*, Honolulu: University of Hawaii Press, pp. 3–26.

Meisner, Maurice, 1974. 'Utopian Socialist Themes in Maoism', in John Wilson Lewis (ed.), *Peasant Rebellion and Communist Revolution in Asia*, Stanford: Stanford University Press, pp. 207–252.

Meng, Xin and Bai, Nansheng, 1988. *Jiagou baindong: Zhongguo nong-cun laodongli de zhuanyi* (*Structural Change: Transfer of Agricultural Labour in China*), Hangzhou: Zhejiang renmin chubanshe.

Millar, James R., 1970. 'Soviet Rapid Development and the Agricultural Surplus Hypothesis', *Soviet Studies*, 22(1), pp. 77–93.

Mills, Edwin S. and Becker, Charles M., 1986. *Studies in Indian Urban Development*, New York: Oxford University Press.

Ming Pao (American Edition), 1984. Nongmin wugong jingshang, zhunxu laohu chengzhen (Peasants Engaged in Industry and Commerce Permitted to Have Town Registration), August 28, p. 8.

Ming Pao, 1988. October 13, p. 9.

Ming Pao, 1989a. September 9, p. 10.

Ming Pao, 1989b. October 29, p. 9.

Ming Pao, 1990a. June 16, p. 45.

Ming Pao, 1990b. October 7. p. 38.

Ming Pao, 1992. February 15, p. 6.

Ministry of Internal Affairs, 1985. *Zhonghua renmin gongheguo xingzheng qu jiance 1985* (*A Handbook of Administrative Regions in the PRC 1985*), Beijing: Zhongguo ditu chubanshe.

Ministry of Internal Affairs, 1986. *Zhonghua renmin gongheguo xingzheng qu jiance 1986* (*A Handbook of Administrative Regions in the PRC 1986*), Beijing: Zhongguo ditu chubanshe.

Ministry of Internal Affairs, 1990. *Zhonghua renmin gongheguo xingzheng qu jiance 1990* (*A Handbook of Administrative Regions in the PRC 1990*), Beijing: Zhongguo ditu chubanshe.

Ministry of Personnel, 1991. *Liudong diaopei gongzuo zhinan* (*A Guide to Job Mobility and Assignments*), Beijing: Gaige chubanshe.

Mosher, Steven W., 1990. *China Misperceived*, New York: New Republic Books.

Murphey, Rhoads, 1975. 'Aspects of Urbanization in Contemporary China: A Revolutionary Model', *Proceedings*, the Association of American Geographers, 7, pp. 165–168.

Murphey, Rhoads, 1980. *The Fading of the Maoist Vision: City and Country in China's Development*, New York: Methuen.

Murray, Pearse, 1981. *Urbanization in the Socialist Countries: A Review*, University of Wisconsin, Unpublished MS thesis.

Murray, Pearse and Szelenyi, Ivan, 1984. 'The City in the Transition to Socialism', *International Journal of Urban and Regional Research*, 8(1), pp. 89–107.

Musil, Jiri, 1980. *Urbanization in Socialist Countries*, White Plains: M. E. Sharpe.

Myers, P., 1970. 'Demographic Trends in Eastern Europe' in US Congress Joint Economic Committee, *Economic Development in Countries of Eastern Europe*, 91st Cong., 2nd Session, pp. 68–148.

Myers, Ramon H., 1986. 'How Well Did U.S. Economists Understand Communist China's Economy?', in Shaw, Yu-ming (ed.), *Mainland China: Politics, Economics, and Reform*, Boulder and London: Westview Press, pp. 421–441.

Nanfang ribao, 1984. August 25, p. 1.

Nanfang ribao, 1988. February 3, p. 2.

Naughton, Barry, 1992a. 'Implications of the State Monopoly Over Industry and Its Relaxation', *Modern China*, 18(1), pp. 14–41.

Naughton, Barry, 1992b. 'Cities in the Chinese Economic System: Changing Roles and Conditions for Autonomy', mimeo.

New York Times, 1992. October 19, pp. A1 and A4.

Ni, Ernest, 1960. *Distribution of Urban and Rural Population of Mainland China, 1953 and 1958*, International Population Reports Series P-95, No. 56. Washington DC: US Department of Commerce.

Nolan, Peter and White, Gordon, 1984. 'Urban Bias, Rural Bias or State Bias? Urban–Rural Relations in Post-Revolutionary China', *Journal of Development Studies*, 20(3), pp. 53–81.

Nove, Alec, 1970. 'The Agricultural Surplus Hypothesis: A Comment on James R. Millar's Article', *Soviet Studies*, 22(1), pp. 394–401.

Odgaard, O., 1990. 'Inadequate and Inaccurate Chinese Statistics: the Case of Private Rural Enterprises', *China Information*, 5(3), pp. 29–38.

Ofer, Gur, 1976. 'Industrial Structure, Urbanization, and the Growth Strategy of Socialist Countries', *Quarterly Journal of Economics*, 90 (2), pp. 219–244.

Ofer, Gur, 1977. 'Economizing on Urbanization in Socialist Countries: Historical Necessity or Socialist Strategy' in Brown, A. A. and Neuberger, E. (eds.), *Internal Migration: A Comparative Perspective*, New York: Academic Press, pp. 277–303.

Ofer, Gur, 1973. *The Service Sector in Soviet Economic Growth: A Comparative Study*, Cambridge, MA: Harvard University Press.

Oksenberg, Michel, 1973. 'On Learning from China', in Oksenberg, Michel (ed.), *China's Developmental Experience*, New York: Praeger Publishers, pp. 1–16.

Orleans, Leo A., 1959. 'The Recent Growth of China's Urban Population', *The Geographical Review*, 49(1), pp. 43–57.

Orleans, Leo A. and Burnham, Ly, 1984. 'The Enigma of China's Urban Population', *Asian Survey*, 24(7), pp. 788–804.

Pannell, Clifton, 1984. 'China's Changing Cities: An Urban View of the Past, Present, and Future', in Ginsburg, Norton and Lalor, Bernard A. (eds.), *China: The 80s Era*, Boulder: Westview Press, pp. 192–221.

Pannell, Clifton, 1987. 'Economic Reforms and Readjustment in the People's Republic of China and Some Geographic Consequences,' *Studies in Comparative International Development*, 22(4), pp. 54–73.

Pannell, Clifton, 1990. 'China's Urban Geography', *Progress in Human Geography*, 14(2), pp. 214–236.

Parish, William L., 1981. 'Egalitarianism in Chinese Society', *Problems of Communism*, 1, pp. 37–53.

Parish, William L., 1987. 'Urban Policy in Centralized Economies: China' in Tolley, George S. and Thomas, Vinod (eds.), *The Economics of Urbanization and Urban Policies in Developing Countries*, Washington, DC: The World Bank, pp. 73–84.

Peng, Xizhe, 1991. *Demographic Transition in China*, Oxford: Clarendon Press.

Perkins, Dwight, 1966. *Market Control and Planning in Communist China*, Cambridge, MA: Harvard University Press.

Perkins, Dwight, 1975. 'Growth and Changing Structure of China's Twentieth-Century Economy', in Perkins, Dwight (ed.) *China's Modern Economy in Historical Perspective*, Stanford: Stanford University Press, pp. 115–166.

Perkins, Dwight, 1990. 'The Influence of Economic Reforms on China's Urbanization', in Kwok, R., *et al.* (eds.), *Chinese Urban Reform*, Armonk: M. E. Sharpe, pp. 78–106.

Perkins, Dwight, 1991. 'The Lasting Effect of China's Economic Reforms, 1979–1989', in Kenneth Lieberthal *et al.* (eds), *Perspectives on Modern China*, Armonk: M. E. Sharpe, pp. 341–363.

Perkins, Dwight and Yusuf, Shabid, 1984. *Rural Development in China*, Baltimore: Johns Hopkins University Press.

PRC: Documents of First Session of the Fourth National People's Congress, 1975. Hong Kong: Joint Publishing Co.

Preston, Samuel, H. 1988. 'Urban Growth in Developing Countries: A Demographic Reappraisal', in Gugler, Josef, (ed.), 1988, *The Urbanization of the Third World*, New York: Oxford University Press, pp. 11–31.

Prybyla, Jan S., 1982. 'China's Economic Development: Demise of a Model', *Problems of Communism*, May–June, pp. 38–42.

Qiao, Xiaochun and Li, Jingwu, 1990. 'Dui disici renkou pucha shizhen renkou huafen koujing de tantao' (A Study of the Criteria of Classifying Population of Cities and Towns in the Fourth National Population Census), *Renkou yu jingji* (*Population and Economy*), 3, pp. 22–28.

Qiu, Chuanying, 1980. 'Guanyu shige chengshi jiuye jiegou qingkuang de tiaocha' (On the Survey of Employment Structure in Ten Cities), *Jingjixue dongtai* (*Bulletin of Economics*), 4, pp. 36–39.

Ran, Maoxing and Berry, Brian, 1989. 'Underurbanization Policies Assessed: China, 1949–1986', *Urban Geography*, 10(2), pp. 111–120.

Ranis, Gustav and Fei, John C. H., 1961. 'A Theory of Economic Development', *The American Economic Review*, 51(4), pp. 533–565.

Rawski, Thomas G., 1979. *Economic Growth and Employment in China*, New York: Oxford University Press.

Rawski, Thomas G., 1982. 'The Simple Arithmetic of Chinese Income Distribution', *Keizai Kenkyu* (*Economic Research*), 33(1), pp. 12–26.

Regulska, Joanna, 1987. 'Urban Development under Socialism: The Polish Experience', *Urban Geography*, 8(4), pp. 321–339.

Renmin ribao, 1979. February 19, p. 2.

Renmin ribao, 1980a. October 16, p. 1.

Renmin ribao, 1980b. December 19, p. 5.

Renmin ribao, 1981. March 31, p. 1.

Renmin ribao, 1984a. March 15, p. 1.

Renmin ribao, 1984b. November 23, p. 4.

Renmin ribao, 1984c. October 10, p. 1.

Renmin ribao, 1985. September 8, p. 4.

Renmin ribao and *Hongqi* Editorial Boards, 1963. 'Guanyu Sidalin wenti' (On Stalin), *Renmin ribao*, September 13.

Ronnas, Per and Sjoberg, Orjan (1993). 'Urbanization, Central Planning and Tolley's Model of Urban Growth: A Critical Review', *Geoforum*, 24(2), pp. 193–204.

Santos, M., 1979. *The Shared Space: the Two Circuits of the Urban Economy in Underdeveloped Countries*, London and New York: Methuen.

Scharping, Thomas, 1987. 'Comment: Urbanization in China since 1949', *The China Quarterly*, 109, pp. 101–104.

Schinz, Alfred, 1989. *Urbanization of the Earth: Cities in China*, Berlin and Stuttgart: Gebruder Borntraeger.

Schwartz, Benjamin, 1973. 'China's Development Experience, 1949–72', in Oksenberg, Michel (ed.), *China's Developmental Experience*, New York: Praeger Publishers, pp. 17–26.

Shabad, Theodore, 1959. 'The Population of China's Cities', *The Geographical Review*, 49(1), pp. 32–42.

Shen, Daoqi, and Cui, Gonghao, 1990. 'Urban Geography and Urban Planning', in Geographical Society of China (ed.), *Recent Development of Geographical Science in China*, Beijing: Science Press, pp. 204–213.

Shrestha, Nanda, 1987. 'Institutional Policies and Migration Behaviour: A Selective Review', *World Development*, 15, pp. 329–345.

Sichuan University, 1982. *Yidu jingji (The Indian Economy)*, Beijing: Renmin chubanshe.

Sing Tao Daily, 1988. June 14, p. 1.

Sit, Victor F. S., 1984. 'Urban Fairs in China', *Economic Geography*, 63(4), pp. 306–318.

Sit, Victor F. S. (ed.), 1985. *Chinese Cities: The Growth of the Metropolis since 1949*, Hong Kong: Oxford University Press, pp. 1–66.

Sjoberg, Orjan, 1992. 'Underurbanization and Zero Urban Growth Hypothesis: Diverted Migration in Albania', *Geograpfiska Annaler*, 74B(1), pp. 3–19.

Skinner, G. William (ed.), 1977. *The City in Late Imperial China*, Stanford: Stanford University Press.

Skinner, G. William, 1964–65. 'Marketing and Social Structure in Rural China', *Journal of Asian Studies*, 24(1), pp. 3–43; 24(2), pp. 195–228; 24(3), pp. 363–399.

Skinner, G. William, 1985. 'Rural Marketing in China: Repression and Revival', *The China Quarterly*, 103, pp. 393–413.

Smith, Graham, 1989. *Planned Development in the Socialist World*, Cambridge: Cambridge University Press.

Solinger, Dorothy, 1985. '"Temporary Residence Certificate" Regulations in Wuhan, May 1983', *The China Quarterly*, 101, pp. 98–103.

Solinger, Dorothy, 1991. 'China's Transients and the State: A Form of Civil Society', USC Seminar Series No. 1, Hong Kong Institute of Asia-Pacific Studies, Chinese University of Hong Kong.

Sorrentino, Constance, 1983. 'International Comparisons of Labor Force Participation, 1960–81', *Monthly Labor Review*, February, pp. 23–36.

South China Morning Post (International Weekly), 1992. December 26.

South China Morning Post (International Weekly), 1993. June 12, p. 11.

Sovani, N. V., 1966. 'The Analysis of Over-Urbanization', in N. V. Sovani, *Urbanization and Urban India*, London: Asia Publishing House.

Spulber, Nicolas, 1963. 'Contrasting Economic Patterns: Chinese and Soviet Development Strategies', *Soviet Studies*, 15(1), pp. 1–16.

Spulber, Nicolas, 1971. *Socialist Management and Planning*, Bloomington: Indiana University Press.

State Council, 1955. 'Guowuyuan guanyu shizhcn liangshi dinghang gongying zanxing banfa de mingling' (State Council's Order of Provisional Measures on the Fixed Amount of Grain Supply in Cities and Towns) in Legal System Bureau of the State Council, 1987. *Zhongguo renmin gongheguo xianxing fagui huibian 1949–1985 (Collection of Current Laws and Regulations in the People's Republic of China 1949–85)*, Volume on finance and commerce, Beijing: Renmin chubanshe, pp. 479–486.

State Council, 1957. 'State Council's Temporary Regulations Regarding Recruitment of Temporary Labourers from the Countryside by Enterprises', *Renmin ribao*, December 14, p. 3.

State Council, 1962. 'State Council's Temporary Regulation Regarding the Use of Temporary Workers in State-run Enterprises', in *Zhonghua renmin gongheguo fagui huibian* (Jan 1962–Dec 1963) (*Collection of Legal Documents in the People's Republic of China*), 23, Beijing: Falu chubanshe, pp. 220–223.

State Council, 1965. 'State Council's Provisional Regulations on Improving the Deployment and Administration of Temporary Workers', in Legal System Bureau of the State Council, 1987. *Zhongguo renmin gongheguo xianxing fagui huibian 1949–1985 (Collection of Current Laws and Regulations in the People's Republic of China 1949–85)*, Volume on Labour and Personnel, Beijing: Renmin chubanshe, pp. 87–89.

State Council, 1981. 'State Council's Regulation Regarding Urban Non-agricultural Individual Economy', in *Siying he geti jingji shiyong fagui daquan (A Practical Encyclopedia of Regulations Regarding Private and Individual Enterprises)*, (1988) Beijing: Renmin chubanshe, pp. 61–64.

State Council, 1982a. 'Directives on the Strict Control of the Flow of Rural Labour Force into Cities to Work and the Conversion of Agricultural Population into Non-agricultural Population', *Guowuyuan gongbao (Bulletin of the State Council)*, February 10, pp. 885–887.

State Council, 1982b. 'Directives on the Strict Forbidding of Unhealthy Tendencies in the Work of Recruiting and Assigning State Workers and Staff', *Guowuyuan gongbao (Bulletin of the State Council)*, June 10, pp. 339–342.

State Council, 1983a. 'Supplement to "State Council's Regulation Regarding Urban Non-agricultural Individual Economy"', in *Siying he geti jingji shiyong fagui daquan (A Practical Encyclopedia of Regulations Regarding Private and Individual Enterprises)*, Beijing: Renmin chubanshe (1988), pp. 65–67.

State Council, 1983b. 'Stipulations Regarding Urban Labourers' Cooperatives', in Ministry of Labour and Personnel (ed.), *Laodong fagui xuanbian* (*A Compilation of Selected Labour Regulations*), Beijing: Laodong renshi chubanshe, pp. 105–108.

State Council, 1984a. 'Several Stipulations Concerning Rural Individual Industrial and Commercial Enterprises', in Ministry of Labour and Personnel (ed.), *Laodong fagui xuanbian* (*A Compilation of Selected Labour Regulations*), Beijing: Laodong renshi chubanshe, pp. 109–117.

State Council, 1984b. 'Temporary Procedures Regarding Hiring of Peasant Contract Workers and Using of Rural Construction Teams', *Zhonghua renmin gongheguo xianxing fagui huibian 1949–1985 Laodong renshi juan* (*Collection of Legal Documents in Use in the People's Republic of China 1949–85: Volume on Labour and Personnel*), Beijing: Falu chubanshe, pp. 208–213.

State Council, 1986. 'Directive Regarding the Adjustments of City Designation Criteria and the Conditions for Putting Counties under Cities' Administration', in Chinese Academy of Social Sciences, *Zhongguo renkou nianjian 1987* (*Population Yearbook of China 1987*), Beijing: Zhongguo shehui kexue chubanshe, pp. 60–61.

State Council, 1987a. 'Villagers' Committees of the People's Republic of China Organization Law', in *Zhonghua renmin gongheguo changyongfa daquan* (*A Collection of Commonly Used Laws in the People's Republic of China*), Beijing: Falu chubanshe, pp. 74–76.

State Council, 1987b. 'Temporary Regulation Regarding Urban and Rural Individual Industrial and Commercial Enterprises', in Ministry of Labour and Personnel (ed.), *Laodong fagui xuanbian* (*A Compilation of Selected Labour Regulations*), Beijing: Laodong renshi chubanshe, pp. 113–117.

State Council, 1988. 'Zhonghua renkou gongheguo siying qiye zhanxing tiaoli' (Temporary Regulation regarding Privately run Enterprises in the People's Republic of China), *Guowuyuan gongbu* (*Bulletin of State Council*), 15, pp. 483–489.

State Council, 1991. *Major Figures of the Fourth National Population Census of China*, Beijing: China Statistical Publishing House.

State Council and State Statistical Bureau, 1983. *10 Per cent Sampling Tabulation on the 1982 Population Census of the People's Republic of China*, Beijing: Zhongguo tongji chubanshe.

State Council and State Statistical Bureau, 1985. *1982 Population Census of China*, Beijing: Zhongguo tongji chubanshe.

State Statistical Bureau (SSB), 1982. *Zhongguo tongji nianjian 1981* (*Statistical Yearbook of China 1981*), Beijing: Zhongguo yongji chubanshe.

State Statistical Bureau (SSB), 1983a–91a. *Zhongguo tongji nianjian* (*Statistical Yearbook of China*), Beijing: Zhongguo tongji chubanshe (various years).

State Statistical Bureau (SSB), 1985b. *Zhongguo gongye jingji tongji ziliao (China's Industrial Economic Statistics)*, Beijing: Zhongguo tongji chubanshe.

State Statistical Bureau (SSB), 1986b. *Zhongguo he waiguo chengshi tongji ziliao (Chinese and Foreign Urban Statistics)*, Beijing: Zhongguo tongji chubanshe.

State Statistical Bureau (SSB), 1987b. *Zhongguo laodong gongzi tongji ziliao, 1949–1985 (Statistical Data on China's Labour and Wages, 1949–1985)*, Beijing: Zhongguo tongji chubanshe.

State Statistical Bureau (SSB), 1988b. *Tabulations of China 1% Population Sample Survey: National Volume*, Beijing: Zhongguo tongji chubanshe.

State Statistical Bureau (SSB), 1989b. *Fenjin de sishinian (The Progressing Forty Years)*, Beijing: Zhongguo tongji chubanshe.

State Statistical Bureau (SSB), 1990b. *Zhongguo laodong gongzi tongji niganjian 1990 (Statistical Yearbook of China's Labour and Wages, 1990)*, Beijing: Zhongguo tongji chubanshe.

Stone, Bruce, 1986. 'Chinese Socialism's Record on Food and Agriculture', *Problems of Communism*, Sept.–Oct., pp. 63–72.

Stren, Richard, et al., 1992. *An Urban Problematique: The Challenge of Urbanization for Development Assistance*, Toronto: Centre for Urban and Community Studies, University of Toronto.

Ta Kung Pao, 1984. (American edition) March 21, p. 1.

Tan, K. C., 1986. 'Revitalized Small Towns in China', *The Geographical Review*, 76(2), pp. 138–148.

Tang, Anthony M., 1984. *An Analytical and Empirical Investigation of Agriculture in Mainland China, 1952–1980*, Mainland China Economic Series No. 4, Taipei: Chung-Hua Institute for Economic Research.

Tang, Jianzhong and Ma, Laurence, 1985. 'Evolution of Urban Collective Enterprises in China', *The China Quarterly*, 104, pp. 614–640.

Tang, Wing-Shing, 1990. 'The Dynamics of Urban Spatial Structure in China, 1949–76', The Chinese University of Hong Kong, Department of Geography, *Occasional Paper* No. 107.

Tang, Wing-Shing, and Jenkins, Alan, 1990. 'Urbanization: Processes, Politics and Patterns,' in Cannon, Terry, and Jenkins, Alan (eds.), *The Geography of Contemporary China*, London and New York: Routledge, pp. 203–219.

Taubman, Wolfang and Winmer, Urs, 1987. 'Supply and Marketing in Chinese Cities', in Chai, Joseph C. H. and Leung, Chi-keung (eds.), *China's Economic Reforms*, Hong Kong: University of Hong Kong Centre of Asian Studies, pp. 331–366.

Taylor, Jeffrey, 1988. 'Rural Employment Trends and the Legacy of Surplus Labour, 1979–86', *The China Quarterly*, 116, pp. 736–766.

Tayor, Jeffery and Banister, Judith, 1991. 'Surplus Rural Labor in the People's Republic of China', in Veeck, Gregory (ed.), *The Uneven Landscape: Geographical Studies in Post-Reform China*, pp. 87–120.

The Nineties, 1992a. August issue, p. 43.

The Nineties, 1992b. October issue, p. 23.

Tian, Xueyuan, 1989. 'Zhongguo chengshi renkou huafen biaozhun wenti yanjiu' (Research on the Question of Classification of Urban Population in China), *Renkou yu jingji*, 1, pp. 3–8.

Tien, H. Yuan, 1973. *China's Population Struggle*, London: Longman Group Ltd.

Tin, Fang, and Lin, Fatang, 1986. *Zhongguo renkou qianyi* (*Migration in China*), Beijing: Zhishe chubanshe.

Tolley, George, 1987. 'Urbanization and Economic Development', in Tolley, George S. and Thomas, Vinod, (eds.), *The Economics of Urbanization and Urban Policies in Developing Countries*, Washington, DC: The World Bank, pp. 15–31.

Tolley, George and Thomas, Vinod, 1987. 'An Overview of Urban Growth: Problem, Policies, and Evaluation', in Tolley, George S. and Thomas, Vinod (eds.), *The Economics of Urbanization and Urban Policies in Developing Countries*, Washington, DC: The World Bank, pp. 1–12.

Tongji gongzuo, 1957. '1949–1956 nian woguo renkou tongji ziliao' (China's Population Statistics, 1949–1956), 11, pp. 24–25.

Tongji University, Chongqing Architectural and Engineering College and Wuhan Institute of Architectural Materials and Technology, 1981. *Chengshi guihua yuanli* (*Principles of City Planning*), Beijing: Zhongguo jianzhu gongye chubanshe.

Tsai, Hsung-Hsiung, 1987. 'Population Decentralization Policies: The Experience of Taiwan', in Fuchs, Roland *et al.* (eds.), *Urbanization and Urban Policies in Pacific Asia*, Boulder and London: Westview, pp. 214–229.

Ullman, Edward L. and Dacey, Michael F., 1962. 'The Minimum Requirements Approach to the Urban Economic Base', in Norborg, Knut (ed.), *Proceedings of the IGU Symposium in Urban Geography, Lund 1960*, Lund: C. W. K. Gleerup Publisher, pp. 121–143.

Ullman, Morris B., 1961. *Cities of Mainland China: 1953–1959*, International Population Reports Series P-95, No. 59, Washington, DC: US Department of Commerce.

United Nations, 1974. *Methods for Projections of Urban and Rural Population*, Population Studies No. 55, New York: United Nations.

United Nations, 1980. *Pattern of Urban and Rural Population Growth*, Population Studies No. 68, New York: Department of International Economic and Social Affairs, United Nations.

United Nations, 1987. *The Prospects of World Urban Population*, Population Studies 101.

Van Ness, Peter and Raichur, Satish, 1983. 'Dilemmas of Socialist Development: An Analysis of Strategic Lines in China, 1949–1981', *Bulletin of Concerned Asian Scholars*, 15(1), pp. 2–15.

Wakabayashi, Keiko, 1990. 'Migration From Rural to Urban Areas in China', *The Developing Economies*, 28(4), pp. 503–523.

Wang, Haibo, 1981. 'Relationship between Accumulation and Consumption', in Ma, Hong and Sun, Shangqing (eds.), *Zhongguo jingji jie wenti yanjiu (Research on China's Economic Structure)*, Beijing: Renmin chubanshe, pp. 562–600.

Wang, Haibo, 1986. *Xin Zhongguo gongye jingjishi (The History of Industrial Economy in New China)*, Beijing: Jingji guanli chubanshe.

Wang, Jici, and Fang, Qing, 1990. 'An Incentive to Immigration from Villages to Town', Paper presented at the Regional Conference, International Geographical Union, Beijing, China, August 1990.

Wang, Shaoguang, 1993. 'The Rise of the Second Budget and the Decline of State Capacity in China,' Paper presented at the University of Washington, January 14.

Wang, Shengxue, 1990. 'Zhongguo chengshi fazhan fangzhen fengxi' (An Analysis of China's Urban Development Policy), *Zhongdeng chengshi jingji (Economy of Medium Cities)*, 3, pp. 46 and 51–55.

Wang, Sijun, 1991. '80 niandai zhongguo renkou chengzhenhua gaiguan' (An Overview of the Urbanization of Population in China in the 1980s), *Zhongguo renkou nianjian 1990 (China Population Year Book 1990)*, pp. 121–127.

Wang, Sijun and Han, Bo, 1989. 'Guanyu chengxiang huafen biaozhun wenti de jidian yijian' (Some Suggestions of the Criteria of Dividing Population of Cities and Towns), *Renkou yu jingji (Population and Economy)*, 1, pp. 14–15.

Wang, Sijun, 1993. 'Zhongguo renkou dili yanjiu de jingzhang' (Development of Research on China's Population Geography), in So, Chak-lam and Chan, Kam Wing (eds.), *Dili yanjiu yu fazhan (Geographical Research and Development)*, Hong Kong: Hong Kong University Press, pp. 353–360.

Wang, Xiangming, 1986. 'Zhongguo renkou de chengzhenhua wenti' (Urbanization Problems in China), in CASS, *Zhongguo renkou nianjian, 1985 (Population Yearbook of China, 1985)*, Beijing: Zhongguo shehui kexue chubanshe, pp. 283–301.

Wang Xiangming, 1988. 'Renkou qianyi he liudong dui renkou chengzhenhua jincheng de yingxiang' (The Impact of Population Migration and Movement on the Process of the Urbanization of Population), *Renkou yu jingji*, 2, pp. 19–31.

Weber, Max, 1951. *The Religion of China*, New York: Free Press.

Wei, Jinsheng, 1989. 'Population Growth of and In-migration to Towns in China in the 1980s and their Determinants', Paper presented at the International Conference on Internal Migration and Urbanization in China, Beijing, December 6–8.

Weisskopf, Thomas E., 1980. 'The Relevance of the Chinese Experience for Third World Economic Development', *Theory and Society*, 4, pp. 283–318.

Weitzman, Martin, 1970. 'Soviet Postwar Growth and Capital-labour Substitution', *American Economic Review*, 60(4), pp. 676–692.

Wen Wei Po, 1986. January 20, p. 20.

Wen Wei Po, 1987a. July 21, p. 2.

Wen Wei Po, 1987b. November 24, p. 3.

Wen Wei Po, 1988a. February 25, p. 1.

Wen Wei Po, 1988b. May 12, p. 2.

Wen Wei Po, 1988c. August 22, p. 1.

Wen Wei Po, 1989a. April 5, p. 17.

Wen Wei Po, 1989b. December 28, p. 3.

Wen Wei Po, 1989c. December 9, p. 5.

Wen Wei Po, 1989d. April 4, p. 5.

Wen Wei Po, 1990a. April 4, p. 15.

Wen Wei Po, 1990b. June 20, p. 33 and June 22, p. 23.

Wen Wei Po, 1990c. June 17, p. 21.

Wen Wei Po, 1991. October 14, p. 3.

Wheelwright, E. L. and McFarlane, B., 1970. *The Chinese Road to Socialism*. New York: Monthly Review Press.

Whitney, Joseph, 1980. 'East Asia' in Klee, G. A. (ed.), *World Systems of Traditional Resource Management*, Silver Spring: V. H. Winston, pp. 101–129.

Whyte, Martin King and Parish, William L., 1984. *Urban Life in Contemporary China*, Chicago: University of Chicago Press.

Wilczynski, J., 1972. *Socialist Economic Development and Reforms*, London: Macmillan.

Williams, Jack F., 1991. 'Urban and Regional Planning in Taiwan', Paper presented at the Second International Conference on Asian Urbanization, New Delhi, India, January.

Wong, Christine, 1988. 'Interpreting Rural Industrial Growth in the Post-Mao Period', *Modern China*, 14(1), pp. 3–30.

Wong, Christine, 1991. 'Central–Local Relations in an Era of Fiscal Decline: The Paradox of Fiscal Decentralization in Post-Mao China', *The China Quarterly*, 128, pp. 691–715.

World Bank, 1980. *World Development Report 1980*, New York: Oxford University Press.

World Bank, 1982. *World Development Report 1982*, New York: Oxford University Press.

World Bank, 1983a. *China: Socialist Economic Development*, Vols. 1 and 2, Washington, DC: World Bank.

World Bank, 1983b. *World Development Report 1983*, Washington, DC: World Bank.

World Bank, 1985a. *China: Economic Structure in International Perspective*, Washington, DC: The World Bank.

World Bank, 1985b. *China: Long-term Development Issues and Options*, Baltimore: Johns Hopkins University Press.

World Journal, 1992a. August 5, p. 10.

World Journal, 1992b. October 1, p. 11.

World Journal, 1992c. November 25, p. 11.

World Journal, 1992d. December 3, p. 11.

World Journal, 1992e. August 6, p. 11.

World Journal, 1992f. December 15, p. 10.

World Journal, 1992g. December 17, p. 10.

World Journal, 1992h. December 28, p. 1.

World Journal, 1993a. January 5, p. 10.

World Journal, 1993b. January 7, p. 10.

Wu, Chung-tong, 1987. 'Chinese Socialism and Uneven Development', in Forbes, Dean and Thrift, Nigel (eds.), *The Socialist Third World*, Oxford: Basil Blackwell Ltd, pp. 53–97.

Wu, Chung-tong and Xu, Xue-qiang, 1990. 'Economic Reform and Rural to Urban Migration', in Linge, G. J. R. and Forbes, D. K. (eds.), *China's Spatial Economy*, Hong Kong: Oxford University Press, pp. 129–143.

Wu, Daowen, 1992. 'Zhongguo chengshihua daolu lilun pingshu' (An Evaluation of Theories on China's Urbanization Path), *Renkou yu yanjiu*, 3, pp. 55–57.

Wu, Keqiang and Zheng, Tao, 1986. 'Dushi zhong de nongmin hetong-gong') (The Urban Peasant Contract Workers), *Liaowang (Outlook)*, December 1, pp. 14–15.

Wu, Xiaoying, 1986. 'Renkou chengshihua: lishi, xianshi he xunze' (Urbanization of Population: History, Reality, and Choice), *Jingji yanjiu (Economic Research)*, 11, pp. 25–30.

Wu, Youren, 1981. 'Guanyu woguo chengzhen renkou laodong goucheng de chubu yanjiu' (A Preliminary Study of the Labour Structure of City and Town Population in China), *Dili xuebao (Acta Geographica Sinica)*, 36(2), pp. 121–133.

Wu, Youren, 1983. 'Guanyu woguo shehuizhuyi chengshihua wenti' (Questions on China's Socialist Urbanization), in Beijing College of Economics (ed.), *Zhongguo renkou kexue lunwenji (Symposium on Chinese Population Science)*, Beijing: Zhongguo xueshu chubanshe, pp. 96–104.

Xu, Huadong, *et al.*, 1985. 'Tan xiao chengzhen de jianzhen wenti' (On the Question of Designations of Small Towns), *Chengxiang jianshe (Urban and Rural Construction)*, 2, pp. 34–35.

Xu, Jianchuan, 1986. 'Woguo chengshi de zhuangkuang yu fazhan' (The Situation and Development of Cities in China), *Jianzhu jingji (Architecture and Economy)*, 5, pp. 32–35.

Xu, Xueqiang, 1983. 'Woguo chengshi guihua gongzuo de fazhan' (Development of Urban Planning in China), Paper presented at the University of Hong Kong.

Xu, Xueqiang and Chu, David, 1986. 'Nuli fazhan woguo de chengshi delixue' (Developing Urban Geography in China), *Jingji dili (Economic Geography)*, 6(1), pp. 10–14.

Xu, Xueqiang and Li, Si-ming, 1990. 'China's Open Door Policy and Urbanization in the Pearl River Delta Region', *International Journal of Urban and Regional Research*, 16(1), pp. 49–69.

Xu, Xueqiang, *et al.*, 1987. *Zhong guo xiaoshizhen de fazhan (Development of Small Cities and Towns in China)*, Guangzhou: Zhongshan daxue chubanshe.

Xue, Muqiao, 1980. *Danqian woguo jingji de ruogan wenti (Current Issues in China's Economy)*, Beijing: Renmin chubanshe.

Yan, Zhongmin and Ning, Yuemin, 1980. 'Woguo chengzhen renkou fazhan bianhua tedian chutan' (A Preliminary Study of the Changes and Characteristics of Urban Population in China), in Hu, Huanyong, *et al.*, *Renkou yanjiu lunwenji (Collected Works on Population Research)*, Shanghai: Huadong daxue chubanshe, pp. 20–38.

Yan, Zhongmin, *et al.*, 1964. 'Shilun Suxi diqu nongye fazhan yu zhongxiao chengzhen de guanxi' (The Relationship between the Agricultural Development in the Suzhou-Wuxi Area and Medium and Small Cities), *Dili xuebao (Acta Geographica Sinica)*, 30(3), pp. 234–246.

Yang, Shuzhen, 1988. 'Woguo xian jiaduan jingji xiezuoqu' (China's Present Economic Co-operation Regions), *Dili Zhisi (Geographical Knowledge)*, 11, pp. 8–10.

Yao, Shimou and Wu, Chucai, 1982. 'Woguo nongcun renkou chengshihua de yichong teshu xingshi—shilun woguo de yinnong yicong renkou' ('A Special Form of Urbanization of Rural Population in China—a Comment on the Population of Both Peasants and Workers'), *Dili xuebao (Acta Geographica Sinica)*, 37(2), pp. 155–62.

Ye, Weijun *et al.* (eds), 1988. *Zhongguo chengshihua daolu chutan (A Preliminary Exploration of China's Urbanization Paths)*, Beijing: Zhongguo zhanwan chubanshe.

Yeh, Anthony Gar-On, 1989. 'Reference Materials on Urban Development and Planning in China', Hong Kong: University of Hong Kong, Centre of Urban Planning and Environmental Management, *Working Paper* No. 44.

Yeh, Anthony Gar-On and Xu, Xueqiang, 1989. 'City System Development in China 1953–86', University of Hong Kong, Centre of Urban Studies and Planning, *Working Paper*, No. 41.

Yeung, Yue-man, 1990. *Changing Cities of Pacific Asia*, Hong Kong: Chinese University Press.

Yeung, Yue-man and Hu, Xu-wei (eds.), 1992. *China's Coastal Cities: Catalysts for Modernization*, Honolulu: University of Hawaii Press.

Yeung, Yue-man and Hu, Xu-wei, 1992. 'China's Coastal Cities as Development and Modernization Agents: An Overview', in Yeung and Hu (eds.), *China's Coastal Cities: Catalysts for Modernization*, Honolulu: University of Hawaii Press, pp. 1–24.

Yeung, Yue-man and Zhou, Yixing, 1987. 'Editors' Introduction', *Chinese Sociology and Anthropology* (special issue on Chinese urbanization), 19(3–4), pp. 3–13.

Yeung, Yue-man and Zhou, Yixing, 1991. 'Human Geography in China: Evolution, Rejuvenation and Prospect', *Progress in Human Geography*, 15(4), pp. 373–394.

Yu, Zuyao, 1981. 'Shangye fuwu jigao' (Structure of Commerce and Service), in Ma, Hong and Sun, Shangqing (eds.) *Zhongguo jingji jie wenti yanjiu (Research on China's Economic Structure)*, Beijing: Renmin chubanshe, pp. 437–466.

Zaslavsky, Victor and Luryi, Yuri, 1979. 'The Passport System in the USSR and Changes in Soviet Society', *Soviet Union*, 6(2), pp. 137–153.

Zelinsky, Wilbur, 1971. 'The Hypothesis of Mobility Transition', *Geographical Review*, 61 pp. 219–249.

Zeng, Yi, 1991. 'Renkou chengzhenghua dui woguo renkou fazhan de yingxiang' (The Impact of Urbanization on Population Development of China), *Renkou xuekan (Population Journal)*, 2, pp. 1–6.

Zhang, Kaimin, 1989. *Shanghai Liudong renkou (Floating Population in Shanghai)*, Beijing: Zhongguo tongji chubanshe.

Zhang, Qingwu, 1987. *Huji shouce (A Handbook of Household Registrations)*, Beijing: Qunzhong chubanshe.

Zhang, Qingwu, 1988. 'Luilun woguo de hukou qianyi zhengce' (A Brief Discussion on China's Household Migration Policy), *Zhongguo renkou kexue*, 2, pp. 35–8.

Zhang, Qingwu, 1989. 'Zhongguo hukou qianyi zhengce de huigu yu sikao' (A Review and Reflection of the Policies of Household Registration Migration in China), Paper presented at the International Conference on Internal Migration and Urbanization in China.

Zhang, Xiaohe, 1991. 'The Urban–Rural Isolation and Its Impact on China's Production and Trade Pattern', *Chinese Economy Research Unit Working Paper*, 4/91, University of Adelaide.

Zhang, Zhuoyuan, 1981. 'Establishing a Rational Economic Structure and Promoting Socialist Modernization Development', in Ma, Hong and Sun, Shangqing (eds.), *Zhongguo jingji jiegou wenti yanjiu (Research on China's Economic Structure)*, Beijing: Renmin chubanshe, pp. 56–98.

Zhao, Yinqing, 1988. 'Zhong chengshihua daolu lilun shuping' (A Theoretical Review of Chinese Road to Urbanization), in Ye, Weijun *et al.* (eds.), *Zhongguo chengshihua daolu chutan (A Preliminary Investigation of the Chinese Road to Urbanization)*, Beijing: Zhongguo zhanwan chubanshe, pp. 399–400.

Zhao, Ziyang, 1982. 'Report on the Sixth Five-year Plan', in *Fifth Session of the Fifth National People's Congress* (1983), Beijing: Foreign Language Press, pp. 109–185.

Zhejiang ribao, 1985. January 5.

Zheng, Guizhen *et al.*, 1985. 'Shanghai shiqu renkou wenti chutan' (An Exploration of the Question on Circulatory Population in Shanghai), *Renkou yanjiu* (*Population Studies*), 3, pp. 2–7.

Zhou, Yixing, 1982. 'Chengshihua yu guomin shengchan zongzhi guanxi de guiluxing tantao' (An Exploration of the Relationship between Urbanization and the Gross Domestic Product', *Renkou yu jingji* (*Population and Economy*), 1, pp. 28–33.

Zhou, Yixing, 1989. 'Zhongguo chengzhen de gainian he chengzhen renkou de tongji koujing' (The Concept of Cities and Towns in China and the statistical definition of urban population), *Renkou yu jingji* (*Population and Economy*), 1, pp. 9–13.

Zhou, Yixing, 1990. 'Evaluation and Rethinking about the National Urban Growth Policy of China,' Paper presented at the IGU Regional Conference, Beijing, August 13–20.

Zhou, Yixing and Shi, Yulong, 1990. 'Guanyu wuoguo shizhen renkou de jige wenti' (Several Questions about Population of Cities and Towns in China), *Renkou yu jingji* (*Population and Economy*), 6, pp. 9–13.

Zhou, Yixing and Sun, Ying, 1992, 'Dui wuoguo disici renkou pucha shizhen renkou bizhong de fenxi' (An Analysis of the Proportion of the Population of Cities and Towns in the Fourth National Population Census of China), *Renkou yu jingji* (*Population and Economy*), 1, pp. 21–27.

Zhu, Baoshu, *et al.*, 1991. 'Nongcun renkou xian shaochengzhen zhuanyi de xindongtai he xin wenti' (New Situation and New Problems Concerning Rural Population Migrating to Small Towns), *Zhongguo renkou kexue*, 1, pp. 49–55.

Zweig, David, 1987. 'From Village to City: Reforming Urban–Rural Relations in China', *International Regional Science Review*, 11(1), pp. 43–58.

Zweig, David, 1991. 'Rural Industry: Constraining the Leading Growth Sector in China's Economy', in US Congress, Joint Economic Committee, *China's Economic Dilemmas in the 1990s*, Vol. 1, pp. 418–436.

Index

AGRICULTURAL POPULATION, *see* Urban population statistics
Agriculture, 4, 9–10, 62–4, 67, 93, 140; reforms of, 47, 98, 108
Anti-urbanism, *see* Chinese model of urban development

'BLIND FLOWS', *see* Migration

CHINESE MODEL: of development, 4, 8–11, 148; of urban development, 2–4, 10–12, 52, 72, 91, 110, 143, 148
Cities: consumer, 10, 72; county-level, 20, 105, 119; definitions of, *see* Urban definitions; directly under central administration, 20; key-point, 105; Open, 106–7; producer, 10, 72, 103, 120; provincial/prefectural level, 20–1, 31–2, 105; separately listed, 106
Collectivization, 9, 37, 55, 57, 62, 62, 69, 77
Commodity grain, 15, 26–8, 39, 122, 124, 140
Communes, 38, 63, 77, 81, 108, 135, 144
Consumer cities, *see* Cities
Cultural Revolution, 40, 59, 76, 113, 124

DAQING, model, 39
Decentralization of administration, 47–8, 106, 118
Demography, *see* Population growth
Deng Xiaoping, 59, 98–9, 151
Desa kota region, 33, 145, 151

ECONOMIC DEVELOPMENT STRATEGY, 16, 59–63, 99, 142; *see also* Chinese model of development
Economic performance, 17, 63–8, 109, 150–1
Employment: urban 28, 42, 47, 87, 111–12, 122–32; *see also* Unemployment

FEINONGYE CHENGZHEN RENKOU (Non-agricultural Population of Cities and Towns), *see* Urban population

Female labour participation, 38, 80–1, 143, 147
First Five-year Plan, 37, 59, 60, 62, 67, 71, 142
Floating population, 33, 44–8, 117, 124, 132, 145, 151
Formal migration, *see* Migration
Free markets, 100–1, 114, 122, 124–5

GRAIN RATIONING, *see* Rationing
Grain supply, *see* Commodity grain
Great Leap Forward, 4, 8, 38–9, 60, 62, 68, 71, 79, 81, 93

HARRIS-TODARO MIGRATION MODEL, 2, 133–4
Hidden economy, 111, 115, 128, 132
Horizontal integration, 27, 104; *see also Shiguanxian*
Household registration system, 13, 16, 28, 35, 41, 76–8, 95, 118, 147, 152; *zili kouliang hu*, 33, 47, 121, 128, 135; law, 63; *nongzhuangfei*, 47–8, 76, 117–19; *see also* Urban population statistics
Huixiang, *see* Rustications
Hukou, *see* Household registration system

INFORMAL MIGRATION, *see* Migration
Individual enterprises, 100, 128–30
Investment, state capital, 60–3, 69, 72, 99, 101–2, 109, 136

KEY-POINT CITIES, *see* Cities

LABOUR MARKET, 77, 152
Lateral integration, *see* Horizontal integration
Litu bulixiang, 110, 127

MARKET TOWNS, 33, 43, 47, 126
Mao Zedong, 10, 38
Marx, Karl, 57
Migration, 15, 54, 69; control of, 37, 41–7, 48, 9, 59, 63, 76–7, 92, 97–8, 138, 151; formal, 47, 117–20, 132; informal, 117, 120–2, 144; 'blind flows', 37, 82, 122, 133–4; temporary, 101, 117, 145; rural-urban